ArtScroll Mesorah Series®

Expositions on Jewish liturgy and thought

The Aryeh Kaplan Reader

Collected essays on Jewish themes
from the noted writer and thinker

Published by

Mesorah Publications, ltd

The Aryeh Kaplan Reader

The gift he left behind

FIRST EDITION
First Impression . . . September, 1983
Second Impression . . . November, 1985
Third Impression . . . January, 1990
Fourth Impression . . . December, 1995

Published and Distributed by
MESORAH PUBLICATIONS, Ltd.
4401 Second Avenue
Brooklyn, New York 11232

Distributed in Europe by
J. LEHMANN HEBREW BOOKSELLERS
20 Cambridge Terrace
Gateshead, Tyne and Wear
England NE8 1RP

Distributed in Israel by
SIFRIATI / A. GITLER — BOOKS
4 Bilu Street
P.O.B. 14075
Tel Aviv 61140

Distributed in Australia & New Zealand by
GOLDS BOOK & GIFT CO.
36 William Street
Balaclava 3183, Vic., Australia

Distributed in South Africa by
KOLLEL BOOKSHOP
22 Muller Street
Yeoville 2198, Johannesburg, South Africa

THE ARTSCROLL MESORAH SERIES®
THE ARYEH KAPLAN READER

© *Copyright 1985, 1990 by* MESORAH PUBLICATIONS, Ltd.
4401 Second Avenue / Brooklyn, N.Y. 11232 / (718) 921-9000

ISBN
0-89906-173-7 (hard cover)
0-89906-174-5 (paperback)

Printed in the United States of America by Moriah Offset
Bound by Sefercraft, Quality Bookbinders, Ltd. Brooklyn, N.Y.

Table of Contents

A Tribute to
Rabbi Aryeh Kaplan ז״ל

Born
יד חשון תרצ״ה
October 23, 1934

Died
יד שבט תשמ״ג
January 28, 1983

Rabbi Yitzchok Hutner, zt'l, one of the leading scholars and Roshei Hayeshivah of the last generation, once said that Elijah the Prophet walks among us in the streets and we do not even take notice of him; as the Prophet said: "He (Elijah) will restore the hearts of fathers to their children, and the hearts of children to their father." The same can be said about Aryeh Eliyahu Moshe Kaplan, for he was on a similar mission of uniting the hearts of the generations.

Aryeh Kaplan's family originated in Salonika, Greece, and according to business records from that country, as members of the Racenati family his forebears were successful as discount bankers. But Rabbi Aryeh's riches were of the spirit that he had derived from the legacy of that once great Jewish center.

By all appearances, he had assimilated into the Ashkenazic Jewish community, having absorbed the Lithuanian method of Torah study from the yeshivos he attended. Indeed, he was ordained by Rabbi Eliezer Yehudah Finkel of the Mirrer Yeshivah in Jerusalem.

In truth, he succeeded in blending together the disparate influences of Torah in Mir, Salonika, Brisk and others...Chasidism, Talmudic dialectics and philosophy, and integrated them into his ever-pure Jewishness. His teachings and writings glow with the full spectrum of Judaism, as a masterwork of art combines many hues in one original work.

In the course of a writing career that spanned only eleven years, Rabbi Kaplan became well-known to thousands of teen-agers and adults alike. His career began with the five booklets of the Young Israel Intercollegiate Hashkafa Series: *Belief in God; Free Will and the Purpose of Creation; The Jew; Love and the Commandments*; and *The Structure of Jewish Law.*

Several other booklets, spanning the entire spectrum of Jewish thought and philosophy, as well as some dealing with basic practice and observance, were published by the Orthodox Union and its youth arm, the National Conference of Synagogue Youth/NCSY. These include: *Tefillin—God, Man and Tefillin; Love Means Reaching Out; Maimonides' Principles—The Fundamentals of Jewish Faith; The Waters of Eden—The Mystery of the Mikveh*; and *Jerusalem—The Eye of the Universe.*

He authored a series of anti-missionary tracts that were published by NCSY, first separately, later combined into one volume entitled *The Real Messiah*. The author's close relationship with the Orthodox Union also included service as editor of its magazine, *Jewish Life*, and director of its Collegiate program.

Rabbi Kaplan was a popular speaker, who addressed every NCSY National Convention since his association with the organization began, missing only the two that coincided with the birth of two of his children. He also spoke with NCSY's New York Region on a regular basis, and essentially became the spiritual adviser of its Brooklyn region. Firmly believing in NCSY's goals of acquainting unaffiliated and alienated Jewish teen-agers with their heritage, Rabbi Kaplan was a prime force behind the teshuvah phenomenon—the return to Jewish observance. "Throughout history, Jews have always been observant," he once remarked. "The teshuvah movement is just a normalization. The Jewish people are sort of getting their act together. We're just doing what we're supposed to do."

Rabbi Kaplan held an M.A. in physics and his work reflected that training. In culling Jewish sources for his books, he once remarked, "I use my physics background to analyze and systemize data, very much as a physicist would deal with physical reality." This ability enabled him to undertake monumental projects, producing close to 50 books, celebrated for their erudition, completeness and clarity. Rabbi Kaplan brought forth numerous other original works ranging from books explaining the deepest mysteries of Kabbalah and Chassidism to a unique

Haggadah combining utmost simplicity and scholarly depth. Some of his works have been translated into Russian and Dutch, in response to the quest of searching Jews.

Rabbi Kaplan's most recent major effort, *The Living Torah*, published by Maznaim Press, is a contemporary English translation of the five books of Moses with maps, notes, illustrations and an annotated bibliography, all compiled by the author in the short period of nine months. *The Living Torah* has been hailed by scholars and students as the most readable and complete English translation of the Torah ever produced.

Rabbi Kaplan often had several projects in the works simultaneously. During the past five years, while compiling *The Living Torah* and new manuscripts on *tzitzis* and the Jewish wedding, Rabbi Kaplan engaged in the monumental task of translating the 17th century classic, *Meam Loez*, from the original Ladino into English. *Me'am Loez* is the enormously influential multi-volume work initiated by the Sephardic Torah giant, Rabbi Yaakov Culi, which expounds the weekly Sidrah, weaving the Midrashic commentary, philosophic discussion, and halachic guidelines into one flowing text. The translation, published by Maznaim, was entitled *The Torah Anthology*, and it had been Rabbi Kaplan's goal to complete it in eighteen volumes, by Rosh Hashanah, 5743. At the time of his death, 15 volumes had been completed.

As his fame grew, Rabbi Kaplan became one of the most popular magazine journalists in the Torah field. In addition to his service with *Jewish Life*, he was a frequent contributor to *The Jewish Observer*. His articles dealt with an unusually broad range of subjects, ranging from the technicalities of *Safrus* (the scribal arts) and the halachically correct writing of a *get* (Jewish document of divorce), to methodology for countering missionaries, and meditation and prayer. His remarkable ability of presenting esoteric information in a popular, lively style won him a wide following. Moreover, the breadth of his knowledge did not suffer from the pitfall of superficiality. Rabbi Kaplan's articles from *The Jewish Observer* form a major part of this book.

His personal example of modesty, *midos tovos*, great human warmth and sensitivity, and total dedication to Torah study and life of *mitzvos*, was an inspiration to the thousands of individuals whom he touched. His home was always open to visitors, great and humble, from every segment of the Jewish community. His Shabbos table was always crowded with guests attracted to the beauty of the Torah life that he lived, and to the endless stream of wisdom and Torah insight which flowed from his lips.

He labored tirelessly, day and night, producing more outstanding works of great and original Torah scholarship single-handedly than teams of other authors working in the field. Yet, he somehow managed to find time for the simplest Jews, perfect strangers, seeking the answers to the spiritual questions in their lives. None were turned away empty-handed. With this burning preoccupation with Torah, which was his mission in life, he was also a devoted husband to his loyal wife, Tobie, with whom he gave love and inspiration to their nine children. May his example be an inspiration, and his memory a blessing.

Past, Present and Future

Gateway to the Past

T HERE IS A *SEFORIM* STORE down the block where I frequently drop in to make purchases to add to my library. In addition to recently printed works, the store had a large number of older items, some in high piles on the very top shelf, well out of reach. Whenever I entered the store, these always aroused my curiosity.

One day, the piles were gone. They had been moved to the basement to make room for the newer books. I finally had an opportunity to examine these old *seforim*, and as I did, I found myself walking through a gateway to the past.

Most of the *seforim* were some thirty years old, but some were much older. Many were pamphlets, published by obscure authors, but others were important classics that are no longer readily available, and older editions of popular *seforim*. I only picked up a few items on this first visit, but eventually I was drawn back, to what was to become an exciting adventure.

A number of *seforim* seemed very old, and I had assumed them to be too expensive. On second thought, I priced a few and, to my surprise, found them to be no more expensive than their modern counterparts.

⊸§ My First Purchase

My first purchase was a *Gemara*, the last volume of a Sulzbach *Shas* (complete set of Talmud), printed in 5518 (1758). It was an uncanny feeling, owning a *sefer* that could have been held by the Vilna Gaon or the Baal Shem Tov! A comparison with my Vilna *Shas* showed no important differences, except in illustrations in *Seder Taharos*. In the older edition, they are larger and more detailed—of considerable help in understanding obscure and difficult texts.

I later learned that the Sulzbach *Shas*, one of the most esteemed editions, was the standard reference until the Vilna *Shas* was published in 5640 (1880). Sulzbach, Germany, had an active Jewish community, and was the site of an important Jewish printing concern between 1669 and 1851. Its *seforim* were renowned both for their accuracy and high quality.

The *Gemara* was fascinating to sight and touch. It has the original binding, in exquisitely hand-tooled leather, with wooden cover boards, and brass clasps for holding it closed. Embossed on the spine is "David Bamberg (the original owner), 1759." The loving care and craftsmanship that went into every facet of the book's construction spoke volumes. A *Shas* such as this cost a working man a year's wages; and the set would then become a valuable part of his estate, lovingly handed down from father to son.

This *Gemara* was printed by Zalman Madfis (Hebrew for "printer") of Sulzbach. I later found a *Machzor* (a prayer book for festivals) printed ten years later in Sulzbach by Reb Itzak ben Leib, son-in-law of Zalman the Printer, who was evidently still alive. Apparently, Zalman had set up his son-in-law in business, and he began with smaller things, such as prayer books and *Machzorim*.

An important feature of every *sefer* is its *haskamos*—letters by prominent *Gedolim* endorsing its publication. This *Machzor* has a *haskamah* by Rabbi Nasanel Weil, known for his major work, the *Korban Nasanel* on the *Rosh*. Rabbi Nasanel passed away in 5529 (1769), just a year after this Machzor was printed.

I was now fascinated by this family of printers. The *Machzor* showed that Itzak ben Leib also had a printing concern in Furth, a printing center for *seforim* between 1690 and 1868; and sometime later, I picked up a *Reshis Chochmah* printed in Furth in 5523 (1763) by this same Itzak. A note at the end of the *Machzor* announces that Itzak has many other *seforim* for sale at reasonable prices on Alexandrus Street in Sulzbach...All these discoveries, however, were made much later, after my collection had increased.

ᦥ The Fine White Paper of Old

My second important acquisition was a *Rashba*, printed in Furth, Germany in 5511 (1751). It was printed on fine white paper and is in almost perfect condition. Using it is a profound experience. I have a newer *Rashba*, but learning in one that was in existence when the United States was still a British colony heightens my awareness of my link with the past. I was learning in a *sefer* over two hundred years old, while its author lived almost another five hundred years before it was printed!

Another early find was an *Eyin Yaakov* (a compilation of Talmudic Aggados), printed in Amsterdam in 5501 (1741). Unlike present editions with commentaries surrounding the text, this edition places them sequentially. Much to my surprise, I found commentaries from Rabbis David Oppenheimer and Avraham Broda of Frankfurt, which are not in my newer editions of *Eyin Yaakov*.

I also found that the *sefer* consisted of two parts, and that the second portion was printed a year earlier. Particularly interesting were *haskamos* on the second part that were absent in the first portion. Most prominent of these is a *haskamah* by Rabbi Yaakov Yehoshua of Cracow—best known for his *Pnai Yehoshua*. There is also a *haskamah* by Rabbi Eliezer of Amsterdam, author of *Ma'aseh Roke'ach*, who, as the printer notes, was then in the Holy Land. The rest of his story is found in *Shivechei Baal Shem Tov* (p.126). Rabbi Eliezer had gone to the Holy Land especially to meet Rabbi Nachman Horodenker, a prominent disciple of the Baal Shem Tov and grandfather of Rabbi Nachman of Breslov.

Also of Chassidic interest is a Rambam—not nearly as old, but equally fascinating—printed in Berditchev in 5568 (1808), with the *haskamah* of the renowned Rabbi Levi Yitzchak. In his *haskamah* he declares his pleasure that the Rambam is being reprinted in his community, especially since it is using "good paper, black ink, and large, clear type"—no small consideration before these items were mass produced. The print is actually clearer and more readable than my Vilna edition, and I have gotten into the habit of using this older Rambam, especially for the *Mishneh L'Melech*, which is more legible in this older edition.

Having done considerable research into the life of Rabbi Nachman of Breslov, I was delighted to find in this Rambam a *haskamah* from Rabbi David Zvi Orbach of Kremnitz. This *gaon* and *tzaddik* was the father-in-law of Rabbi Nassan of Nemerov, the chief disciple of Rabbi Nachman. Although Rabbi David Zvi had been an important leader in his generation, virtually nothing is known of him today outside of Breslover circles. This *haskamah* is significant to me as the only writing I have ever seen from Rabbi David Zvi; it records that he was important enough for his *haskama* to appear in a Rambam.

⊷§ Detective Work

All these *seforim* were fascinating, but easy to identify. I later came across items that required some detective work, especially so where the title pages were missing.

The first such *sefer* that I acquired looked like a *Gemara* or *Rif* with the text printed in large square Hebrew characters, except that it was surrounded with the *Ma'adanei Yom Tov* and *Divrei Chamudos*, instead of *Rashi* and *Tosafos*. It was obviously a *Rosh*, but with no title page, how could I tell when and where it was printed?

It was definitely pre-1867, the year that the acid process of making paper from wood-pulp was invented, for wood-pulp paper yellows rapidly and becomes brittle. Prior to this, paper was made from rags, and such paper has a distinctive soft feel, retaining its color and strength for hundreds of years. That is why *seforim* hundreds of years old are often in better condition that those printed a few decades ago. This mystery *Rosh* was definitely printed on the older rag paper, and closer examination revealed that it was most probably the handmade paper used in the 1700's.

More important—until 1820 *seforim* were printed completely by hand. It was considered both an art and sacred task, and all involved would print their names on the last page. Fortunately, this signature page was still intact, with the names of the *zetzer* (typesetter) and the *druker* (press operator) signed as living or "now working" in Furth. The first part of the puzzle was unraveled: This *Rosh* had been printed in Furth.

To discover the actual date of publication, I had but to consult Ben Yaakov's *Otzar Haseforim*, a remarkable book listing each edition of every *sefer* printed until 1863. Looking up the *Rosh* and *Maadanei Yom Tov*, I found that the only edition ever published in Furth was printed in 5505 (1745). I now knew exactly which edition I had.

The publisher of this *Rosh* was Zvi Hirsch, son of Reb Chaim of Furth. The copy of the *Rashba* mentioned earlier was printed in Furth in 1751, just six years later, and its publisher was "Chaim son of Zvi Hirsch z'l." During the interim, Reb Zvi Hirsch had passed away, and the publishing house had been taken over by his son Chaim.

⋲§ The "Yom Tov" Puzzler

While delving into this volume, I discovered another interesting fact. The *Ma'adanei Yom Tov* was written by Rabbi Yom Tov Lipman Heller, best known as the author of *Tosefos Yom Tov* on *Mishnayos*. Yet, in his introduction, Rabbi Yom Tov calls his commentary on the *Rosh* "*Ma'adanei Melech*" (not *Ma'adanei Yom Tov*). Behind this name change is an interesting story. The first edition of this commentary was published by the author in Prague in 5388 (1628), but it was denounced by the author's enemies before King Ferdinand II as anti-Christian and anti-government. As a result, in 1745, the Furth publishers feared they would not gain the necessary government permission to print the second edition. They therefore decided to change the title to "*Ma'adanei Yom Tov*," and included a note that no anti-Christian or anti-government sentiments were in the work. This second edition was the one that I had purchased.

The Berlin "Yerushalmi"

A second mystery *sefer* that I obtained was one that had been rebound, and bore the label, "*Talmud Yerushalmi, Seder Nashim*, Berlin." The title page was missing, and there was no signature page at the end of the volume. I was hard pressed to even verify that it had been printed in Berlin.

A quick comparison with my Vilna *Yerushalmi* showed that the two commentaries surrounding the text on the page were the *Korban HaEidah* and the *Shiurei Korban*. In the Vilna *Yerushalmi*, this latter is printed in the back, rather than on the page. In addition, the paper again showed me that his *sefer* was at least two hundred years old.

Carefully examining the volume, I discovered that the binder had inadvertently (?) placed *Nedarim* at the end rather than *Kiddushin*—which should be the last *Mesechta* in the volume. There on the last page of *Kiddushin* was a clear signature of the typesetter and press operator: Yisroel ben Moshe of Breslau, "now engaged in the holy work in Berlin the capital." The *sefer* had indeed been printed in Berlin.

Ben Yaakov reports that the only time the *Yerushalmi* had been printed in Berlin was in 5517 (1757), and that this edition had been published by Rabbi David Frankel, author of the *Korban HaEidah*—then rabbi of Berlin. He was quite wealthy, and had the wherewithal to print his own commentary, this being the edition that I had in hand.

Rabbi David Frankel had originally been rabbi of Dessau, and when he moved to Berlin, he brought along a favorite pupil, Moses Mendelsohn. The differences between master and disciple are remarkable. Today, anyone studying *Yerushalmi* finds the *Korban HaEidah* indispensable, while Mendelsohn's works are all but forgotten. I came across a few ancient copies of his *Bi'ur*; highly controversial in their time, they have not been reprinted for over a century, and are now virtually unconsulted.

Sheimos Hunting

With my new interest in old *seforim*, I sought to add to my collection, but limited funds severely circumscribed my search. I then had a stroke of luck. A few individuals heard of my interest and permitted me to look through their *sheimos*—old *seforim* designated for burial. This was no Cairo Genizah, but if one knows what to look for, fascinating finds can be made.

The first batch of *sheimos* came from the flooded basement of an old *seforim* store, and had been sitting around for years. Many of the *seforim* were mildewed, and as I searched I had to cover my face with a handkerchief to protect my lungs from the dust.

⋖§ An Ancient Nach

My first important find looked like a leather-covered lump of paper. Taking great care not to tear anything. I was able to open the volume, and recognized the book of Joshua, with Rashi, and an old Yiddish commentary. The *sefer* was badly water damaged and the first few pages were missing, but it was clearly very old. By trial and error and with much painful effort I learned to separate the stuck pages without tearing them. It was a tedious process, and for several weeks, whenever I wanted to relax at night, I would separate a few pages.

At the end of the Book of *Melachim* (Kings), I was greeted with a pleasant surprise. The *sefer* had a second title page—not unusual among old *seforim*—with the place and date of publication: Wilhelmsdorf, 5449 (1689). Here in my hands was a *sefer* printed before the Baal Shem Tov was born! Also, the Yiddish commentary, *Hamagid*, which was a compilation of classical commentaries and Midrashim, was written by Rabbi Yaakov ben Yitzchok of Yanov.

Before long, I discovered that the author of *Hamagid*—who had died in 5386 (1626)—also wrote *Tz'enah Ur'enah*, a popular Yiddish commentary on the *Chumash*. His *Hamagid*, following the same style, is on the later books of the Bible. According to Ben Yaakov, the last time this *sefer* was printed was in 5478 (1718), and it is thus virtually unknown today. (I later discovered an abridged edition, published in Kapost in 1818, not mentioned by Ben Yaakov.)

⋖§ The Commentary from Ismir

In another batch of *sheimos* I found what may be my most valuable acquisition. It was folded in half and covered with mildew from years in a damp basement, but it looked promising and I took it home. Carefully straightening out the pages and cleaning off the mildew, I discovered that I had a complete *sefer*, including the title page: *B'nei Chayay*, by Rabbi Chaim Algazi of Ismir, printed in 5477 (1717) in Ortokoi, near Constantinople. It is a commentary on the Four *Turim* (forerunner of our *Shulchan Aruch*), and according to Ben Yaakov, was printed just this one time.

I had never heard of either the *sefer* or its author. Going through the *sefer*, I found that the author frequently quotes as his master Rabbi Chaim Benveniste, author of the *Knesses Hagedolah*. Another of his teachers was Rabbi Shlomo Algazi, who served as chief rabbi of Egypt for forty-eight years.

Rabbi Chaim Algazi was born in Ismir, Turkey, had served as rabbi of Rhodes, and in his old age returned to Ismir as chief rabbi. *B'nei Chayay* was then edited by his granddaughter's husband, Rabbi Aaron Alfandri, author of the *Yad Aaron*. This *sefer* thus opened up an entire chapter in Sephardic Jewish history, and was of special personal interest, since my grandfather was born in Ismir.

‑§ Enter "The Seven Shepherds"

The jewel of my collection is a small *sefer* also found in a *sheimos* sack designated for burial. I had been going through old *siddurim* and pamphlets, when suddenly the unusual square shape of a small *sefer* caught my eye. It was a copy of *Amudeha Shivah* by Rabbi Betzalel Darshan of Slutzk, in almost perfect condition. When I looked at the date, I could hardly believe my eyes: "Prague, 5434 (1674)." This *sefer* was over three hundred years old!

The *sefer* consisted of discussions and *derashos* regarding the "Seven Shepherds": Abraham, Isaac, Jacob, Moses, Aaron, David and Solomon. As with most unfamiliar *seforim*, I first examined the *haskamos*. Most prominent was that of Rabbi David ben Shmuel of Ladmir, the author of the *Turei Zahav* on the *Shulchan Aruch*. Another was from Rabbi Moshe ben Yitzchok of Lublin, son-in-law of the *Maharsha*, and author of the *Mahadura Basra*. One of the printers signed at the end of the volume is Reb Avraham, son of "*Horav HaKadosh*, Rabbi Aaron of Uman.*"

At first I learned little about the author of this small *sefer*. The *haskamos* mentioned that Rabbi Betzalel was from Kobrin, and the *Shem HaGedolim* states that he had written other *seforim*, the most important being *Korban Shabbos*, published in 5451 (1691). Other references mentioned that besides Slutzk, he had been *Maggid* (preacher) in Boskovitz and Premishla. Then I recalled seeing his name in the *Lubavitcher Rabbi's Memoirs* (Vol. 1, p. 208): In his travels, Rabbi Zechariah Yeruchem of Nemerov had visited this very same Rabbi Betzalel! Also prominent in the account are the authors of *haskamos* on this *sefer*, such as Rabbi Zvi Hirsch of Brisk and Rabbi Naftali Hirsch Ginsburg of Pinsk.

My copy of *Amudeha Shivah* was from a second edition, the first having been published in Lublin in 5426 (1666). According to Ben Yaakov, this *sefer* was printed for the third and last time in Dyhernfurth in 5453 (1693). A few phone calls to extensive libraries convinced me that I may well have the only copy of this *sefer* in the United States.

Some people might consider this inconsequential, but there is something very special about owning any *sefer* over 300 years old, even if it were not rare or valuable. We all are aware of how ancient our heritage is, and even the briefest visit to the Holy Land provides one with visible proof of this, stretching back thousands of years. Still, our sages teach us that "hearing is not the same as seeing," and, as in the case of many other things, a constant reminder is most helpful.

I must also emphasise that this relatively rare *sefer* was found in a sack of *sheimos*, consigned for burial. Had I not gone through these *sheimos*, it would have been permanently lost, together with a number of other interesting *seforim*. This should provide an object lesson that before any *sheimos* are buried, they should be gone over by someone familiar with old *seforim*.

Although many of these *seforim* do not have a high monetary value, they form part of our irreplaceable heritage from Europe, a world that no longer exists. Anything buried and lost from this heritage is lost forever.

⋖§ Private Lives

Most interesting about old *seforim* is the private history and lore they reveal. The name of an owner long gone stares up at you, and you wonder who he was, and how the *sefer* passed from hand to hand. Sometimes a string of names is found, as in one *sefer* presented as a gift in 1798, 1845, and again in 1932. Another *sefer* was owned by M.J. Loeb, and the inscription tells us that in 1870 he lived in Beaumont, Texas—just 25 years after Texas had joined the Union. If one had the time, he could spend many hours merely studying the inscriptions in *seforim*.

A striking example is a *Machzor* that I have, printed in Offenbach in 5563 (1803). This *Machzor* belonged to Samson Sichel, and in the back, we find an entire family history. A daughter Miriam was born in 1860, Gittel a year later, and a son, Berman, in 1863. The births of three other sons, Hirsch, Avraham and Yonah, are also noted. Then, in blurry, tear-stained letters, we find the record of the death of three of these children; and later, in happier strokes, the wedding dates of the other three. The last entry was in 1900, when the family apparently was preparing to emigrate to America. One could construct an entire family history from these notes alone.

Compared to some great collections, my accumulation of old *seforim* is not extensive, nor does it contain any really ancient samples. It is not a collection worthy of a great museum or library, but rather one to which an ordinary individual with limited resources can aspire. Before becoming involved with these *seforim*, my library was meant to be learned, and most of my *seforim* were in constant use. These older *seforim* occupy a high shelf, and while occasionally used for learning, they mostly serve as a special inspiration. Somehow, they make the ages in which they were printed and written all the more immediate.

Treasures

S INCE MY FIRST GROPINGS through musty basements, I have found
that there are many people who share my interest in the fascinating
world of antique *seforim*, and that many extraordinary private collections exist. Just two blocks from my house, I found an individual who
has an extensive collection of *seforim* printed over three hundred years
ago. Equally fascinating are the *seforim* stores of Manhattan's Lower East
Side, but with limited funds, serious buying is out of the question.

Nonetheless one can find much of interest—even with very
limited resources—if one's eyes are open. On a "field trip" not too long
ago, my nine-year-old daughter, Avigail, found a *Choshen Mishpat*
printed in Amsterdam in Elul 5458 (1698)—just two weeks before the
Baal Shem Tov was born. Even my six year old son, Michah, found a
first edition of the *Tiferes Yisrael* on the *Mishnah*, perfectly intact,
printed in Hannover in 1830. Very proud of their "finds," the children
have a greater interest in the contents of these *seforim*.

There is a very wide range in people's knowledge of antique
seforim. Experts can, with a single glance, tell where and when a *sefer*
was printed. By contrast, the vast majority of the public has close to no
knowledge whatsoever of the rich history of our *seforim*.

Undoubtedly, this is because almost everything that the average
person needs is currently in print, whereas in the not-too-distant past,
many important *seforim* could be found only in ancient editions.
Nonetheless, an older *sefer* can provide insights not available in newer
editions.

The Jewish Observer—May 1976

✑ An Uncensored Gemara

A good example of this: I recently dug up (quite literally) an old *Gemara Nedarim* from a bin of old *seforim* consigned for burial. The first forty pages were missing, but the type style and the printer's marks indicate that it was probably printed in Amsterdam in 5404 (1644). Since so many editions of the Talmud were printed, it will take more research to verify this date, although it seems likely for a number of reasons.

Most interestingly, this old *Gemara* was not censored. Shortly after the first printing of the Talmud, Christian scholars began to study it for passages they deemed objectionable. They censored these pages from subsequent editions, often deleting entire paragraphs—both from the Talmud itself, and from its commentaries. In addition, before any *sefer* could be published, it was submitted to a censor for approval. Thus, for a long time, the entire tractate of *Avodah Zarah*, which appears to criticize other religions, could not be printed at all.

Most of these deletions were published in a small pamphlet, known as *Chasronos HaShas*. Although the wording of the deletions is provided, they are often difficult to place in proper context. An important example of this is the entire discussion of the Talmudic doctrine that "The law of the government is the law" (*dina demalchusa dina*). In his commentary on *Nedarim* (3:11), the *Rosh* (Rabbi Asher Yechiel) cites the opinion of earlier authorities who sharply limit the scope of this rule. This discussion is very important to a Torah understanding of how to interact with a duly-constituted non-Jewish government, but it is deleted from most editions of the Talmud. Thus, it is not to be found in the Vilna *Shas*, which is the edition now most commonly used and reprinted. But in this ancient fragment of a *Gemara*, the discussion can be found in its entirety.

✑ Four Pages from 1575

For a long time, I would delight in the mere discovery of a *sefer* from the 1600's. Anything earlier seemed to be in the province of libraries, museums, or advanced collectors with unlimited funds. My lucky finds did include items three hundred years old, but this seemed to be the outer limit.

Then once, when sifting through a stack of old covers and loose pages put aside for burial, I came across four strange-looking pages from the Rambam's *Mishneh Torah*. The only commentary on this edition was the *Kessef Mishneh* plus, on one page, the *Maggid Mishneh*. What had happened to all the other commentaries usually printed with the Rambam?

Of the major indices of antique *seforim*, the most important is Ben Yaakov's *Otzar HaSeforim*, which attempts to list every *sefer* printed through 5623 (1863). Another is Chaim Dov Freidberg's *Beis Eked*

Seforim, which is more up-to-date and also provides the number of pages of many editions. This latter feature is often of great help identifying an edition when all else fails.

A quick check of these indices told me that the *Rambam* with only *Kessef Mishneh* had been printed only once—in Venice in the year 5335 (1575). Even during his lifetime, Rabbi Yosef Karo was recognized as a giant among giants. His *Shulchan Aruch* is the accepted code of Jewish Law, and his commentary *Beis Yosef* on the *Tur* is considered among the greatest analytic works on *halachah* (Jewish Law) ever written. He was considered the greatest sage in his generation and people from all over the world sent him questions for his decision.

In his old age, the "*Beis Yosef*" (as he is called) began his last work—the *Kessef Mishneh*, a commentary on the *Rambam*'s monumental *Mishneh Torah*. Although the *Rambam*'s code encompasses the entire body of Talmudic law, he did not cite any sources, and unless one knew the entire Talmud by heart, it was impossible to determine the context from which all of these laws were extracted. An earlier commentary, the *Maggid Mishneh,* was of some help, but it only covered six of the fourteen books of the *Rambam*'s code.

Upon completing the *Kessef Mishneh*, he sent the manuscript to Rabbi Menachem Azariah of Fano, a renowned Kabbalist and author of *Asarah Ma'amoros,* then rabbi of Venice. Since Venice was a great center of Jewish publication, the *Beis Yosef* requested that Rabbi Menachem Azariah see that his commentary was properly printed.

Overjoyed to have the merit of printing a work of the *Gadol HaDor*, the leading figure of his generation, Rabbi Azariah personally paid for its publication. He took it to Bragadini, a prominent printer, and the first volume came out in 5334 (1574). While the *Beis Yosef* lived to see the first three volumes published, the fourth was printed in 5336 (1576), shortly after his death. Thus, incidentally, we are currently celebrating the four hundredth anniversary of the printing of the *Kessef Mishneh*.

Here in my hands, I actually had a few pages of this *Kessef Mishneh*, whose printing had been commissioned by the author himself. Perhaps he had even touched it! Or if not, maybe this copy had been handled by the great Rabbi Menachem Azariah of Fano. To us, people of that generation are legendary. Handling even a piece of paper—a leaf from a book—that was directly associated with them makes their presence all the more real.

⁓§ The Strange Tanach

A few months later, I was searching a Brooklyn *seforim* store, for several items currently out of print. I noticed a pile of old *seforim* in a dusty corner, and never one to miss such an opportunity, looked them over carefully. At the very bottom of the pile was an old *Tanach*, the later Prophets. The cover had been largely eaten away by worms or termites, but the inside was in good shape. It was only lacking the first and last signature (the section of page made from one large printed sheet), making it impossible to identify from the title page or from printer's marks at the end.

In a dark corner, I also found an old copy of the *Mishnas Chassidim*, where the missing first and last page had been filled in by hand. Overcoming the natural trepidation spawned by limited funds, I asked the owner to price these two books. He had to consult his partner and suggested that I call in a few days. When I did, I was pleased to discover that both books would only cost a few dollars. I brought my latest finds home where I could examine them at my leisure.

First, I noticed that the *Tanach* was printed on crisp, firm paper, like that of a dollar bill—the fine linen paper that was used for many early *seforim*. Next, that the pages were not numbered—very significant, since page numbers were introduced to *seforim* in the mid 1500's. Until that time, only signature numbers had been used.

The *Tanach* already appeared to be an interesting and exciting find. To better identify it, I checked the commentaries. The books of Isaiah and the Twelve Minor Prophets contained the commentaries of *Rashi* and *Ibn Ezra*, while Jeremiah and Ezekiel had *Rashi* and the *Radak*. I consulted the standard indices to see when books were printed with these commentaries.

Sure enough, it was the second *Mikra'os Gedolos* ever printed dating back to 5283 (1523)—the first one had been published five years earlier. But more important, it was the first edition of the *Ibn Ezra* on the Prophets ever printed!

◆§ Type and Justification

To verify my findings, I showed the *sefer* to Mr. A.L. Frankel, who, together with his father, David, was once one of the world's most prominent dealers of antique *seforim*. He backed my conclusion, indicating a few distinct features that distinguish the Venetian type styles. This was my first introduction to analysis of type styles, an important tool in dating printed materials.

He also pointed out another feature—the way the lines were justified. In printing terminology, justification simply refers to making the margin even. Lines inevitably vary in their number of letters, and if no effort is made, some would be longer than others. In modern printing, justification is accomplished by varying the space between letters and words. On this page, for instance, the less letters on a line, the greater the space between words. Also, some words are hyphenated and completed on the following line.

In Hebrew, the division of a word at the end of a line is not permitted, making this all the more difficult. In sacred scrolls, justification is accomplished by widening certain letters known as (sic) dilatabiles. In other early manuscripts, however, scribes completed a short line by inserting the first letter from the next line.

Until more sophisticated methods of justification were introduced, early printers adopted this method, squaring off the margin by inserting the first letter from the following line. This is usually a distinct hallmark of the very early *seforim*, since this method of justification was largely discontinued in the mid-1500's. Nonetheless, I recently came across a *Teshuvos Rashba* printed in Vienna, 1812, where this technique was employed.

ᴥ§ Seforim from Venice

Venice is generally not thought of as an important Jewish city, but during the 1500's it was. Around 5269 (1509), German invasions drove many Jewish refugees into Venice. They were too many in number to be expelled, so in 5276 (1516), they were herded into nearby "New Foundry." This had important philological implications, for the Italian expression for "New Foundry" is *Ghetto Nuovo*, and many authorities attribute the word "ghetto" - for a segregated Jewish quarter—to this episode. Yet so many young people today do not even realize that the original ghetto-dwellers were Jews!

During this era, Venice emerged as a prime world center of *seforim* printing—especially due to the activities of Daniel Bomberg. The first edition of the Talmud was printed here, establishing the pagination and style for all subsequent editions. This had special value to me, since this also occurred in 5283 (1532), the very year my *Tanach* was printed.

Seforim are not meant to be museum pieces, but are of greatest value when they are actually used. I therefore make frequent use of this *Tanach*. The paper is highly durable and the print is crisp and clear—much better than any present edition. Once, very late at night, I was looking up something in the *Ibn Ezra*. Before I realized it, I was just turning pages, contemplating all the history that has taken place in the 450 years since this volume was printed:

When it was printed, Rabbi Yosef Karo was still a young man, and had only begun writing his *Beis Yosef* a year earlier. Rabbi Moshe Isserles, the *Rama*, was only three years old. Rabbi Moshe Cordevero (the *Ramak*), dean of the Safed school of *Kabbalah*, was only a year old. Neither the *Ari* nor Rabbi Chaim Vital had even been born. The great population shifts that moved the center of Judaism from the Mediterranean lands to Eastern Europe were just beginning.

Turning the pages, I could almost see the years flying by. Who had held this volume? Had it been in the hands of the *Radbaz*, the *Maharal*, or the *Shach*? Was it in the library of Rabbi Eliahu Mizrachi or the *Shelah*? Had the Alshich or the *Metzudos David* made use of it while writing their commentaries? The very possibilities seemed to forge a physical link with these giants.

Of course, there was no direct evidence of such contact. The only name that I found in the volume was that of Yosef ben Yaakov Vega, whom I am still trying to identify.

⮊ The Incunabulum

Meanwhile, I had not devoted much attention to the other volume, even though it had some interesting features. It was obviously a copy of the *Mishnas Chassidim*, a Kabbalistic text by Rabbi Emanuel Chai Rikki, containing the commentary *Mafte'ach Olomos* by Rabbi Moshe of Dragatshein. Even though it had no title page, time and place were easy to ascertain, since the only edition was printed in Zalkiev in 5505 (1745).

The first and last signatures were missing, and had been replaced by handwritten pages—the only available means then for replacing missing leaves. Judging from the paper and writing style, the handwritten pages were inserted in the late 1700's.

In addition, a small manuscript, containing several chapters from the *Sefer Gilgulim*, was bound at the beginning of the book. The writer noted that he copied these chapters from an edition of *Sefer Gilgulim* printed in Frankfurt-Am-Main in 5444 (1684). Obviously, the book was out of print, and writing by hand was his only means of obtaining a copy. The next edition of the *Gilgulim* was printed in Zalkiev in 5534 (1774), so it can be assumed that the manuscript was written before then.

Even though the practice is forbidden, binders often used leaves from old *seforim* in binding newer volumes. In this case, the binder had used two leaves from a *Mishnayos Nega'im* as end papers, the papers attaching the book to its cover. Initially, I did not pay them much heed, but one evening I examined these end-papers more closely, and immediately realized that the leaves contained parts of the *Mishnah* with the *Rambam's* commentary—and nothing else. But when had the *Mishnah* been printed with nothing but the *Rambam's* commentary? A quick look at the indices gave the answer: Naples in 5252 (1492) and Venice in 5306 (1546). But which one was it?

This was raising exciting possibilities. If it was the Naples edition, it was not only from the first edition of the *Mishnah* ever published, but it was also an *incunabulum*. Incunabulum refers to a book printed before 1500, and to collectors, these are the rarest and most valuable items. This is true of books in general, but since so many *seforim* were destroyed in persecutions and pogroms, Hebrew incunabula are particularly rare.

Before I could properly examine these two leaves, I had to remove them from the covers. Very carefully, I removed the covers and soaked them in a large pan, meticulously separating the paper from the cover boards. Laying paper towels under the leaves so that they would not tear, I gingerly lifted them from the pan. There before me were two intact leaves, in good condition, containing the eighth, ninth and tenth chapters of *Nega'im*.

How was I to determine from which edition they had come? Then it struck me: In the margin of my big "Yachin U'Boaz" Mishnayos, there were Chilufey Girsa'os—variant readings. Two of the most important editions cited were those of Naples and Venice. I would only have to see which one fitted my copy.

Carefully checking the variant readings, I found that my copy conformed exactly to the readings of the Naples edition. It was indeed an incunabulum: two leaves from a sefer printed in 1492, the year best known for the discovery of America and the expulsion from Spain. As an added coincidence, I discovered this incunabulum on Columbus Day!

◌ More on the Leaves

My first information regarding this edition came from the introduction to the "Yachin U'Boaz," that there were only ten known copies of this Mishnayos in existence. Further information came from David Frankel's catalogue of "Hebrew Incunabula," itself a rarity that I had found among some sheimos. Here I found that this edition had been the last sefer printed in Naples by Joshua Solomon Soncino, completed on May 8, 1492. Since many anti-Christian sections—omitted or changed in later editions—are contained in their complete form in this edition, it was subject to particular attack. I also discovered that only two copies of this rarest edition of the Mishnah are known to exist in the United States, and these in major libraries.

Owning one kindled in me an interest in Hebrew incunabula in general. The first book had been printed by Guttenberg around 1455, and just twenty years later, the first Hebrew book, a Chumash with Rashi, was printed in Reggio, Italy. The very next Hebrew text to be printed—a year later—was the Tur, which in those years—before the Beis Yosef—served as the most popular code of Jewish Law. By 1500, close to a hundred different books had been printed.

The invention of the printing press may well have been the hashgachah (Divine governance's) measure for perpetuating the mesorah after the dispersal of the thriving Jewish community from Spain in 1492...Similarly, some have pointed out that the introduction of the photo-offset process in the 1940's was a Divine measure for replacing the millions of sacred volumes that were destroyed in World War II, and could never have been reprinted by conventional means.

In all the world, only a thousand examples of Hebrew incunabula are known to exist—that is, approximately ten copies of each sefer printed. The rest were either worn out and buried, or destroyed in the periodic book burnings, characteristic of those times. Among surviving incunabula, most are now in major libraries or museums, with only a handful still in private hands.

✑ Open Eyes

All this demonstrates that for one who keeps his eyes open, there are still many treasures to be found, even without spending much money. Such treasures are often unidentified and are buried as *sheimos*...lost forever.

This is not only true of *seforim* hundreds of years old, but even of those printed a generation or two ago. Many such *seforim*, printed in Europe, are still in use in synagogues and private libraries, but as they become worn, a good number are being buried. How long will it be before a *sefer* printed in Vilna in 1890 will also be considered a rare treasure? It is something that comes from a world that no longer exists, and once it is gone, it is gone forever.

I would encourage young people who are building *seforim* collections to include some older editions, if only to preserve them for future generations. Providing a tangible link to the giants of the past, these *seforim* will be objects that our children and grandchildren will treasure.

Rabbi Yaakov Culi, זצ״ל

"IT MAKES YOU FEEL LIKE becoming a better Jew."
    This was the first reaction of a friend after examining several chapters of *MeAm Loez*, which I had recently begun to translate into English. His words did not surprise me. While working on the book, I too had felt tugs at my heartstrings, and I found myself saying blessings with more feeling, being just a bit more careful of my religious obligations. The *sefer* is indeed like a magnet, drawing a person closer to Torah.

    For close to two hundred years, *MeAm Loez* enjoyed unparalleled popularity among the common folk of Sephardic Jewry. A large and expensive set was often given as a gift to a new son-in-law, much as a *Shas* (set of the Talmud) is today. In many synagogues, the regular evening Torah-study session between *Minchah* and *Maariv* centered on this book, and a number of groups were formed for the express purpose of studying it. It is said that Rabbi Chaim Medini, famous as the author of the encyclopedic work *Sedei Chemed*, would join such groups, so greatly did he value its wisdom.

    Nowadays *MeAm Loez* in Hebrew has become a popular Bar-Mitzvah gift. Nevertheless, many yeshivah students seem to shun it, as part of a common prejudice against anything written in the vernacular—for the *MeAm Loez* was originally written in Ladino.

    True enough, this work was specifically written for the common man. Far from talking down to the common man, however, the author uplifts the reader with a rich anthology of Torah thought from the Talmud, Midrash, *Zohar*, halachic literature, and philosophy, together with in-depth discussions and analysis.

The Jewish Observer—April 1977

◆§ The Author

The author of *MeAm Loez*, Rabbi Yaakov Culi, had enjoyed a reputation as one of the giants of his generation. He was born in Jerusalem in 1689 to Rabbi Machir Culi (1638-1728), a well-known scholar and saint who was a scion of one of the leading Jewish families of Crete (Candai). Crete had belonged to Venice, but in 1645, the Turks invaded this island, and laid siege to its capital and chief cities. This siege lasted for twenty-five years, one of the longest in modern history, and resulted in almost two hundred thousand casualties.

When the Turks were finally victorious in 1669, the island's economy was in shambles, with the Jews suffering most of all. Fleeing with his remaining wealth, Rabbi Machir eventually settled in Jerusalem around 1688. Here he found a city of scholars, boasting such luminaries as Rabbi Chezkiel di Silva (author of *Pri Chadash*) and Rabbi Ephraim Navon (author of *Machaneh Ephraim*). Leading the community was Rabbi Moshe Galanti, who had been appointed as the first Rishon LeTzion, Chief Rabbi of the Sephardic Jews, in 1668. Rabbi Machir was drawn to another prominent sage, Rabbi Moshe ibn Chabib, and soon married his daughter.

Their first son, Yaakov, was born in 1689, a time of great upheaval in Jerusalem. It began with one of the worst famines in memory, causing many to flee to other locales. A second, even more severe blow to the Jewish community was the death of the illustrious Rabbi Moshe Galanti. This Torah giant had been an undisputed leader for twenty years, and his passing left a great void in the community. His place was filled by Rabbi Yaakov's maternal grandfather, Rabbi Moshe ibn Chabib.

◆§ His Grandfather's Legacy

As a child, Rabbi Yaakov showed great promise, rapidly gaining reputation as a prodigy. He was raised on his grandfather's knee, and by his sixth year, was questioning some of his Talmudic interpretations. Although he was only seven when Rabbi Moshe ibn Chabib died, the memory of his grandfather deeply impressed him for the rest of his life.

A year later, tragedy struck again, when his mother died. His father soon remarried and the family moved to Hebron, and then to Safed. Here the young genius advanced rapidly in his studies, and began the major task of editing his grandfather's numerous writings. Probing his father and other local rabbis for information, he became aware of the gigantic stature of Rabbi Moshe ibn Chabib.

Among the things that he learned was that his grandfather had been born in Salonica in 1654, descending from a famed family with origins in Spain. Among his ancestors were Rabbi Yosef Chabiba (circa 1400)—the author of the *Nimukei Yosef*, and Rabbi Yaakov ibn Chabib

(1459-1516—the author of the *Eyin Yaakov*). His grandfather had lived in Constantinople for a while, and then came to Jerusalem at the age of sixteen. In 1688, when but thiry-four, he was appointed head of the great Yeshivah founded by Moshe ibn Yeush, a philanthropist friend from Constantinople. When Rabbi Moshe ibn Chabib died at forty-two, he had already earned a reputation as one of the greatest sages of his time.

◀§ The Constantinople Venture

Rabbi Yaakov was determined to publish his grandfather's works. Since adequate printing facilities did not exist in the Holy Land at the time, he went to Constantinople, where he had hoped to find financial backing for this task. He arrived in the capital of the Ottoman empire in 1714.

A sensitive young man of twenty-four, Rabbi Yaakov was aghast at conditions in Constantinople. True, the city had many sages who toiled day and night to uplift the community, as well as a great Kolel (institute of advanced study), known as the Hesger, but in general, community life was sinking. Constantinople had been a center of Shabbatai Tzvi's false Messianic movement, and more than any other city, it had suffered from this heretical spirit. Jewish education was virtually nonexistent, and most of the populace was barely literate in Hebrew. People did attend synagogues, but beyond this, Jewish life was on the verge of total disintegration.

Winning support from a Chaim Alfandri, he began work on his grandfather's classical work *Get Pashut*, a profound treatment of the extremely complex laws governing Jewish divorce (see "A Get in Monsey," elsewhere in this volume). This was finally printed by Yitzchak Alfandri, a relative of Chaim, in 1719 in Ortokoi, a suburb of Constantinople. (The only other *sefer* I know published in Ortokoi is *Bnei Chayay*, in 1717. This is described in "Gateway to the Past," elsewhere in this volume.)

◀§ Disciple of the "Mishneh LaMelech"

At this time, the undisputed leader of Sephardic Jewry was Constantinople's Chief Rabbi, Rabbi Yehudah Rosanes (1658-1727). He learned of the brilliant scholar who had come to town, and before long, had appointed him to his *Beis Din* (rabbinical court)—no mean accomplishment for so young a man. Rabbi Yaakov Culi soon became the prime disciple of this leader of world Jewry.

Rabbi Yaakov had just finished printing his grandfather's *Shemos BeAretz*, when tragedy struck the Jewish community. His great master, Rabbi Yehudah Rosanes, passed away on 22 Nisan (April 13), 1727. During the mourning period, the sage's house was looted, and a number of his manuscripts were stolen. The rest were left in a shambles, scattered all over the house. Assuming authority rare for a man his age, Rabbi Yaakov Culi undertook the responsibility of reassembling these important writings and editing them for publication.

During the first year, he completed work on *Perashas Derachim* a collection of Rabbi Yehudah's homilies. In his introduction to this book, Rabbi Yaakov Culi mourns the loss of his great master...But his main work had just begun: Rabbi Yehudah had left one of the most significant commentaries ever written on the Rambam's *Mishneh Torah*, the monumental *Mishneh LaMelech*.

Rabbi Yaakov spent three years carefully assembling and editing this manuscript. Contemporary scholars struggle through the lengthy, profound sequences of logic found in this commentary; to be sure, the editor was in perfect command of every one of these discussions. Where certain points were ambiguous, or where additional explanations were required, Rabbi Yaakov added his own comments in brackets. In 1731, the work was completed and printed as a separate volume. Just eight years later, it was reprinted with the *Mishneh Torah*—below the *Rambam's* text, on the same page—one of a half dozen commentaries accorded this singular distinction.

Today, the *Mishneh LaMelech* is included in all major editions of the *Rambam's* code. Studying it, one also sees Rabbi Yaakov Culi's bracketed commentaries and notes. At the beginning of every printed *Rambam*, one can find his introduction to this work. Thus, at the age of forty, he had already won renown as a leading scholar of his time.

⋰§ His Own Life Work

Having completed the publication of the works of both his grandfather and his master, Rabbi Yaakov began to search for a project that would be his own life work. There is no question that he could have chosen to write the most profound scholarly work, joining the ranks of so many of his contemporaries. Instead, he decided to write a commentary on the Torah for the unlettered Jew. As he writes in his preface: This might strike many of his colleagues as strange. Why would he, a scholar of the first water, write a work for the masses? Surely one of his stature should address himself to the scholarly community! But apparently he was otherwise motivated: How could he engage in scholarship when he saw Jewish life disintegrating all around him? How could he close his eyes to the thousands of souls crying out for access to the Torah?

⋰§ Ladino — The Language of his Work

As his vehicle of expression, Rabbi Yaakov chose Ladino, the common language spoken by Sephardic Jews. Ladino is to Spanish as Yiddish is to German. Written with Hebrew letters, it looks very strange to the untrained eye; but with a little experience and a good Spanish dictionary—it rapidly becomes comprehensible.*

Ladino was developed among the Jews of Spain. As long as the Jewish community flourished there, Ladino was written with the Spanish alphabet, with a liberal sprinkling of Hebrew thrown in. It was not very different from the language used in much of today's Torah literature, where Hebrew is intermingled with English.

After the Jews were expelled from Spain, they gradually dropped use of the Spanish alphabet, and began writing it with Hebrew letters, which they knew from their prayers. At first there was no literature in this language; it was used primarily in correspondence and business records. The first books in Ladino appeared in Constantinople—a translation of the Psalms in 1540, and one of the Torah in 1547. A few years later, the first original work was published in this language, *Regimiento de la Vida* (Regimen of Life) by Rabbi Moshe Almosnino.

While a few other classics, such as *Chovos HaLevavos* (Duties of the Heart) and the *Shulchan Aruch* had been translated into Ladino, the amount of Torah literature available to those who did not understand Hebrew was extremely sparse. It was this vacuum that Rabbi Yaakov Culi decided to fill. As he points out, even such major works as the Rambam's commentary on the *Mishnah*, and Saadiah Gaon's *Emunos VeDeyos* (Doctrines and Beliefs) had been written in Arabic, the vernacular in their time. But no work of this scope had ever been attempted in the vernacular.

◆§ The Scope of MeAm Loez

What Rabbi Yaakov had planned was nothing less than a commentary on the entire Bible, explaining it from countless approaches. Where the Scripture touched on practical application of the Law, it would be discussed in length, with all pertinent details needed for its proper fulfillment. Thus, for example, when dealing with the verse "Be fruitful and multiply," the author devotes some fifty pages to a discussion of the laws of marriage, including one of the clearest elucidations of the rules of family purity ever published in any language.

Then, as now, considerable money could be gained in publishing a successful book. Here the saintliness of the author comes to the fore. In a written contract, he specified that all the profits realized from sales of the book were to be distributed to the yeshivos in the Holy Land, as well as the Hesger Kolel in Constantinople. He would only retain for

---

*In my own efforts to translate *MeAm Loez*, I found the Hebrew, itself a translation from the Ladino, unwieldy—every ambiguity seems multiplied tenfold. Struggling with the Ladino original was far more fruitful, and with a little experience, the words started to take form. Thus, ג׳ודיזמו, a very strange and foreign-looking word when sounded out, was the Spanish word for nothing more strange than Judaism.

Another expression that took me by surprise, סיניור דיל מונדו, when sounded out, yielded *Senor del Mondo*—"Master of the Universe."

himself the standard commission given to charity collectors.

The work was originally planned to consist of seven volumes, encompassing all the books of the Bible. In the two years that the author worked on it, he completed all of the book of Genesis (*Bereshis*), and two-thirds of Exodus (*Shemos*), a total of over eleven hundred large printed pages. (In the current Hebrew translation, this fills over 1800 pages.) Then, at the age of 42, on 19 Av (August 9), 1732, Rabbi Yaakov Culi passed away, leaving his work unfinished.

The contemporary Sephardic sages saw the strong positive effect *MeAm Loez* was having on the community, and thus sought others to complete the work. Rabbi Yaakov had left over voluminous notes, and these would be incorporated into the continuation. The first one to take on this task was Rabbi Yitzchak Magriso, who completed Exodus in 1746, Leviticus in 1753, and Numbers in 1764. Deuteronomy was finished by Rabbi Yitzchak Bechor Agruiti in 1772. These latter sages followed Rabbi Culi's style so closely that the entire set can be considered a single integral work.

Never before had a work achieved such instant popularity. But even greater than its popularity was its impact. Thousands of readers who had been almost totally irreligious suddenly started to become observant. A new spirit swept through Sephardic communities, similar to that engendered by the Chassidic movement upon Ashkenazic Jewry a half century later. Very few *sefarim* in modern times have had such a great impact on their milieu.

⊷§ Reprints and Translations

The *MeAm Loez* was reprinted at least eight times, in cities around the Mediterranean region. The volumes were so heavily used that few copies of the older editions are existent—they were literally worn out, just like a *Siddur* or a *Chumash*. An Arabic translation published under the name of *Pis'shagen HaKasav*, was prepared by Rabbi Avraham Lersi, and was published in various cities in North Africa between 1886 and 1904. An edition of *Bereshis*, transliterated into Spanish letters, was published in 1967 by the Ibn Tibbon Institute at the University of Granada, Spain.

Although this was one of the most popular volumes in Sephardic countries, it had been virtually unknown to Ashkenazim, who generally do not read Ladino. With the destruction of most Ladino speaking communities in World War II, the number of people who could read the *MeAm Loez* in the original diminished. Translation of the entire set into Hebrew in the late 1960's finally brought it to the attention of the contemporary Torah world. Although the original name of the *sefer* was *MeAm Loez*, in the Hebrew edition, the word "*Yalkut*" (Anthology) was added. One reason for this was the fact that certain portions, which the translator felt were not pertinent to our times, were omitted.

In naming his work, Rabbi Yaakov Culi based the title on the verse, "When the Jews went out of Egypt, the house of Jacob from a strange-speaking people (*MeAm Loez*), Yehudah became His holy one, Israel His kingdom" (Psalms 114:1). Through the medium of this book, he had hoped that his people would emerge from the shackles of ignorance. Yehudah in his own reference alludes to Yehudah Mizrach, a Constantinople philanthropist, who underwrote the costs of the printing of the first edition. His reference to the last phrase in this verse was then meant to be a prayer that his work would bring Israel to once again become part of "His kingdom."

He succeeded, perhaps beyond his fondest dreams. A half century after his death, Rabbi Chaim Yosef David Azulai (the *Chida*) wrote of him, "He was expert in the Talmud, codes and commentaries, as we can readily see from his book *MeAm Loez*, which he wrote to bring merit to the multitudes. Fortunate is his portion."

Battle for Survival

R AMBAM, RABBI YOSEF KARO (who wrote the *Shulchan Aruch*), Rabbi Isaac Luria (the Ari-Zal, leading 16th Century Kabbalist)—these
are the towering names in Judaism's glorious heritage...names in which
all of Jewry takes deepest pride. All were Sephardim.

Today, Sephardic Jewry is threatened with extinction—not just
cultural extinction as Sephardim, but total extinction as Jews. Yet, little
of our information, discussion and concern focuses on this segment of
Jewry. In Israel, where the majority of its citizens come from Sephardic
and Arab lands, the awareness is somewhat sharper, and there are active programs aimed at maintaining the Jewish fidelity of the Sephardim, some geared more specifically for the preservation of the Sephardic heritage.

Hundreds of thousands of Sephardic Jews live outside of *Eretz
Yisrael*, many of them recently uprooted from old communities where
they had been secure in their Jewish heritage. Today, they flounder
without fast anchorage in the values of their past.

Teaching Sephardic children should be a very distinct undertaking. First, their rich Sephardic heritage of *minhagim* (customs) and
Torah leadership are to be perpetuated. In addition, the Sephardic
temperament should be taken into account. This can mean preserving
a *t'mimus* (wholesomeness) that has flourished for centuries without
being exposed to the more corrosive elements of Western culture. It
can also mean taking into account the capacity of Sephardim for ex-

The Jewish Observer—January 1975

treme reaction to an encounter with Western "sophistication" and mores—witness the Black Panther movement in Israel today.

A network of schools especially geared for Sephardic children has existed since 1944, and it is now being extended to accommodating them in new surroundings. This article is a survey of the Ozar Hatorah network.

~§ The Old Pattern

Since the latter part of the 19th century, the only widespread education system serving youth in Sephardic lands was secular, under the auspices of the Alliance Israelite Universelle. Organized in 1860, one of AIU's aims was to set up training programs for backward Jewish communities. The emphasis was on secular education and French culture, with little regard for religious or Jewish education—with the net result that the process of assimilation was hastened.

For the most part, the world Jewish community seemed hardly aware of these communities; and members of the indigenous leadership, having completed their studies in France, sincerely believed that the road to salvation lay in cultural assimilation, looking upon Jewish religious studies as something of the past. Thus, Casablanca, for example, had a Jewish population of 80,000 in the early forties, but no community school. Funds were not lacking, but no one devoted time and effort to organize such schools. In various degrees, this same pattern prevailed thoughout North Africa and Asia Minor.

~§ The Founders

Viewing this situation, a group of dedicated laymen met under the leadership of Mr. Isaac Shalom, of blessed memory, a well-known Syrian born manufacturer in New York City, who was a magnanimous contributor to all Torah causes, Ashkenazi and Sephardi alike; and Mr. Joseph Shamah of Israel. They were later joined by Mr. Ezra Tuebal of Buenos Aires, originally from Aleppo, Syria. These men acted on the initiative of Reb Shraga Feivel Mendlowitz, of blessed memory, who is known as the guiding hand behind the growth of Torah in the United States, through Mesifta Torah Vodaath (which he led for decades), Torah Umesorah (which he founded), as well as numerous other institutions. Mr. Mendlowitz (as he insisted on being called) urged Mr. Shalom to recreate in Sephardic lands the Torah Umesorah plan of establishing a Torah Day School in every American community. Mr. Shalom and company recognized the need for immediate action and set about creating a cohesive network of schools without counterpart in America, by virtue of central funding and control.

An initial $400,000 was raised, primarily by Isaac Shalom and Ezra Tuebal. An office was opened in Jerusalem, and large sums were allocated to assist existing educational institutions, especially primary religious schools. After the establishment of the State of Israel, twenty-nine schools were opened there by the organization, but when the Israeli government assumed responsibility for most primary education, and Chinuch Atzmai emerged as custodian of most of the religious schooling, Ozar Hatorah closed its operations in the Holy Land.

Iran

The first country outside of Israel where Ozar Hatorah set up schools was Iran, where 80,000 Jews lived. Most of these lived in spiritual and physical poverty, cut off from the centers of Jewish learning for many generations, and with little knowledge of the basic principles of Judaism. Local religious leadership had been virtually wiped out (in pogroms in the 19th century) and surviving leaders had shockingly little Jewish knowledge. Study of Talmud had been forgotten, and it was doubtful if a single fully qualified rabbi existed in the entire country.

The ignorance of the average Jew was abysmal. In the city of Meshed, for example, the entire Jewish community of 20,000 went underground and officially became devout Moslems. Only in the 20th century, when the late Shah reinstated religious liberty, did they openly return to Judaism, but with no knowledge of what it was all about. Other communities were not much different. The Alliance Israelite Universelle had set up schools in the main centers and in some small towns, but only half an hour per day was devoted to teaching prayers, and then only in primary grades.

Ozar Hatorah appointed Rabbi Isaac Lewi as director of its Iran operation. He traveled extensively throughout the country, visiting small towns and villages. Wherever he could find someone who knew Hebrew, he opened a school, using whatever accommodations were available, no matter how primitive or unsuitable. An arrangement was also made with the AIU, whereby Ozar Hatorah would provide ten hours per week of Jewish education in all AIU primary schools, maintaining responsibility for both teachers and curriculum. This arrangement is still in effect.

When it became obvious that the Torah education of Iran would require more funds than Ozar Hatorah could provide, the American Joint Distribution Committee was approached for a subsidy. JDC opened its own office in Teheran, providing a general assistance program which included school lunches, medical aid, and a substantial education subsidy.

Today, Ozar Hatorah maintains a network of forty schools in Iran, servicing 8600 pupils. A yeshivah teachers' training school in Shiraz has graduates in Ozar Hatorah schools across Iran. The Jewish population of Iran remains stable at around 80,000 due to a high living standard and the enlightened attitude of the Shah, with no trend toward emigration. Assimilation has to some degree been halted by the work of Ozar Hatorah, and the spirit of Jewish consciousness in Iran has to a large degree been revitalized.

❧ Libya and Syria

Tripoli, Libya, had a Jewish population of 29,000 at the end of World War II, but only a few hundred pupils attended the religious schools, and the study of Torah had all but ceased. After the war, Yeshivah Neve Shalom was opened through the efforts of the chief rabbi of Tripoli, and the student body grew to eighty. A teachers' seminary was also founded, and Ozar Hatorah sent teachers from Israel to provide intensive courses. Jewish soldiers stationed there during the war had also organized a Hebrew School, but it was now faced with many problems, primarily a shortage of funding and staff. Ozar Hatorah sent teachers from Israel, and also assisted with part of the budget.

With the raising of Jewish consciousness in Tripoli, the entire community immigrated to Israel in 1950-51. No youth remained behind, and Ozar Hatorah closed its Tripoli operation.

The founders of Ozar Hatorah were born in Syria, and with its post-war Jewish population of 14,000, this became an important base of operations. Two primary schools are still operating in Damascus and Aleppo, with 350 pupils each. In 1971 the Damascus school was singled out by the governmental education department as the school with the highest marks—all pupils tested passed final primary school examinations with honors.

❧ Morocco

Morocco was very different from Iran when Ozar Hatorah began operations there in 1947. Far from being indifferent to religious education and tradition, the majority of Moroccan Jews were fully conscious of their heritage, and proud of the influence of Moroccan Jewry when Fez (Fas) was a center of Talmudic scholarship—serving as the base of the *Rif* (Rabbi Yitzchak Al-Fasi) and the *Rambam*. Up until the 19th century, this tradition of Jewish learning remained strong.

Since the 1890's, the French Alliance Israelite Universelle has been providing education geared to the needs of the contemporary labor market. Young Moroccan Jews obtained sufficient French education to become white collar workers and bank clerks, but very little Jewish education. Virtually nothing was done to qualify new rabbinical leaders to replace the learned rabbis of previous generations, and schools of higher Jewish learning existed only in Marrakesh, Menkes, and Sefrou. Meanwhile, thousands of Jewish children had no education at all, secular or religious, and roamed the streets, dirty, ill-fed and unhealthy.

Nonetheless, the majority of Moroccan Jews remained true to their heritage, and when Ozar Hatorah entered the area, they responded enthusiastically. Within a short time, committees were formed in most Jewish communities, with a central coordinating body in Casablanca. Existing Talmud Torahs and Yeshivos were given financial assistance and new ones were created. Here too, the Joint Distribution Committee gradually took over a major portion of the financial burden.

The creation of the State of Israel brought about a change in the Moroccan Jewish community. Although not especially harassed, many of its members looked towards a better life in Israel, and by 1966, some 100,000 had emigrated. Thousands more went to France, looking for a better economic future. Despite this massive emigration, however, the number of students in Ozar Hatorah schools has increased.

Today, the situation in Morocco is fairly stable. Ozar Hatorah currently maintains 23 schools there, and out of a total Jewish population of 32,000, some three thousand students, or 60% of the school-age population, attend these schools.

ـۃ France

Today, France presents one of the great educational challenges confronting World Jewry. Unlike Iran, Syria and Morocco the situation in France is not at all stable. The intermarriage rate in France is over 60%—as high as 80% in smaller communities—and at the present rate, the Jewish community can become extinct within two generations. An intensive identity-through-education program is urgent.

ـۃ The French Past

France has one of the oldest Jewish communities in Europe, and was famed as a seat of Jewish learning during the time of Rashi and the Tosafists. The community suffered a significant decline over the centuries as a result of the Crusades, persecution, and plague; and during World War II, over 90,000 French Jews perished in the death chambers, leaving a post-war population of 150,000.

Over the past fifteen years, this relatively small population has been inundated by almost half a million North African Jews, mostly from Algeria and Tunisia, with a sprinkling from Morocco, Libya and Egypt. Educated in French, and with the same rights as overseas French citizens, these "Pieds Noirs" ("black feet," a French term usually applied to the descendants of French settlers in North Africa), as they were called, settled mainly in the Paris area, Lyons, Marseilles, Nice and Toulouse, completely altering the Jewish complexion of these communities. Many settled in communities in southern France where no communal structure had ever existed.

Among these immigrants the situation is particularly appalling. Of some 120,000 Jewish school children between six and sixteen, only some 4,000 attend Jewish schools. Many of these immigrants do not comprehend the relevance of their Jewish heritage, and are overwhelmed by the advanced, sophisticated non-Jewish environment that they encounter. The indigenous Jewish community feared that the massive new influx of immigrants would lead to new anti-Semitism. This, in turn, led the older community to strive even harder to assimilate, as well as to disassociate itself from the newcomers.

The French Jewish leadership that did work to help found their efforts unequal to the situation; the immigrants outnumbered the natives three to one. Many local communities were largely assimilated and made little effort to preserve the Jewish identity of the refugee chldren. The Fonde Sociale, the old established official body that looks after Jewish interests and is entrusted with Jewish education, suffers from a lack of funds, since the lion's share of money raised goes to Israel, with only a small fraction returned to the French community.

Assimilation is so rampant that a process that took four generations in America is taking place in a single generation among these immigrants. Most were religious when they came to France, and the majority still maintain *kashrus, taharas hamishpachah* and synagogue attendance, but observance is rapidly waning, with Sabbath observance the first thing to go. The generation gap is enormous, and many children who intermarry have parents who strictly adhere to the tenets of Judaism.

Even though the immigrants are Sephardim, they get along very well with their Ashkenazic counterparts, and in many ways, those who are religious have succeeded in vitalizing Jewish life in France. In many areas, they are the most insistent in demanding religious institutions, Hebrew schools, and kosher meat. Thus, in Montmartre, Paris, there are currently over thirty kosher butcher shops which cater mainly to the Sephardic immigrants. And even though most immigrants are lower-middle or working class and state schools are free, they pay comparatively high tuition fees to send their children to Jewish schools.

Thus, even though the situation is critical, fertile ground does exist for spreading Torah education. The immigrants do respond with great interest, encouragement and commitment. Even teachers are available, trained both in Morocco and France. What is lacking, however, is seed money and people to get things started.

Ozar Hatorah came into France in 1961, opening its first school in Lyons. Since then, its program has expanded dramatically, and it currently runs twelve schools in France, with an enrollment of 1400—double that of last year. Half of its maintenance budget of $1.2 million is raised by the French community, with the rest provided by Ozar Hatorah. Still, the number of schools is inadequate, and a number of important communities have no schools at all.

Thus, for example, Nice had a population of 20,000 Jews, mostly from North Africa. Yet, it was not until 1971 that this community opened a kindergarten, primary school, and Talmudic Studies Center, with the help of Ozar Hatorah. The effect was so dramatic that one of the parents, who had a thriving law practice, decided to close his office and devote his full time to Torah study.

Marseilles had a population of 80,000 Sephardic Jews, but no communal center, and only a small Akiba School run by the Jewish Agency. A Mr. Philip Cohen bought a house, surrounded by a large tract of land, with borrowed money, and established a Kollel with ten married men. Soon a kindergarten and primary school were also started. When two large organizations paid off his debts, he borrowed more money to start a secondary school. The skeleton of a four-story building has been completed for this purpose, but $400,000 is needed before it can be completed.

Sarcelles, a Paris suburb, has 2000 Jewish families, who recently purchased a large tract of land to build four school buildings at a cost of $1.5 million. The first structure should start going up imminently.

As the number of secondary school graduates increases so does the need for higher Jewish education. There are a handful of yeshivos in France, and many Ozar Hatorah graduates go on to higher Torah study. There is also a school for women teachers in Strasbourg, and plans exist for a school for male teachers as well. One of the most interesting yeshivos is run by Rabbi Eliahu Abithol, especially set up for post-graduate university students. There are currently 40 students in this three year course, many who are graduate students in medicine, mathematics, law and other disciplines.

For most university students, the situation in France is considerably worse than here in the United States. A delegation of 500 students from the University of Nice recently came to the heads of the community, complaining about the total lack of Jewish facilities on campus, and asking for at least a Jewish canteen. This, however, only highlights the lack of Jewish facilities for university students outside of Paris, since there is no official organization to meet their needs. Montpellier, a university town with 1200 Jewish students, has neither kosher food nor a center for spiritual guidance. The same is true of Grenoble, another important university town.

The four thousand students currently attending Jewish school represent the French Jewish community's main hope for the future. Still, they represent less than two-thirds of one percent of the total Jewish population, and less than three percent of the school age populace. A tenfold increase would be needed to guarantee survival, and much more if the community is to flourish and grow. If nothing is done, *chas veshalom*, we may witness the demise of the entire French speaking Jewish community, once one of the most vital segments of world Jewry. This is a responsibility that cannot be taken lightly.

☙ Future Plans

Among the future plans of Ozar Hatorah is the opening of a network of schools throughout North and South America. With more than half a million Jews, schools are still severely lacking in South America, and much effort is necessary if assimilation is to be abated. Montreal has over 50,000 Moroccan Jews, yet it has but one school for them with less than 200 students, and even this is insufficiently supported. In many Western Hemisphere communities funds are available, and all that is needed is organization and people to coordinate the effort.

Our sages teach us that all Jews are responsible for each other. As long as the spiritual life of any Jew is in jeopardy, none of us can be at ease.

Key 73 and
The Vulnerable Jew

U NTIL RECENTLY, CHRISTIAN MISSIONARY activity directed toward Jews was almost a joke. We were aware of their efforts and the materials that they were distributing, but we were also aware that almost all of it ended in the trashcan. In those days, the total number of conversions numbered less than a dozen annually, and in the entire country there could not have been more than a few score *meshumadim* (apostates) calling themselves "Jewish Christians."

In the past two years, however, this situation has changed radically. Almost everyone is now aware of the missionaries' remarkable and disturbing progress. They have been making significant inroads on the Jewish collegiate scene, and converts now number in the thousands. What was once a disturbing joke is now a cause for much concern within the Jewish community.

A far cry from the seedy naive approach of previous decades, these modern missionaries are now launching a slick, hip campaign. They offer brochures and pamphlets that are strictly "with it." They have begun a concentrated campaign through the media, and have found a generation of value-hungry Jewish youth ready to swallow their bait. Millions of dollars are presently being expended in this effort.

The Jewish Observer—June 1973

✑ Key 73

Although not directed especially at Jews, Key 73 raises a major point of concern in the Jewish community. It is active on a national scale, launched with a major television special, and has a mass appeal that is bound to reach a large number of Jews of all ages. There is no question that this will strengthen existing missionary activity, and provide an atmosphere where more and more of our youth are exposed to Christian doctrines. In order to appreciate the problem, it is important to understand the history, purpose, and scope of Key 73.

Key 73 has been called one of the most ambitious projects in the modern history of Christianity, aiming at overwhelming the United States and Canada with the Christian message. It is supported by most major Protestant denominations, as well as a good number of Catholic dioceses.

✑ The Scope

The planned scope of Key 73 includes programs of Bible study, public prayer, door-to-door visits by Christians to their nonbelieving neighbors, and similar activities. It is projected that these programs will be carried out on the local level by some 200,000 Christian congregations. The national Key 73 headquarters in St. Louis is meanwhile putting together films and brochures, as well as radio, television and newspaper advertisements, promoting the cause of Christianity. All this is being financed by a fund-raising drive that is expected to raise several million dollars.

✑ The Genesis

Key 73 grew out of a 1967 editorial in *Christianity Today*, which called upon all Christians to pool their efforts to promote the faith. Billy Graham and other prominent ministers were struck by the idea, and held a meeting in Washington, D.C. to discuss it. They picked 1973 as the earliest practical target year.

An offshoot of this was the Christian Consciousness Revival, held two years ago in Dallas, Texas, and attended by some 75,000 young people. A number of top evangelists met and set a goal of Christianizing both America and the world within ten years. A great deal of attention was directed toward the Jews, and millions of dollars were pledged toward missionary activities in this direction. This was the birthplace of many missionary activities directed toward the Jews.

These missionary groups are not spontaneous uprisings. They are part of a well-financed, well-organized *shmad* effort. Worse yet, they have been notoriously successful.

⊰§ The Vulnerable Jew

At no time in history has the young Jew been as vulnerable to the enticements of Christian missionaries as at the present.

To begin with, the Jewish collegiate is the victim of an educational system that has utterly failed to teach him Judaism as a viable lifestyle. As a rule, his Jewish education consisted mostly of history and language, totally lacking in insights into the depths of Torah and *hashkafah* (religious philosophy). In discussing their Jewish education, most collegiates look back at it as a totally negative experience. Too many of our educators seem totally unable to communicate a sense of meaningfulness, relevancy, and excitement in their teaching of Judaism. In the non-Orthodox community the problem has assumed overwhelming proportions, but even our own synagogue schools are guilty of failing to impart to our children any deep understanding of Torah and *Yiddishkeit*.

Not finding any ideological outlet in Judaism, the contemporary Jewish youth has turned to other avenues. He has become active in every new cause, whether it was civil rights, the free speech movement, anti-war protests, Black Panther rallies, Biafra or Bangladesh. He has experimented widely with grass, hash and acid. He shuttled from one cause to the next, from one fad to another. He is a child of his generation, desperately seeking roots and searching for meaning in life. He feels exhausted and alone, yearning for something that will make life worth living.

We find our Jewish youth flocking to dozens of disciplines and creeds. They are found in the ranks of Hindu consciousness, transcendental meditation, Zen, Subud and Yoga. Beyond these, they have explored the entire landscape of pop therapies and enthusiasms. Desperately searching youth are ready to turn every passing idea into an object of faith. The *Whole Earth Catalogue*, tarot cards and the *I Ching* all have served as fundamental texts for our deluded Jewish youth.

All of these expressions indicate a profound need for religious values and experience. Of these, the "new" Christianity has been the most recent, popular and obvious expression of this need.

⊰§ The Appeal of Christianity

All these disciplines and creeds tend to satisfy our youth's driving need for certainty, purity and involvement transcending the self. Christianity has become more popular than the others because it provides all this and more. The missionaries come bearing instantaneous, push-button forgiveness of sin, and an apparent end to all guilt and self-disgust. They offer companionship in a lonely world and authority in a society that has become progressively more rootless and permissive. They can explain and justify present suffering in simplistic terms, and at the same time, offer the hope that good will triumph. Lulled in the bosom of Christianity, a confused boy or girl can once again become an innocent child.

Beyond this, Christianity has also been made a very enticing part of the youth culture. Plays and movies such as *Superstar* and *Godspell* contain themes with which Jewish youth can easily identify. Songs explicating Christian values, once the fare of Sunday morning church programs, now find their way into the Top 40. Almost subliminally, these values have become part of our youth culture, leaving our rootless youth particularly vulnerable to the message of the missionaries.

◆§ "Judaism? — We Did it Already!"

The ultimate tragedy is that many of these youths will search everywhere for an answer except in Judaism. They feel that they know about Judaism—they have gone to Hebrew School—and they feel no compulsion to re-explore it. The picture that they have been given of Judaism is so negative in their eyes that it is not even worth considering.

A prominent Jewish thinker once suggested that much of our alienation problem would be solved if all our Hebrew Schools and Talmud Torahs were shut down. This would at least leave our youth with the opportunity to search for *Yiddishkeit*. While I would not advocate anything quite so radical, our ideas concerning Jewish education—especially on the non-Yeshivah level—certainly need a major overhaul.

We find our youth yearning increasingly for the transcendental. But what efforts have been made to teach our children the transcendental elements of Judaism? How much stress is placed on *Hashem* as the basis of our religion? How much is taught about the spiritual nature of the *mitzvos*?

Our youth are overburdened with feelings of guilt and alienation. But what percent of our curricula deal with the fundamental concepts of *teshuvah*? How much emphasis is placed on the profound differences between Judaism as a lifestyle and that of middle-class America? How much is taught about *kedushah* and *taharah* (sanctity and purity)? Unfortunately, the very elements sought most by our youth are often dismissed by our educators as being "too religious."

Judaism obviously does have the answers. Every believing Jew knows this. Judaism and Torah have provided us with meaning and depth for more than three thousand years in every possible culture, and have been eminently successful in meeting myriad challenges. But unless we can communicate this to our youth, they will remain increasingly vulnerable to the efforts of the missionaries—and worse.

The Iceberg

Although the missionary problem is very grave, it is merely the tip of the iceberg. True, it is a very dramatic problem and we are losing thousands of our youth to these missionaries. Yet, for every young boy or girl that converts to Christianity, there are over a hundred lost to Judaism in any number of other ways. An alarming and growing majority of our youth is being claimed by intermarriage, assimilation and general alienation. When reports tell us that eighty percent of our youth never go to synagogue, even on Rosh Hashanah and Yom Kippur, something is dramatically wrong. When we find that almost half of our youth are intermarrying, then we know that we are faced with a problem of awesome dimensions. The missionaries exist but they are only a small facet of this problem.

In some ways the missionary movement and Key 73 might ultimately be good for the Jewish community. Undeniably, those whom we lose represent an irrevocable tragedy. Nonetheless, even evil will contain an element of good and can further *Hashem's* goals. And the missionary movement can have a positive aspect if it awakens us to the larger problem facing the Jewish community.

Our situation is not unlike the person who is ill but unaware of it—even when he learns that all is not well, he delays seeking treatment. But when symptoms get worse and pain sets in, he seeks a physician. The symptoms may be most painful, but when they force the individual to seek treatment, they may ultimately save his life.

There is absolutely no question that American Jewry is mortally sick, dying a slow death, and very few of us are doing anything about it. Of course, *Yiddishkeit* is flourishing in some communities, but this represents but a miniscule percentage of the total Jewish population. The rest of American Jewry is almost terminally ill, while the religious community continues its business as if nothing unusual were happening.

Suddenly we find ourselves suffering unbearable pain—witnessing Jewish boys and girls converting to Christianity. Should this evil push us to try to cure the disease, then it may also prove to be a blessing in disguise. If we start seeking a cure, then there may be hope for Jewry as a whole.

Diagnosis: Domination of the Inauthentic

The first step, of course, is to carefully diagnose the disease, of which *shmad* is only one symptom. The blurring of lines between authentic Judaism and spurious innovations represents a larger and more serious aspect of this disease. Our youth can all too readily see through the sham of non-authentic ideologies sold under the banner of Judaism, and they then tend to dismiss the authentic together with the spurious. We must reject this falsehood, and make it clear that there is only one authentic Torah Judaism, and that it alone offers meaning and purpose in the truest sense of the word.

◆§ Isolation of the Torah Community

Another aspect of the disease has been the isolation of the Torah community and its indifference to the plight of American Jewry at large. The general feeling was, "As long as my own children go to yeshivah—as long as they grow up to be *shomrei mitzvos*—then everything is all right." There were some concerned groups, such as NCSY and Lubavitch, but they represented only a very small portion of Torah Jewry's resources. It was only when we began to feel the threat to our children that we have begun to react.

It is sad but true that we have not been our brothers' keepers. There are many detailed laws, stemming from *mitzvos* of Torah origin, directing us to speak up when we see others going astray. It is time that we began to study and know these *dinim*. The *Gemara* tells us that when the *Beis Hamikdash* was destroyed, even the most righteous of men were killed because they made no effort to lead their brethren to the true path. The Rambam comments that *Hashem* had promised that they would survive, and that this was the only time that He ever annulled a good decree. The point is that our responsibilities extend beyond our doorsteps.

Recently, such *gedolim* as Rabbi Moshe Feinstein and Rabbi Gedaliah Schorr spoke out, saying that even yeshivah students should devote some time in helping bring others back to *Yiddishkeit*. In the case of yeshivah students a *heter* is needed to permit them to take time from their sacred studies toward this end. But those not immersed in Torah study certainly have always had the obligation to be concerned for the uncommitted. Every one of us must find his way of responding to the unspoken cry for help that is in the hearts if not on the lips of our estranged brothers.

◆§ Judaism Without Religion?

In many ways, the missionary problem affords us a unique opportunity to teach Judaism as a religion. In the past, those advocating the religious aspects of Judaism often represented an uncomfortably small minority in the total Jewish community. The vast majority found their area of concern in Zionism, social action, and fund raising. Many young Jews were never given any opportunity whatsoever to confront Judaism as a religion.

The missionaries, however, are selling religion, and can therefore only be fought with religious truth. At a recent meeting, a prominent

Reform leader declared that only the Orthodox can effectively combat the missionaries. The students attracted to the missionaries are those who have an interest in religion. Only the truths of Judaism can provide a potent antidote.

Our anti-missionary activities may therefore force many students to confront their Jewishness for the first time in a purely religious light. We are prompting a most basic question from them. While declaring that their being Jewish is directly opposed to Christianity, we leave one question unanswered: What does being Jewish favor?

↝ Attacking the Cause by Strengthening Jewish Awareness

It is obvious that any success on the part of the missionaries is closely related to the widespread intellectual and spiritual paucity on the part of our youth. We must move to reverse these trends, especially through educational youth programs. Our leaders must encourage Jews of all ages to seek a broader and deeper understanding of our great Torah teachings, imbibing a new Jewish awareness. This cannot be a mere intellectual exercise, and much more is needed than logical proof and demonstrations. The missionaries do not try to appeal to logic. They are quite aware of the holes in their arguments. But they are very skilled in the use of experiential involvement and emotional appeal.

↝ Judaism: Feel It and Think It

We must counteract this with an experiential involvement and emotional appeal for Judaism. This, of course, must be combined with an intellectual approach. The study of Torah is one of the most important doors to Judaism, and it is intellectually both logical and stimulating. But another very important approach is to allow students to "taste and see" what true Judaism is all about.

The two most successful organizations in reaching out to uncommitted Jewish youth have been NCSY and Lubavitch. These organizations have brought literally thousands of teen-agers and collegiates back to *Yiddishkeit*. It is interesting to note, however, that they both share the same basic approach. They do not just "speak" about *Shabbos* and *davening*. They take students and expose them to a *Shabbos*, allow them to participate in real *davening*, give them a feeling of the intrinsic beauty of Judaism. Given this with a little sound *hashkafah*, a surprising number of our youth suddenly discover Judaism as a live option.

Another important element that both these groups share is peer influence. It is good and well for a rabbi or teacher to preach about Torah and *Yiddishkeit*, but our youth must also see it exercised as a live option by their contemporaries. It is truly amazing what can result when one places a non-committed young Jew in contact with his religious peers in a controlled atmosphere. For many, seeing their contemporaries turned on to *Yiddishkeit* is a startling revelation, and it is usually *more effective* than the best rabbi or teacher.

Another effective program involves inviting youngsters to spend Shabbos and holidays in religious homes. This gives them the opportunity to view Judaism as a lifestyle that is both appealing and meaningful; and it gives the guests an opportunity to formulate a mental image or goal of how they will conduct their own adult lives in the future. This is something that can be instituted in many synagogues with a minimum of expense and effort. A good example of such a program exists in Hartford, where several dozen homes are regularly opened to college students, with remarkable success.

In general, every Jewish community will have to make its own appraisal of the challenges posed by missionary activity. Alienation, however, is a universal problem, and must be faced as such. Each community must do what it can, taking its own unique problems and resources into account.

⊷§ Fighting the Missionaries: Limitations

When confronted with missionaries engaged in their work, we must be careful not to overreact. It is very alarming to hear reports of individual conversions, but we have no evidence that the missionaries are having an overwhelming impact on our Jewish youth. As mentioned earlier, it is more a part of the gloomy overall picture of Jewish alienation. On the other hand, we must also realize that every Jewish soul is infinitely precious, and that no effort should be spared to stop the work of the missionaries.

Stopping the missionaries, however, is no easy task. They are both dedicated and obstinate. In some cases, strong-arm tactics have been successful, but there is always the danger of *Chilul Hashem*. These very strong-arm tactics often give the missionaries ammunition in declaring that Judaism is morally and spiritually bankrupt.

We must also keep in mind the *din* that it is forbidden to engage a Jewish *apikorus* or apostate in debate. It can be very tempting to try to beat the missionaries at their own game of Biblical "proof." We must, however, remember that this is *their* game. Missionaries are often closed-minded fanatics. They are trained to respond to arguments with pat, almost memorized answers. If they cannot handle an objection, they will deflect it by raising another point, and still another. Even when you win, you often lose.

Missionaries often try to engage Jews in debates, especially where they find a public forum. Most of these missionaries spend months training for such debates. They know the passages from the Prophets used for their "proofs" much better than most yeshivah graduates, even though their overall knowledge of Scripture may be meager. If one is not especially trained in this field, he may find himself totally at a loss in dispelling these "proofs." There are several excellent publications, such as the *Otzar Vikuchim*, which utterly refute all their arguments and claims, but even these are best used by trained personnel, and then, only where there is a genuine possibility that a convert may be won back to Judaism.

It is very important not to publicly attack or abuse these missionaries. They relish the aura of martyrdom that this gives them, and often use it to their own advantage. In general, their style is likely to be cool and friendly. It is best to respond in kind, displaying a firm, calm and secure conviction of one's faith in Judaism.

ঙ The Direct Confrontation

There is always the question of what to do when directly confronted with the problem of conversion. What does one do when confronted by a Jew who has converted to Christianity? How should one react? How can one help?

Where feasible it is best to contact organizations actively involved with this problem. They have personnel trained to deal with converts, and have an excellent record of success. Very often, they are able to turn a *meshumad* around and make him into an observant Torah-Jew. Although the names and addresses of these organizations cannot be publicized in print, they can be reached through any of our major national Orthodox organizations.

There are times, however, when one cannot make use of these organizations. One might then find himself in a position where he can have a positive influence on a *meshumad*, and there are several points that should be remembered. As long as there is a definite chance to win him back, we have the obligation to try.

The first thing to do when placed in such a situation is to gain an understanding of the issues involved. There is some good material available from such organizations as NCSY, and it can often be used to good advantage.

The *din* states that one should not engage a *meshumad* in debates, and on a practical level, this has been found to be excellent advice. Such debates most often only serve to harden the convert's position and make the gap all the more difficult to bridge. The best thing to do is to politely hear him out, and let him talk until he gets it out of his system. The only verbal response to the argument need be "*Ani maamin be'emunah shleimah*—I believe in Judaism with perfect faith," and express personal concern. Most *meshumadim* are hungry for friendship, and will readily respond to a warm approach.

In speaking of people such as these, the Rambam tells us that we must "draw them with words of peace, until they return to the strength of the Torah." He does not advise us to engage in debates or arguments. The experience of most groups engaged in anti-missionary activity has demonstrated the wisdom of the Rambam's advice and has shown it to be the most successful approach.

Where a major problem exists, communities should set up their own anti-missionary task forces. There is a small band of professionals that is able to set up training programs in this area. Here again, these can most readily be contacted through our national Orthodox organizations.

Another area where our national organizations can help is in the generation of study materials. Some anti-missionary material is now available, but there is need for much more. As we learn by experience, we must update these materials and make them reflect our increased sophistication in dealing with this problem.

Even more important is the necessity for materials explaining the basics of Judaism. The best way to counterattack the missionary effort is by stressing the positive values of Judaism. Here again, good materials are needed, and only too few exist today. It might be a good idea to renew the "Jewish Pocket Book" concept, with the widest possible distribution. Our national organizations can be of great help in financing, publishing and distributing such materials.

❧ Summary

The American Jewish Community is facing a great crisis, an important symptom of which is the current missionary problem. Unless some action is taken, we stand to lose as much as ninety percent of our youth in the next two generations. Even the most ardent Torah Judaism will find difficulty in thriving in an environment where the majority of Jews are totally alienated from their roots. With the exception of maintaining our Yeshivos and Bais Yaakovs, this problem deserves the highest priority in the Jewish community.

Who Shall Render

the Decisions?

IN A YISSACHAR-ZEVULUN relationship, one person supports another who is devoting his time and energies to Torah study, thereby gaining a share in the merit of the scholar's sacred endeavors. A number of businessmen have been putting this concept into practice on a fairly large scale, involving Torah scholars totally immersed in some of the most difficult areas of Torah study. The story of the formation of one such group and the course it is charting is a fascinating one.

⋅§ The Piecework Drop-Out

It began six years ago. A successful investment broker, whom we shall refer to as "Mr. Zeb," had set aside time each morning for personal Torah study with Yochanan, a young man whom he knew as one of the most promising young scholars in a nearby *kolel*. One morning, Mr. Zeb found Yochanan somewhat fatigued—even his mind, usually sharp as a razor, seemed dull. Mr. Zeb chose not to comment, but when the situation persisted for a week or two, he inquired if anything was amiss.

Yochanan shrugged off the question, but when Mr. Zeb pressed the point, he admitted that he had taken a part-time job, from 4 to 9 each evening, doing piecework. His family had expanded, and without some extra income, he simply could not survive.

Piecework! Mr. Zeb was aghast. This young man, a most promising Torah scholar—possibly a future *gadol* (Torah giant)—was forced to take time off from his Torah studies to do piecework! How much longer

The Jewish Observer—June 1978

would Yochanan be able to continue his studies at all, at this rate?—And if he entered the business world, what a loss this would be!

"How much do you need?" asked Mr. Zeb.

"With an extra $80 a week, we could get by." Nothing further was said at that session.

That night, Mr. Zeb could not sleep. For the lack of a miserable $80 a week, the Jewish people stood in danger of losing a potential leader...a mere $4000 a year. Perhaps he could even take the money out of his own pocket. Business had been good that year...but a $4000 bite out of an individual's income is still a major sum.—Yet, how could he just sit by and do nothing?

At that time, Mr. Zeb's eldest daughter was entering her teens. In not too many years she would marry. One of Mr. Zeb's fondest dreams was that her husband would be a *talmid chacham* (Torah scholar) who would continue studying after their wedding. It would be his greatest pleasure to support his son-in-law while he studied Torah. Somehow, the money would be there.

But that would be years hence. The *kolel* man's problem was right now. What if he strained his finances and took the $4000 a year out of his pocket? The bite would hurt, but wouldn't it be worth it? Was his present-day responsibility toward *Klal Yisrael* (the entire Jewish people) any less than his future responsibility toward the man, still unbeknown to him, whom his daughter would someday marry?

By morning, he had made up his mind. After his session with Yochanan, Mr. Zeb asked, "If I were to give you the $80 each week, would you be able to study full-time without interruption?"

The young man was flustered. "But you're my friend! How could I ever take money from you? I know your business is good, but you're not *that* wealthy. I couldn't take such a favor from you."

"I'm not *giving* you anything. Think of yourself as having a highly successful business, and I want to buy in. What you'll be giving me is much more valuable than what I'll be paying. If anything, you'll be doing me a favor.

"Some men," Mr. Zeb continued, "are willing to place their money in a bank and merely let it draw interest. I was never like that. Whenever I had extra money, I always looked for a business deal where I had a direct hand in earning my profits. I try to give generously to important charities, but this is just putting money in the bank. My partnership with you will give me a chance to have a direct hand in the 'business,' and allow me to grow with you."

Reluctantly, Yochanan agreed, and a classical Yissachar-Zevulun partnership was formed. During the initial few months, the $80 a week was not that easy for Mr. Zeb to provide. Luxuries to which his family had grown accustomed had to be foregone, and when business was slow, the pinch actually hurt. But then, inexorably, his business began to improve. Before long, his income had increased so that the $4000 a year had been more than adequately replaced.

⊷ Moshe — the "Milkman"

At this time, Moshe, another of Mr. Zeb's friends, was also experiencing financial problems in *kolel*. His family was also growing, and he too needed additional income.

Moshe learned of a milk route that in two or three hours per day could yield just enough, while allowing him to spend most of his time at study. Then another offer came: a major Brooklyn yeshivah would engage him as a *maggid shiur* (lecturer) to older students. It was tempting, since it would allow him to remain in the Torah world full-time.

Moshe consulted a prominent Chassidic leader who knew him well. He advised the milk route: "I know your capabilities. You have great promise as a scholar. If you take the milk route, you will spend the rest of the day studying Torah at your present high level. But if you take the yeshiva job, you will remain a teacher. Teaching Torah is important but your gifts demand something else from you."

Moshe took the milk route. A few weeks later, Mr. Zeb bumped into Moshe delivering his milk. Mr. Zeb was shocked. That a superior scholar should be forced to take off several hours from his study to deliver milk was a major tragedy in Mr. Zeb's eyes...Before long, Moshe joined Yochanan as Mr. Zeb's second partner.

⊷ The Crucial Years

Our sages teach that when one expends money for any charity, including support for Torah study, Providence pays it back with interest. This is the only area in which it is even permissible to test God. Mr. Zeb had drawn his business partner into his Torah investments, and the results became a concrete example of this principle. The business was now expending over $10,000 a year in support of Torah scholars, and at the same time, their business had so expanded that they were ready to increase their obligations further.

"Everytime we made a business deal," Mr. Zeb explained, "we had our Torah partners in mind. If a deal would prove unsuccessful, not only would we be losing money—we might, Heaven forbid, also be losing Torah."

And the dividends grew for both Mr. Zeb and an expanding group of Yissachars, making a marked difference to them during the most crucial years in an individual's advancement toward greatness.

Most yeshivah students terminate their formal studies in their early twenties, usually when they get married. A small proportion of the total yeshivah population continues in *kolel* after marriage, some studying into their late twenties. By then, the pressures of supporting a family usually impel them to seek other means of livelihood. Thus, very few students can practically afford to study Torah full-time into their thirties and beyond.

Our sages teach that out of every thousand students who enter the *beis Hamidrash*, one will emerge as a true Torah leader. The other thousand are by no means unimportant. They provide leadership on many levels—as yeshivah lecturers, teachers, rabbis, scribes, and often as businessmen who support Torah. But out of the *elef* (thousand), there is always the *echad*—the one who can be expected to become one of the unique Torah leaders of all Jewry.

The knowledge and insight that this *echad* must develop are so vast as to defy simple description. Whereas a person can develop into an appreciable Torah scholar by his early thirties, the true leader must remain totally immersed in Torah for many more years, perhaps until he is well into his forties, or even later. His education is an investment that all Jewry must make if it is to have future Torah leadership.

The Chofetz Chaim (Rabbi Yisroel Meir Kagan) was the leading Torah sage of the early part of this century. It is well-known that he did not enter the public arena until the last thirty years of his life, when he was well into his sixties. He merited living past ninety, and during his last thirty years, in addition to guiding world Jewry through several major crises, he also wrote some of the most important Torah classics.

The Chazon Ish (Rabbi Avraham Yeshayah Karelitz) was once asked, "Wouldn't it have been better for the Chofetz Chaim to have begun his public life earlier? Just think how much more he could have accomplished!"

Replied the Chazon Ish, "Had he begun earlier, he would never have been the Chofetz Chaim. The pressures of public life would have prevented him from developing into the Torah giant that could provide true leadership."

One *gadol* explained, "The recent cataclysm of *Churban Europe* almost destroyed the body of the Jewish people. Until now, our job has been primarily to rebuild the body. This has been done by the many yeshivos, girls' Torah schools and *kolelim* that have been built. But now we must rebuild the head. We must provide for future Torah leaders."

◆§ A Desperate Need

When Mr. Zeb embarked on his career of aiding young *kolel* men, he had no particular goal in mind. But a number of events were to help crystallize his goals. One of his neighbors was involved in an important *din Torah*, and wanted the case to be adjudicated strictly according to Torah law, as set forth in *Choshen Mishpat*, the section of the *Shulchan Aruch* (Code of Jewish Law) dealing with monetary laws. After approaching a number of prominent rabbis, he discovered that he could not find one sufficiently expert in *Choshen Mishpat* willing to decide the case on its purely legal merits. (There were, of course, men who could, but they were either without the time or the energy required to engage in the protracted litigation that such a case would involve.)

Mr. Zeb then learned about a meeting attended by Rabbi Moshe

Feinstein and a number of other prominent *Roshei Yeshivah* (yeshivah heads). During the session, Reb Moshe remarked, "People are constantly asking me questions. My phone rings every five minutes. In time, I would like to turn over the phone to someone else. Please provide me with someone."

The report of Rabbi Feinstein's words made a profound impression on Mr. Zeb, and he discussed the problem with other prominent Torah figures. A Torah giant such as Rabbi Feinstein is constantly called upon to make decisions that can determine the course of Judaism for generations to come. Despite his advanced years, Reb Moshe was handling a load that would stagger many a younger man. But he was also concerned about decisions yet to be made. Where were the young men currently being trained to take the reins?—To whom could he "turn over the phone"?

A Torah leader deals with many areas of Torah scholarship, and all are important. Among them is the work of the *poseik*—the authority on Jewish law—who is equipped to apply Torah principles to practical cases. Only he can determine the Torah's answers to the myriad halachic questions confronting each generation. While many young Torah scholars do have expertise in various areas of Torah law, a true *poseik* must have thorough knowledge of all four parts of the *Shulchan Aruch*, as well as the Responsa—the huge body of case law that has developed around its every paragraph in the course of centuries. Rare is the young man so equipped.

ᴈᵹ Helping the Process

As these concepts were presented to Mr. Zeb, an idea began taking shape in his mind: At times, the natural process by which the One emerges from the Thousand needs prompting and support. In fact, it is sometimes necessary to use extraordinary means to stimulate the end-result—to produce the outstanding Rosh Yeshivah, *poseik*, or authoritative scholar that would have emerged on his own in a more leisurely era. Mr. Zeb decided to concentrate on preparing *poskim*.

Discussions with *rabbanim* had revealed that a young man, who had already obtained *semichah* (rabbinical ordination on portions of *Yoreh De'ah*, one section of the Codes), could complete the rest of the *Shulchan Aruch* in depth in approximately ten years. By the end of that period, he would be qualified to render opinions in every area of Jewish law. During these ten years, the young man would have to be totally free of all financial worries. This meant paying him considerably more than the usual *kolel* stipend, approximating the salary of a better-paying teaching job.

Mr. Zeb discussed the idea with several business associates, and he found two colleagues, each willing to support a young man for ten years. With the other man who already was his partner, they formed a nucleus of four. Thus, the *Mechon HaHora'ah* was born.

This was a serious undertaking, not an enterprise for mere dilettantes. Young men taken into the Mechon—all *musmachim* (ordained), with the highest recommendations from their Roshei Yeshivah—were required to sign a written agreement to spend ten years in Torah study, and to complete all four sections of the *Shulchan Aruch* in this time. Periodic examinations, both written and oral, would be given to measure their proficiency. Fellows of the Mechon would also have to write *teshuvos* (responsa) on test problems, so as to gain practical experience in rendering decisions.

During a recent visit to the Mechon, I found eight young men studying, in pairs, so involved in *Choshen Mishpat* that they hardly noticed my entry. They were well into the second section, an extremely difficult area of Torah litigation (*To'an Ve'nitan*). Mr. Zeb showed me the written examination that the young men had recently completed on the previous section, on *Halva'ah* (loans). It is highly unlikely that many people other than the members of that small group of Torah scholars could pass such a test...Eventually, they will be equipped to decide future *dinei Torah* (litigations) either by strict interpretation of the law or binding arbitration, whichever the contestants specify.

✑ The Holy Land's Needs

Having successfully established the Mechon in the United States, Mr. Zeb turned his efforts to the Holy Land. There was a pragmatic reason for this: the lower cost of living in Israel would permit the same amount of money to go much further than in the United States. And the need in Israel was certainly equally great.

In one area it may even be greater. While there are a number of Ashkenazic Torah leaders, the ranks of the Sephardic Torah leadership have dwindled almost to the vanishing point. Of the Sephardic authorities extant, many work for the Israeli government as part of the *Rabbanut*, and religion and politics do make for an uneasy mixture.

The raw material is there, for there are many brilliant Sephardic students enrolled in Israel's yeshivos and *kolelim*. But these budding leaders are without the wherewithal to study for the many years needed for them to blossom. Again, by prodding his business associates, Mr. Zeb was able to find enough Zevuluns to support fourteen Sephardic Yissachars.

Most important, these young Sephardim are maintaining the purity of their heritage. Many Sephardic scholars who study in Ashkenazic institutions find their Sephardic Torah heritage washed away in their Ashkenazic surroundings. Deeply involved in the works of the major Sephardic *poskim*, the group in Jerusalem shows promise of providing the leadership to lift their communities to the Torah heights for which they were once famed.

❧ The Broker's Office

After seeing the Mechon, I visited Mr. Zeb's relatively modest office, where the Mechon's paper work is done, eliminating overhead expenses. "I don't want to run an institution," explained Mr. Zeb. "I am nothing more than a Torah broker. I try to match people with Torah capability with business men who will support them."

Although the Mechon has avoided publicity, its activities are becoming known in the Torah world. The Mechon is giving its *kolel* men a structured program with a definite goal: if they excel in their studies, they will have a specific role to play in meeting the needs of *Klal Yisrael*. The mere existence of such a place has therefore raised the sights of many Torah scholars. Several institutions are contemplating emulating its approach, although each will be putting stress on a different area of greatness in Torah. In fact, one relatively new *kolel* has set up a format for its members to complete *Shas* (the entire Talmud) in depth over a given number of years.

❧ Points West

Who knows from where future Torah leadership may come? Mr. Zeb was recently visiting the Hebrew Institute of California, in Santa Clara, a yeshivah for late-starters. The yeshivah dean told him of "Nesanel," who had begun his studies just two years earlier, and was obviously a boy of rare caliber, quick comprehension and excellent retention.

But now the boy had a practical problem. His father demanded that he leave his Torah studies for a college career. This was not a matter of ideology with the father, but merely a question of how his son would support himself if he intends to devote himself full-time to Torah study.

Mr. Zeb did something that he had never before done. He gave Nesanel a conditional contract: If after he marries he will obtain *semichah* and otherwise meet the qualifications, he would give him a ten-year contract as a fellow of the Mechon. With the document in hand, Nesanel was able to convince his father to allow him to continue his full-time Torah studies.

❧ The Institutes of Advanced Study

The secular world has its Institute for Advanced Study in Princeton, renowned as the place where Einstein was able to work undisturbed. At the Princeton Institute, the world's leading scholars grow without having to compete in the market place. The secular world realizes that intellectual leadership is essential to a nation's survival. This concept should be all the more obvious to *Klal Yisrael*, for Torah study is the very life-staff of our people, and Torah knowledge provides the primary source of guidance.

Before World War II, there were literally hundreds of Torah giants, often unsung, scattered in communities across Europe. In his relentless pursuit of the Final Solution, Hitler destroyed metropolises and *shtetlach*—their rabbis and teachers, guides and *poskim*, yeshivos and *shtieblach*. Now the contemporary Jewish community is in the process of developing a new generation of Torah giants of its own.

If a person would have provided the financial support for the Chofetz Chaim or Chazon Ish to become what they did, imagine his merit! But there are people today who may be providing the means for the emergence of the Chofetz Chaims and Chazon Ishs of the future.

A Time for Action

❧ The Priority

FIRST CORRECT YOURSELF, and then correct others (*Sanhedrin* 18a). It is indeed a great *mitzvah* to bring others close to Torah. First, however, one must strengthen his own commitment to Torah.

Yeshivah years are a time when one must concentrate on self-improvement. During one's youth, one must make Torah study his full-time occupation, striving for greatness in Torah. Even traits generally considered negative, such as envy, must be harnessed to further one's growth in Torah, as the *Gemara* advises: "Envy among scribes increases wisdom" (*Baba Basra* 21a). Like King David, his cry must be "My soul thirsts for You" (*Tehillim* 63:2). This must supersede all other involvements. Only after one has developed his own powers in Torah can one assume responsibility for others.

This sequence is reflected in our prayers, when we ask God to give us the power "to learn and to teach." First we must learn, then we can teach others.

Today, however, a crisis situation exists, and it is most acute. While there were times when we could keep ourselves distant from forces of darkness, they are now closing in, even threatening the most sheltered communities of those loyal to Torah. In addition, many people estranged from Torah are searching for the truth of Torah. These are exceptional times. We must therefore examine our accepted priorities to determine who is to be charged with the responsibility of battling to better our situation and under what conditions.

The following essay is based on a call to action issued by Hagaon Harav Moshe Feinstein, Shlita, to Yeshivah students. The Jewish Observer—June 1973

✍ Prerequisites: Accepting Authority of the Torah Leadership

The first step in this examination is the establishment of guidelines. Rules must be strictly adhered to, even when bringing people close to Torah, and unless one follows them, he can do more damage than good.

The most basic rule is to follow the directives of our Torah leadership, especially in the area of *kiruv rechokim* (reaching out to those estranged from *Yiddishkeit*) where there is always a temptation and rationalization to compromise and to make concessions. While every discipline has its experts, and people generally recognize that one can only succeed if he follows their advice, in *kiruv rechokim* there are too many self-styled experts, who believe that they know more than *Gedolei Torah*. Too often, their ideas can accomplish more harm than good. Worse yet, they consider such matters outside the expertise of our Torah leaders and feel that they are not obligated to follow their teachings, even making light of their advice. This approach, in itself, is as great an evil as that which they are setting out to overcome, for it does violence to a central aspect of the Jewish commitment: the authority vested in the Torah leadership of each generation, as an integral part of *Torah Shebe'al Peh* (the Oral Law).

The *Gemara* tells of a heathen who came to Hillel to be converted to Judaism (*Shabbos* 31a). The heathen was willing to accept both the Written Torah and the Oral Law—as Rashi explains—but he refused to recognize the interpretations of Shamai and Hillel as part of the Oral Law spoken by God. Nonetheless Hillel accepted him. Hillel was confident (Rashi explains) that once he taught the heathen, the latter would come to depend upon him. Rashi's explanation of this incident illustrates that belief in the Oral Law is totally dependent upon the acceptance of the teachings of the *Gedolei Hador* (giants of the generation).

This authority must be granted to the leaders of each generation, regardless of their relative merit to leaders of other generations—'Yiftach in his generation is like Shmuel in his'' (*Rosh Hashanah* 25b). Even though the prophet Shmuel was undoubtedly greater than Yiftach, the latter still merited ultimate respect as the Torah leader of his own generation. Greater sages have existed in earlier times, but our obligation is to follow those of our age.

One who does not accept the Torah leaders of his generation cannot claim to believe in the Oral Law. Thus a person who does not subjugate himself to our Torah leaders, even though he may be religious in every other respect, is not qualified to lead others in *kiruv rechokim*.

✍ Who Can Lead the Searchers?

When presented with the opportunity to engage in endeavors outside of his personal growth, the *ben Torah* will normally defer to others. He assumes that there are others who are equally qualified to handle the problem at hand, if not more so. Now that so many irreligious people are seeking truth, we might hope that there are enough interested parties who are qualified to meet their needs. Unfortunately, this is not so, for the very ones who claim to offer them truth are often further from it than the seekers, and might even be described as being ensnared in an idolatry of sorts.

The Torah warns "Do not turn to the idols" (Vayikra 19:4), which the Gemara explains as a reference to conceptual idols, ideologies not based on the Torah (Shabbos 149a). Unless one follows the Torah meticulously, he can even make idols of his own ideas. This unstructured and uninhibited "freedom of thought" is frequently the hallmark of many who are engaged in enlightening those who are seeking, and unquestionably disqualifies them from the task.

Yet those who seek guidance must be led by someone. He who leads others must be extremely firm in his faith. He must not follow his own whims, but must base his entire ideology on God's Torah. He must be meticulous in adhering to the teachings of our Torah leaders, and must not be misled by false ideologies or foreign methodologies. This leaves us none but the ben Torah, whose spiritual stamina is fortified by the Torah as taught by the heads of our great yeshivos. Only he is equipped to address the masses and return them to the truth.

◆§ The Reluctant Redeemer

But the yeshivah student may insist that he can offer the world much more by devoting himself fully to his Torah studies, his primary obligation. One is not permitted to interrupt Torah study for any mitzvah, unless it is a personal obligation (such as tefillin or reciting Shema). Indeed, our People's greatest teacher and prime redeemer, Moshe Rabbeinu, actually would have preferred to abstain from leading the Jewish People from bondage to freedom. He realized that he could accomplish much more through his personal involvement in Torah.

The Midrash tells of Moshe's unwillingness to assume leadership in four major assignments: pleading to Pharaoh for the release of Bnei Yisrael, splitting the sea, ascending Mount Sinai to receive the Torah, and entering the newly erected Ohel Mo'ed (tabernacle). In each of these cases Moshe stood aside until God commanded him to lead: "You must, for there is no one else!"

Thus, the yeshivah student's predilection to abstain has a precedent. But by the same token so does the necessity that he become actively involved, in exceptional circumstances. As Moshe responded to the voice of authority when it told him that he must because there was no one else, so too must our yeshivah students. As mentioned before, there are no others who are qualified for the task. Under such circumstances, Torah study must also be interrupted.

Another factor that enlarges the obligation on those who are capable of bringing others closer to Torah is the fact that many people who are far from a Torah life can be categorized as *tinokos shenishbu,* that is, people held captive by gentiles since infancy (*Yoreh De'ah* 159:6). It is a *mitzvah*—an obligation—to bring such individuals back to the Torah and Judaism (*Mishneh Torah, Hilchos Mamrim* 3:3). When there is no one else to accomplish this, then one must even take time from his Torah studies to do so.

In summary, one must emulate Moshe, who was a leader because he had no choice.

ᴈ§ The "Teach or Learn" Dilemma

There is always the defense against active involvement in teaching others: "Must I sacrifice my own growth?"

The *Gemara* teaches us: "A man and his son must both study Torah. When possibilities exist for only one, a man's personal needs take precedence to his son's" (*Kidushin* 29b, *Yoreh Deah* 245:2). One may not even take time from his own Torah studies to teach his son, unless he knows that his son's potential is greater than his own. This is a highly significant point: If one's own studies take precedence over teaching his own child, then they certainly take precedence over teaching strangers.

Yet we find that Rabbi Preda had a student with whom he review-ed each lesson four hundred times. As a reward for this, four hundred extra years were allotted to his life, and everyone in his generation was guaranteed a place in the World to Come (*Eruvin* 54b).

One would assume that Rabbi Preda could have gained more knowledge had he used this time for his own study. To be sure, when one teaches, he also learns, in keeping with Rabbi Chanina's statement: "I have learned much from my teachers, more from my companions, and most of all from my students" (*Tanis* 7a). Rav Chanina's maxim, however, obviously did not apply to a student such as Rabbi Preda's. In addition, no one can grow exclusively from teaching; each individual must also study for himself.

What is apparent from this is that even though an individual's own studies take precedence over another's, he must still find time to teach others.

ᴈ§ In Search of a Time-Formula

A major question remains, however: "How much time can and must one devote to this task?"

A rule of proportions for giving of personal resources to others can be inferred from the laws of charity. (We find a similar parallel in *Tanna DeBei Eliahu Rabbah* 27.) A person must have enough to take care of his own personal needs before he gives charity (*Tur Yoreh De'ah* 151). Nevertheless, this is not to be taken so literally as to totally exempt a person who does not have everything he needs from giving charity (*Yoreh De'ah* 248:1). There is always some measure that one must do for others.

The same is true of our own Torah needs. Beyond question, one's primary obligation is to his own studies. One can never say that he has amassed enough to meet his personal needs, for Torah "is longer than the earth and broader than the sea." One must therefore give his own studies precedence, but this must not be absolute. One must also act on behalf of others.

As in charity, where one has an obligation to give a tenth of his income to the poor, so must one spend one tenth of his time working on behalf of others, bringing them close to Torah. If one is endowed with greater resources, he must correspondingly spend more of his time with others.

❧ The Pitfalls of Our Times

One cannot contemplate involvement with fellow Jews in more worldly circumstances, even for the higher purpose of winning them to a Torah commitment, without taking note of the risks and pitfalls that abound today. It is in place to issue words of caution as well as words of encouragement in this regard.

Today's situation has special pitfalls peculiar to our times. Many people feel that they can partake of the worldly along with Torah. They do not realize that this world is the portion of Eisav, and not of Yaakov (*Devarim Rabbah* 1:17). They want to indulge in all worldly delights, in a kosher manner; should a commodity or activity carry a kosher label, they even consider it a *mitzvah* to pursue it. This brings people to lose valuable time from their Torah studies, and in some respects the situation has reached tragic proportions. Most certainly, then, if one hopes to bring others to Torah, he must make Torah the primary focus of his life. It is thus incumbent upon us to divorce ourselves from worldly pursuits to the greatest extent possible. Our sages went so far as to contemplate completely destroying all evil urges (*Yetzer Hara*). They did not fully execute this plan because a measure of *Yetzer Hara* is essential for the continuance of the course of nature. Nonetheless, they sought to reduce pursuit of worldly desires to the greatest degree possible.

When faced with this warning to avoid entanglements in worldly pleasures and distractions, one might well be reluctant to engage in any pursuit other than Torah study—even for the ultimate purpose of bettering the lot of others through *kiruv rechokim*. But the current situation makes urgent demands upon us, for "It is a time to work for God, they have abandoned Your Torah" (*Tehillim* 119:126). Indeed, one must devote the major portion of his time to Torah study, but there are times when we must set Torah study aside and implement Torah action for God's sake, to bring the truth to others.

When one does this in the manner prescribed by our Torah leadership, then God will give him strength so that association with people estranged from our religion will not harm him.

When one follows the ways of Torah, he is indeed protected by God from all harm. It is in this spirit that the Torah tells us: "Yaakov came complete to the city of Shechem" (*Bereishis* 33:18). Rashi comments that he returned from Lavan complete in body, possessions, and Torah. He had followed the way of the Torah, and no harm could befall him.

A "Get" in Monsey

✑ What is a Get?

THERE ARE FEW JEWISH PRACTICES that require as much precision as the issuing of a *get* (Jewish bill of divorce). In concise words, the Torah prescribes the procedure: "He shall write for her a bill of divorce (*sefer krisus*), and give it into her hand" (*Devarim* 24:1). The *Targum Onkeles* translates "bill of divorce" into Aramaic "*get peturin*" (which is usually shortened to "*get*"). The detailed procedures emanating from this passage are all part of the Oral Law, spoken at Sinai.

Although the Torah permits divorce, it is certainly not a matter to be taken lightly; according to the Midrash, when a divorce takes place the very stones of the *mizbe'ach* (Temple Altar) weep for the tragedy. In addition to the human element, divorce is a grave matter because it deals with the sanctity of family life, which plays so supreme a role in Judaism, from premarital restrictions, through the details of marriage law, and the regulatory requirements of *Taharas Hamishpachah* (Laws of Family Purity). In Jewish life there is no such thing as "an innocent affair."

In halachic (legal) terms, breaking the bond between man and wife represents a most radical change of status. Until the *get* is given, the marriage bond retains its full force—in terms of both the sanctity of the union and its proscriptive ramifications; a breach of marriage fidelity is nothing less than adultery, subject to the most severe penalties. Once the *get* takes effect, however, the former "*eishes ish*" (wife) is totally released from restrictive laws of marriage.

The Jewish Observer—December 1976

Everyone involved in preparing a *get* must be fully aware of the vast responsibility of producing such a powerful legal instrument. Reflecting the serious nature of a *get*, Jewish law requires that it be written with the utmost precision. Even the letters must be shaped in exact accordance with the laws of Torah script...Not unlike a radio, where even a single misconnected wire results in a failure of reception, even a single "misconnected" letter will prevent a *get* from dissolving the marriage bond.

The entire Talmudic tract of *Gittin* is devoted to the laws governing the *get*. These laws are codified in 150 plus pages (*amudim*) in the standard printing of the *Shulchan Aruch* with literally thousands of responsa (*teshuvos*) devoted to the topic. The Rabbi supervising a *get* must be an expert in the major areas of these laws of *gittin*.

Special attention is given to the precise spelling and designation of all names in a *get*, not only of the principal parties, but also of the places referred to in the *get*; for these are crucial to the exact identification of the people involved, and to those responsible for the writing of the *get*. There is an extensive body of halachic literature governing this particularly difficult field. It could be said that through these laws, in a sense, the name of every city in the world can become part of Torah.

The body of *halachah* governing the *get* can thus serve as an example of how the Torah includes and elevates all aspects of life—including the relationships between men and women, even touching the places where they dwell.

*   *   *

"So you wrote a *get* in Monsey. What's so impressive about that?"

I was overhearing what sounded like typical pre-Minchah banter. The other fellow, a bearded young man who seemed in his early thirties, was very excited. Even though there had been a Jewish community in the Monsey area (in suburban Rockland County, about forty miles northwest of New York City) for some seventy-five years, this was the first time that a *get* had ever been written there. Drawn into the conversation, I became fascinated, and invited the young man to my home, where the conversation continued until late in the night. My reward was some unexpected insight into an area of Jewish Law regarding which very little is generally known.

ᴇ§ The Time has Come ...

It had begun about three years ago, when the Kolel HaRabbanim, A Monsey-based institute devoted to the study of religious laws governing marriage and divorce, was going through the laws regarding the writing of the names of cities in *gittin* (*Even HaEzer* 128). Some students inquired as to how the city of Monsey would be treated in a *get*, and were surprised to learn that no *get* had ever been written there.

This led to a theoretical investigation, attempting to apply to the actual case of Monsey the principles that they had been learning.

A host of unanswered questions brought Rabbi Leib Landesman (who was telling me this story) along with other Kolel members to the door of Rabbi Yaakov Kamenetzky, who also lives in Monsey. In the course of the discussion, it emerged that some people hesitate to give a necessary *get* because they do not want to bother traveling to New York City. A case was discussed where a somewhat religious woman was divorcing a non-religious man, and he would only give her a *get* in Rockland County.

Only after many hours of persuasion would he consent to go to New York City. Upon hearing this, Reb Yaakov said that the time had come to set up the means for writing *gittin* in Monsey. "Besides," he said, "Monsey has already become a major Orthodox Jewish community and must be prepared to service other communities. It is only fitting that Monsey should be equipped to write *gittin*."

◄§ No Trivial Task

Arranging for *gittin* to be written in a city is no trivial task. The precise pronunciation and Hebrew spelling of the city must be determined, along with two identifying marks, such as adjacent bodies of water and the source of the community's water supply. Normally, the *Rav* of the city would make a preliminary investigation and then on that basis submit his opinion to leading authorities (*gedolim*) for approval. A *Rav* would only rely on his own judgment in a dire emergency, and even in such a case, he would later subject his opinion to the scrutiny of leading rabbinical authorities, for the writing of an approved *get* establishes a binding precedent, with grave implications: If a woman should remarry without a proper *get*, her children subsequently born are *mamzeirim* (illegitimate), and this in turn can have tragic effects for many generations afterwards. It is therefore forbidden to alter such things as the spelling of a city or its identifying marks from *get* to *get*, since this would cast aspersions on earlier *gittin* as well as on the status of children later born to the women divorced with the previously written *gittin*. Thus, the first *get* written in a city is all important, since its precedent may be binding forever.

Even a *Rav* of the status of Rabbi Yaakov Kamenetzky would not take the responsibility of determining these rulings on his own. He suggested that all the pertinent facts be investigated, and that they be presented to Rabbi Moshe Feinstein for approval.

◄§ Search for the Boundaries of Monsey

First to be investigated were the precise boundaries of Monsey. When writing a *get* there, one had to be certain that he was inside the city proper. One problem was that Monsey is not incorporated, and therefore does not have a corporate boundary. Rabbi Leib Landesman, dean of Kolel HaRabbonim, discussed this problem in *shul* one morning, and one of the congregants volunteered that he went hiking every Sunday with the Planning Director of Rockland County.

A meeting was set up in March, 1975, and the Planning Director agreed to investigate the matter. A week later, he sent Rabbi Landesman a census map, which provided the most official definition of the boundaries of Monsey available. A visit to the postal authorities, however, produced a second map, on which the boundaries were defined somewhat differently. The first question: which of these two maps should be accepted as authoritative?

Careful study revealed an inconsistency in the postal map. According to this map, several apartment buildings would be in Monsey proper. This, however, was impossible, since Monsey was unincorporated, and county zoning prohibited apartment buildings in unincorporated areas. By contrast, the census map showed these buildings to be in the adjacent incorporated village of Spring Valley. The corporate limits of Spring Valley were investigated, and these were found to conform to the census map. It was therefore decided to accept the census map as more authoritative. Reb Yaakov, however, suggested that they only use areas that were unquestionably in Monsey according to both maps. One does not take any chances regarding *gittin*.

⇜ How do You Spell "Monsey"?

Another question involved the precise pronunciation of the city. Some people pronounced it "Monsey," with the "o" corresponding to the "o" in "monster," while others pronounced it "Munsey," as in "Monday." If it were pronounced *Monsey*, it would have to be spelled מנסי, without an *alef*, while if it were pronounced *Munsey*, the Hebrew spelling would be מאנסי, with an *alef*. (As a general rule in *gittin*, an *alef* denotes a *kametz*.) Since residents used both pronunciations, this presented a problem.

The need for such precise determination is not at all far fetched. Over two hundred years ago, there was a question as to whether a certain city should have its name spelled Piltz פילץ or Pilttz פילטץ, with an extra *tes*. A leading halachic authority of the time concluded that even such a minor variation in the spelling of the name can render a *get* invalid (*Noda Bihuda* 88). As stated the precise reference to a place must be unequivocal, to avoid any doubt as to the exact location and the principals involved in the *get*.

Careful investigation revealed that most of the older residents pronounced the name of the city "*Munsey*." This was supported by a search through the records of the Rockland County Historical Society, which revealed that the city had been named after the Munsee Indians, a tribe of the Delaware family . . . Even an Indian tribe had influence on how a *get* should be written!

Most important, however, was the fact that in Yiddish, the pronunciation was invariable "*Munsey.*" There is a rule that whenever a slight variation exists between the Jewish and non-Jewish version of a city's name, the Jewish pronunciation be used (*Even Haezer* 128:4, in Hagah). It was finally decided to use the pronunciation *Munsey*, and to spell it מאנסי, with an *alef*.

◄§ The Geographic Features

Before a *get* can be written in a city, certain identifying marks must be determined. These normally consist of adjacent bodies of water and the source of the local water supply. In the case of Monsey, such identification was particularly important, since there are two other cities with the same name: Muncie, Indiana, and Muncy, Pennsylvania. Even though these are spelled differently in English, these cities were also named after the Munsee Indians.

It would seem to be easiest to simply write "Monsey, New York." However, political divisions such as states and countries are never used in *gittin*, because they are arbitrary and subject to change. The usual practice is to use an adjacent river or lake as a distinguishing mark, for such natural features are considered permanent.

There are no prominent bodies of water near Monsey, and therefore, further investigation was necessary. If an identifying landmark could not be found, *gittin* could not be written in Monsey. A visit to the Rockland County Drainage Agency revealed several minor streams in the area, as well as a large pond, known as Lake Suzanne.

Initially, it seemed best to explore the small rivers that appeared to be close to Monsey. One young man making an on-site inspection of one of these streams inadvertently trespassed on posted property and was stopped by the police. Imagine trying to explain to an Irish cop that he was surveying the stream in order to write a Jewish bill of divorce!

In the end, however, it was learned that the larger streams stop short of Monsey proper, while the smaller ones that do enter Monsey do not have well-defined names. It was therefore decided to concentrate on Lake Suzanne.

This lake had only come into existence some thirty years earlier. It had originally been a swamp, fed by a small stream and springs on its north side. The owner of the property, Mr. Ellish, had dammed one end of the swamp, making it into a lake. Since it was situated on Suzanne Drive, it came to be called Lake Suzanne.

There was some question, however, as to whether this lake was permanent enough to be used as an identifying landmark. Since it was the only possible body of water that could be used, this was a crucial question. A call to the Army Corps of Engineers confirmed that this lake could not be drained or filled in without government permission, since it was part of a major watershed. Further investigation revealed that property owners bordering the lake had water rights written into their deeds. When the owner of an island in the lake once wanted to drain it temporarily to facilitate the installation of sewer pipes to the island, a number of property owners sued to prevent even such a temporary draining. All this was enough to give the lake sufficient permanent status.

Armed with all this information, three Kolel members made an appointment with Rabbi Moshe Feinstein. The major points were briefly discussed, but Reb Moshe announced that he would not even begin without consulting Rabbi Yaakov Kamenetzky. He immediately placed a call to Reb Yaakov, and they agreed to discuss the question fully after a forthcoming meeting of the Moetzes Gedolei HaTorah—the Council of Torah Sages of Agudah Israel of America (where the question of a special Martyrs' Day for the Six Million was to be discussed).

After the meeting, Reb Moshe and Reb Yaakov were joined by the three Kolel members and Reb Moshe's secretaries. Another question immediately arose regarding Lake Suzanne. The lake is fed by a stream, and the water then flows out through the opposite end of the lake. Since the water is constantly flowing, according to *halachah*, the lake is nothing more than a wide spot in the stream. Still it could not be called the "Suzanne River," since its official name is "Lake Suzanne." After an involved discussion of all pertinent precedents, Reb Moshe suggested that it be referred to as נהר ליק סוזען "Lake Suzanne River." After more than a year's background digging, the two Torah giants could agree on the initial wording: "Monsey, a city situated on the Lake Suzanne River..."

◈§ Whence the Water?

The final feature to be determined was the source of Monsey's water supply. This necessitated a visit to the Spring Valley Water Company, which maintains some five artesian wells in Rockland County. It was learned that the company maintains a grid system, where water can be shunted from one place to another as needed, Normally, however, most of the water used in the Monsey area came from local artesian wells. An examination of the large system map indicated that at least one of these wells was located in Monsey proper.

◈§ "Waters of a Well" or "of Wells"?

Another question arose: Was there just one well in Monsey proper, or were there more than one? If there were only one, the proper wording would be "situated on the waters of a well (*mei be'er*)," while if there were more than one, it would be "waters of wells (*mei be'eros*)." Reb Moshe instructed the young men to determine this precisely, and then to bring in all pertinent maps for his inspection.

A call to the Spring Valley Water Company produced a detailed map indicating all the wells in the Monsey area. The map showed two wells that appeared to be within the boundaries designated for Monsey, but this could not be determined for sure without a personal inspection. The first well, on Grove Street, was easy to find, and was clearly within the designated area. The second one, however, was more difficult to locate. It was off the highway at the end of a little-used dirt road. But was it actually within the halachic boundaries of Monsey? If it was, on one map, but not on the other, serious problems would remain unresolved. It was possible that after all this work, it would still be impossible to write *gittin* in Monsey.

The distance of this well from recognized landmarks was carefully measured, and it was located on both the census and postal maps. Sure enough, according to both maps, it was within the borders of Monsey. It was thus established that there were two wells in Monsey proper.

When this information was brought to Reb Moshe, he wrote the following: "In — במאנסי מתא דיתבא על נהר ליק סוזען ועל מי בארת Monsey, a city situated on the Lake Suzanne River, and on the waters of wells".

He said, however, that he would not render a decisive opinion until other major authorities (*gedolim*) formally agreed with him. He was especially concerned that such agreement come from Chassidic authorities, for he did not want to establish a precedent that would be binding on them without their consent. For this purpose, Reb Moshe wrote the text again on a piece of his official stationery:

במאנסי מתא דיתבא על נהר ליק סוזען ועל מי בארת

✑ Winning Approval

Obtaining such an agreement was not all that easy. Some rabbis simply did not want to presume to be the first to give consent. One deferred, saying that he was not sufficiently versed in American geography and the English language. Another indicated that he would like to formally agree, but limitations imposed by advancing age made it impossible for him to assume the responsibility of doing the necessary research. All felt the tremendous weight of responsiblity that goes with setting up a city for *gittin*. As one sage noted, even Brooklyn had not been set up for *gittin* until some forty years ago.

The first one to grant consent was Rabbi Yechezkel Roth, the Satmar *Dayan* (Rabbinical judge). But even he did not do so easily. He was bothered by the reference to Monsey as "*mossa*"—which some authorities explain as meaning "city." For hundreds of years, *gittin* have described the place of the writing of the document as a *mossa*, and the description would, of necessity, have to be an apt one. In emergency circumstances, a *get* could be written on the *ad hoc* basis in a village, and the setting would then be listed accordingly as a *k'far*. Otherwise, the *get* could not be written. True, a town with a population of over one hundred has the halachic status of a "city," and would not be called a *k'far*, a village. There is a major opinion however, that if people usually call a place a town or village, one cannot refer to it as a "city" in a *get* (*Divrei Chaim, Shemos Gittin, Shaar Shinui Mekomos* #10). Monsey's status as one or the other had to be determined. Rabbi Roth requested two weeks to research the question.

When the Kolel members returned to the Satmar *Dayan*, they discovered that he had actually written a *teshuvah* (responsum) on the subject. Careful research had indicated that the opinion stating that an entity usually called a village could not be referred to as a city only referred to a village in a totally rural area. Without question, a suburban area, even if unincorporated, has the halachic status of a city (*mossa*). Thus, not only was a decision rendered for Monsey, but a precedent was established for all suburban areas.

To these names were added those of Rabbi Moshe Stern, the Debretziner Rav; Rabbi Moshe Neuschloss, Rav of New Square; and Rabbi Nathan Horowitz, a leading Monsey Rav. The first *get* was written in Monsey on 24 Cheshvan, 5736 (October 29, 1975). In the following year, over fifteen additional *gittin* were written there, with people coming from as far as Connecticut and Pennsylvania.

◆§ Seven Short Words ... And 30,000 Divorces

This extensive investigation involved nothing more than seven short words in the *get*. All this effort had been necessary merely to establish exactly how Monsey should be written and identified. But there are numerous other difficult points in a *get*. The names of both the man and woman must be spelled precisely; this includes both the Hebrew names and transliteration into Hebrew of all English names and nicknames by which they are known. A *get* must be written by a competent *sofer* (scribe), since many of the same laws apply in the same manner as they do in the case of *tefillin* and *mezuzos*. The laws governing *gittin* are among the most complex in the entire *Shulchan Aruch*, and a *get* must therefore be prepared only under the supervision of the most proficient experts; which brings to mind an extremely critical problem:

If the overall divorce rate in America can be applied to the Jewish community, there are some 30,000 Jewish couples getting divorced every year. Assuming that intermarriages are shorter-lived than intra-Jewish marriages, and that they assume a large proportion of the figure, at least 10,000 Jewish couples divorce each year. How many of them are not aware of the requirements for the writing and delivering of a *get*? And that without one, the woman is still married to her first husband, and any children she bears by another man will be *mamzeirim*?

An awesome responsibility to avert the mushrooming of this type of tragedy falls on the shoulders of the Jewish community:

• The broad public must be made aware of the need for a *get* when a divorce is contemplated.

• Scribes and qualified rabbis must be prepared for the task. Is it conceivable that there are enough people sufficiently learned and well-trained to supervise and write 10,000 *gittin* every year?

• Efforts should be made to make the writing of *gittin* accessible to all who may require it. The precedent of writing *gittin* has already been set generations ago in most American cities—San Francisco, New Orleans, Kansas City, Omaha. Today, however, we are short of qualified personnel to carry on the precedent, when the need arises.

The stones of the *mizbe'ach* still weep when a *get* is delivered, but the very foundations of the *Beis HaMikdash*—the sanctuary of Klal Yisroel—shake when the family breaks up without the benefit of a *get*.

Technology
in Service of Torah

WHILE IT IS ALMOST INEVITABLE that every advance in technology ushers in new problems in its wake, this may seem to be especially true in the Torah context. Undoubtedly, the complexities that arise from new discoveries, inventions, and manufacturing processes can at times make *Shabbos* observance and vigilance in regard to *kashrus*, for example, more difficult. With ingenuity and perseverance, however, man can put technology to work *for* him and use its blessings to solve problems in the very realms where it initially caused them to appear. This has been the goal of the Institute of Science and Halachah, located in Jerusalem's Bayit Vegan section. Indeed, this Institute—which is a non-profit organization, dedicated to seeking out ways to bring modern technological processes into conformity with *halachah*—has made the hallmarks of the industrial revolution—invention and technological refinement—the tools for resolving extremely difficult challenges to living a full life in consonance with the Torah's demands.

ᴖ Front-Page News

The Institute has been in the news several times as of late. One of the forty-three points in the Begin coalition agreement with Agudath Israel called for a review of the hundreds of *hetterei avodah*, which "permit" businesses and factories to operate on *Shabbos*—in spite of the legal re-

The Jewish Observer—October 1980

quirement that they be closed—when the government was satisfied that considerations of "national security or undue hardship" call for such dispensation. Under the new agreement, the Institute of Science and Halachah was assigned the task of reviewing each such *hetter* to determine whether a hardship indeed exists, and if so, to find ways in which Sabbath violation could be avoided.

More recently, the spotlight was on Professor Lev, founder and head of the Institute, when he led a commission, appointed by Jerusalem's Mayor Teddy Kollek, assigned with the task of surveying the northern tier of the city where the disputed Ramot Road brings Sabbath-desecrating traffic to the very feet of the religious communities nestled on the hillside—Kiryat Sanz and Ezras Torah, among others. It was Lev's task to determine whether the controversial road follows the most direct route for a road from Ramot to Jerusalem-proper (the surveying team came up with a far different route from the existing one); and how the sights and sounds of the present roadway could be sheltered from view and earshot of the offended communities until a new road would be opened. (Here, too, the Science and Halachah team came up with an inventive design for an acoustical half-tunnel that would shroud the uphill side of the roadway.) Unfortunately, it is not in the Institute's realm to stop the flow of traffic or close roads on the Sabbath; but within certain parameters, it can reduce problems even when it cannot solve them categorically.

The illustrations that follow are further examples of how, with the proper approach, as pursued by the Institute of Science and Halachah, technology can be a positive factor in a Torah society, rather than a source of problems.

◆§ The Steel Problem

"Steel City" is a non-Sabbath observing steel mill in the northern Israeli city of Acco. It operates an arc furnace that processes scrap steel and makes it into concrete reinforcement rods, a product widely used in Israel's booming construction industry.

The arc furnace is an immense cauldron (or "pot") the size of a standard living room, holding sixty tons of scrap metal. Attached to the huge cover of this "pot" are six carbon electrodes, each about eighteen inches wide and four feet long—half of them positive, half of them negative. An arc is struck from the positive to the negative electrodes, heating the metal to 2000 degrees F. When a batch is melted and refined, the pot is tipped over by a crane, pouring out the steel into appropriate molds.

Steel is the only material strong enough for such a crucible; yet the heat must be intense enough to melt the steel scrap in the pot without melting the pot itself. This problem is solved by coating the inside of the pot with "refractory material," usually an eight-inch layer of firebrick held together with the heat-resistant cement.

It is a universally accepted practice to constantly keep the heat in the crucible, for if the firebrick is heated and then cooled, it is exposed to thermal shock, and is likely to crack and deteriorate—possibly damaging the crucible beyond repair. Shutting down a steel plant and starting it up again, therefore, is a process that takes at least several days, so as to cool down and reheat the refractory bricks gradually enough not to damage them.

Not surprisingly, when Dr. Menachem Hartman of the Institute sat down with the directors of Steel City to discuss the possibility of closing down for *Shabbos*, their initial reaction was: "Impossible. There is no way a steel plant could be closed down one day a week!"

This did not close the issue. Dr. Hartman calculated the cooling rate of the firebricks and concluded that there was no need to allow the bricks to cool down over *Shabbos*: With the heat retained over the twenty-four hour period, there would be no thermal shock when the furnace was started again on Saturday night. This could be accomplished if the crucible's cover were kept closed, and a gas heater were installed and kept burning inside; the temperature of the pot would not go down more than a few hundred degrees, eliminating any danger that the firebricks would crack. With this relatively minor adjustment, the plant could be closed for *Shabbos*.

When the proposal was taken to the plant's directors, they were skeptical: Yes, it looked fine on paper, but would it really work? They simply could not take risks with expensive machinery, for if the calculations turned out wrong, the damage would be irreparable. They told the Institute that they would only consider using such a method if another plant had been successful with it.

Thus, the scientific resolution of the problem was merely the first step. Letters were sent to every steel plant in the world: "Did you ever shut down for one day a week? How did you do it?"

Initially, the responses reflected the conventional wisdom that it was impossible or very difficult to shut down an arc furnace, until a letter from Kobe (Japan) Steel reported its own successful experience: In the 1960's Japan was engaged in a program to cool down its overheated economy, and cut production. By government order, Kobe Steel was to close one day a week. The letter outlined the procedure it had used—tightly closing the furnace to prevent heat loss, and installing a gas heater, exactly as had been proposed by the Institute. In fact, after a time, Kobe's engineers concluded that even the gas heater was unnecessary. The firebricks retain heat so well that in a twenty-four-hour period, they only cool down a few hundred degrees and that was not enough to damage them.

It was later learned that United States Steel also occasionally closes down its electric furnaces for twenty-four-hour periods, merely keeping the furnace tightly closed.

It would have been nice to conclude this chapter with a report that Steel City is now closed for *Shabbos* and that its one hundred employees no longer violate the sacred day. Not yet. But at least it is now known that this is a possibility.

⊷§ The Nylon Spin-Off

The basic premise of the Institute of Science and Halachah, then, is that there is no industrial process that is incompatible with *Shabbos* observance. Its successes are such that the spin-off from its research is frequently beneficial to the industry itself.

One example of this is the nylon crimping factory, where threads of nylon are put through a crimping process, and then heat-treated to keep the twist in the yarn. This is important to give nylon—by nature a smooth, stiff, plastic-like material—the characteristics of bounce and body, so that it can be used for clothing and the like.

Again, the assumption has always been that such a plant had to run continuously twenty-four hours a day, seven days a week. When the plant is shut down, many of the delicate filaments snap, and re-threading the machinery is a tedious task that can take several days. So great is the loss that results from shutdown, that many plants have their own auxiliary electric power plant to maintain the machinery without interruption in the event of a power failure.

Closing down such a plant for *Shabbos* seemed out of the question—until the Institute began studying the process. It was discovered that problems arose because the plant was normally shut down by simply turning off the motors. This abrupt stoppage of the filaments caused many of them to break. The solution was simple: Merely place a control on the motor to cause it to slow down gradually, and then run for a while at dead slow speed. The machinery could then be shut down without any breakage at all. This not only allowed a plant to close for *Shabbos*, but also made it much simpler and cheaper to close the machinery for repairs.

Here the story has a happier ending. There currently is a *Shomer Shabbos* nylon-crimping plant in Brooklyn using this method—and a major Israeli plant is considering adopting it, as well.

Of course, not every problem is that simple. There are processes, such as the manufacture of nylon yarn, that are not as easy to shut down. In such cases, the Institute is working with computers and microprocessors that may be able to run such plants on *Shabbos* with only a minimal number of supervisory personnel—non-Jews, at that.

⊷§ The Hospital

Much of the Institute's research is focused on overcoming the difficulties of running a hospital, without unnecessarily violating *Shabbos* restrictions—concentrating on Jerusalem's Shaarei Tzedek. This involves a broad range of problems ranging from keeping records to warming food on *Shabbos*.

The importance of meticulous record-keeping in a hospital needs no elaboration. Yet not every patient nor every bit of information justifies violating the Sabbath by writing. There are many makeshift methods of recording data without actually writing, but many of them are clumsy or cumbersome. One ingenious approach developed by the Institute is based on the halachic definition of writing as involving the making of a permanent mark. Research and invention came up with a slowly fading ink that is legible during the first day it is used, but totally disappears after three days—offering a permissible means of temporary record keeping on *Shabbos* for a patient who is ill, but not dangerously so.*

One of the most interesting problems involved designing a device to call nurses on *Shabbos*. In the past, the patients used a manual bell on *Shabbos* to signal their need for assistance or attention. Although there is a rabbinical prohibition against ringing a bell on *Shabbos*, this does not apply to a person sick enough to be hospitalized. But a bell represents many problems of its own: if the patient's room is any distance from the nurse, she may not hear it. Or, the patient may not be strong enough to ring it loudly enough to be heard. And when it is rung loudly, it may disturb other patients. Moreover, the mere fact that the patient has been granted permission to perform a usually prohibited task because of his illness can be demoralizing.

Discussing the problem with some of the most prominent halachic authorities of our time, the Institute was told that an electrical device could be used by patients on *Shabbos*, as long as two restrictions were kept in mind: First, the device could not involve heating a filament white hot—as in a lamp bulb—since that is considered equivalent to making fire on the Sabbath. Second, the switch activating the device could not turn on the electrical current directly—only indirectly.

What could best be used instead of a light? The Institute devised a small, highly-reflective tab that is raised by an electromagnet. When in an upright position, the tab reflects the fluorescent lights in the corridors. Since there is no heating of a filament, as there is in the standard lightbulb, the first guideline was fulfilled. Furthermore, after tending the patient, the nurse simply flips the tab back down rather than extinguishing a light, as is standard in conventional signal devices.

Dealing with the second requirement proved more difficult. It called for the invention of an entirely new device—the *gramma* switch. This is a switch that turns on an electrical current indirectly—by *gramma* (Hebrew for causation).

The *gramma* switch works with a small light and a photo-electric

---

*[Use of this special ink circumvents the Scriptural prohibition of writing with a permanent ink. Nevertheless, writing with a fading ink is rabbinically proscribed (see *Shabbos* 104b and *Shulchan Aruch Orach Chaim* 340:4). Therefore the permissibility of using this special ink is limited to the medical records of hospital patients and cannot be extended to other situations.—Ed.]

cell. The light goes on for a thousandth of a second, several times a minute, and if the light reaches the cell, it turns the switch on. Ordinarily, however, a plate of metal blocks the light from the cell, preventing the switch from being activated.

However, when a patient pushes the button, he is pushing aside the metal plate. Hence, the light will then be able to shine on the cell, thus turning on the switch. The patient is not turning on the switch, but merely removing an object preventing the switch from being turned on automatically. As a further precaution, the switch is designed not to react to the first light pulse, but the third one. Thus, the switch is not activated until several flashes after the patient pushes the button, further separating his action from the indirect result it permits to take place.

Of course, under normal circumstances one would be forbidden to use such a switch on *Shabbos*. But in the case of a person sick enough to be hospitalized, halachic authorities have permitted its use.

* * *

The individual cases are very fascinating, and much progress in *Shemiras Shabbos* has been made due to the efforts of the Institute. But more important, the time will soon be with us when all Jews will be *Shomer Shabbos* and it will be a universally recognized necessity to run a *Shomer Shabbos* modern industrial state. Yes, even after the advent of *Moshiach* plants will manufacture steel and nylon (see *Rambam* and the *Shelah*). One can well imagine that these plants will use many of the processes developed by the Institute of Science and Halachah.

The Festivals

Rosh Hashanah Thoughts

Sounding the
Shofar of Mercy

ROSH HASHANAH RECALLS the *Sixth Day of Creation* on which God formed Adam (the first man). That event constitutes the true foundation of the world, for this development of mankind was the ultimate purpose and the fulfillment of God's desire to make an existence on an earth that was previously desolate and void.

It was following this Sixth Day of Creation that God surveyed all that He had done and termed it "very good." Since this Sixth Day is the key with which we initiate the New Year (Rosh Hashanah) in the Jewish calendar, it is appropriate that we too spiritually start off our activities with the recognition of the inherent potential of "very good" that also lies before us.

In the special prayers that we recite during the festival of Rosh Hashanah, there is an emphasis on the fact that "This is the day which is the beginning of Your creation, a remembrance of the first day" and that "Today is the birthday of the world."

If we accept the vital importance of man's creation on the Sixth Day by Hashem, then it is indeed possible for us to comprehend the validity of the above two verses which appear prominently in the special *Machzor* (Prayer Book) for Rosh Hashanah.

⊸§ A Gemara Dispute

Nevertheless, a very interesting dispute does develop in the Talmud which would seem to cast several questions as to what our proper at-

This article was originally transcribed from Rabbi Kaplan's lecture notes, for publication in the Crown Heights Chronicle—September 1982.

titude and understanding should be with regards to the important festival of Rosh Hashanah.

In the talmudic tractate of Rosh Hashanah, there is recorded an argument between the sages as to just when the Six Days of Creation of the world actually occurred.

One opinion holds that God completed His creation on Rosh Hashanah (the first day of Tishrei), after having begun the process earlier on the twenty-fifth day of Elul.

A second view however insists that these Six Days of Creation took place during the first six days in the Hebrew month of Nisan. This is the seventh month of the Jewish calendar and it comes out in the spring when we joyfully celebrate the *Yom Tov* (festival) of Passover.

At first glance, it would seem that the final, accepted opinion in this dispute as to when Creation actually occurred would have to be that of Tishrei. After all, it is on the first day of Tishrei that we observe Rosh Hashanah and in our prayers declare, "This is the day which is the beginning of Your creation."

Nevertheless, the actual decision rendered by the sages in this talmudic dispute is that the Creation of the world was in reality completed in the month of Nisan, not Tishrei! Last year (1981), we recognized the validity of this fact when we recited the special "*Birchas HaChamah*" (Blessing over the Sun) on the fourth day of Nisan.

⋖§ Birchas HaChamah

The *Birchas HaChamah* is an unusual blessing which is uttered once every twenty-eight years when, according to Jewish tradition, the sun returns to the exact point in its orbital journey that it occupied at the moment when God initially created it at the outset of the fourth day (Wednesday).

The fact that religious Jews all over the world recited the *Birchas HaChamah* on the fourth day of Nisan verifies the second opinion in the Gemara's argument as to when Creation was completed.

If this is indeed so, the obvious question must arise as to why then do we celebrate the pinnacle (God's formation of mankind) of Creation on Rosh Hashanah (which falls on the first day of Tishrei) and not on the seemingly more appropriate sixth day of Nisan.

The answer to this dilemma is that actually both opinions in the talmudic dispute are correct and, furthermore, neither contradicts the other. Briefly, *Tosafos*, one of the major commentaries to the Talmud, points out that with regards to the Creation of the world, there were two distinct yet related aspects to God's handiwork.

At first, during the month of Tishrei, the idea came to God to create the world. The world could thus be said to have come into being by Divine thought. Yet, the concepts of these thoughts were not finalized by God into completed deed until the subsequent month of Nisan had arrived.

✑ Hashem/Elokim: Mixing Mercy with Justice

In his major commentary on the Torah, Rashi also discusses this connection by questioning the significance of the first words in the Bible (Genesis 1:1)—"In the beginning God (*Elokim*) created the heavens and the earth."

Elokim when referring to God relates to His Divine attribute of strict justice, while the name of *Hashem* in turn emphasizes the Divine attribute of mercy.

Rashi wonders why in the first verse of the Torah only the term "*Elokim*" is used. Yet, later on after completing the description of the events of the Six Days of Creation, the Bible (Genesis 2:4) writes—"...in the day that *Hashem Elokim* made the earth and the heavens."

In the first case, just the name "*Elokim*" with its connection to strict justice is employed. However, in the second verse, the combined name of *Hashem Elokim* which refers to both the Divine qualities of mercy and strict justice is utilized to explain the account of the world's Creation.

The answer that Rashi provides also alludes to the two Creations of the world by God—the first by His thought during the month of Tishrei and the second which relates to His completed action during the month of Nisan.

Rashi declares that (in Tishrei) God initially as Judge (*Elokim*) intended to create the world and place it under the attribute (rule) of strict justice. But, He realized that the world could not thus endure. Therefore, He later on (in Nisan) gave precedence to Divine mercy and mixed it together with the previous aspect of Divine justice. Only with this combination of both mercy and justice could God's thought of Tishrei be viable and brought down during Nisan into completed deed.

The second verse (Genesis 2:4) refers to God's Creation of the world in Nisan. Furthermore, by placing the attribute of mercy (*Hashem*) before that of justice (*Elokim*), the verse emphasizes the stronger role that Divine mercy played in the formation of the world.

Let us review what has just been stated. When we analyze the Creation of the world which occurred in Tishrei, we understand that it was a development based on *Elokim*'s thought which was enveloped through His aspect of *Din* (Judgment).

What is the prevailing quality of the *Yom Tov* of Rosh Hashanah? It is indeed that of "judgment," for we do call the festival—"*Yom HaDin*" (the Day of Judgment).

By studying the liturgy of the prayers that we recite during Rosh Hashanah and in examining the emotions that evolve in our hearts during our observances of the festival, it is clear that this concern for the quality of "justice" is truly preeminent.

◆§ The Zodiac of Libra

To gain a deeper insight into the significance of this aspect, we can ask ourselves the insightful question as to what is the *mazal* or astrological sign of the month of Tishrei. The answer is Libra. The zodiac of Libra is interestingly enough represented by the balancing of the scales of justice.

This would tend to reemphasize the point that the first Creation of the world by God's thought, which was completed on the first day of Tishrei (Rosh Hashanah), was performed as already stated under the attribute of Divine justice.

This world that *Elokim* created by thought in Tishrei was entirely dominated by judgment and it was "very good" and perfect.

Unfortunately, the potential of theory which is perfect is not always carried out likewise into action. Recognizing this reality, *Hashem* in Nisan was forced to add Divine mercy and thus allow the actual world to endure in deed.

To further elaborate on this combination of the attributes of justice (Tishrei) and mercy (Nisan), we can turn our attention to the shofar which is sounded on the festival of Rosh Hashanah.

◆§ The Shofar Mitzvah

To hear the blast of the shofar is the primary *mitzvah* of this day. In fact, the *Shulchan Aruch* (the Code of Jewish Law) has determined that if one must make a choice of either praying in a synagogue that has a *minyan* (a quorum of ten adult male Jews) but lacks a shofar or in a synagogue that lacks a *minyan* but has a shofar, the individual is obligated to forsake the benefits that come from communal prayer and should rather go to where he can hear the call of the shofar.

It is thus quite clear that hearing the shofar sounded on Rosh Hashanah plays a most significant role in our celebrating the festival. Our sages declare that the sound of the shofar exerts a pivotal influence in directing the heart of the Jew towards returning to *Hashem* in *tshuvah* (repentance).

Why is it that this instrument is so important to the Jew and that it dominates the service of Rosh Hashanah? What does this horn of a ram, an adult male lamb, actually represent? The Talmud states that the shofar is symbolic of the ram that was sacrificed by our forefather Abraham in the place of his son Isaac. (It should be noted at this point that this very significant episode of the *Akeidah*, an incident which continues to influence Jewish history today, occurred also on a day that was Rosh Hashanah.)

The Bible relates the account of how, after waiting for many years to have a child by his wife Sarah, Abraham was finally blessed with the birth of Isaac when the patriarch was well advanced (one hundred years old) in age.

Then after being told by God that it would only be through Isaac that he would be truly blessed and that his spiritual legacy would be passed on through the generations that his son would beget, Abraham is commanded by God to take his beloved Isaac and bring him up to Mount Moriah and prepare him as a burnt offering.

◄§ Abraham's Kindness

This was a major challenge for Abraham to overcome as he was naturally possessed by a tendency to perform kindness to others. The Torah (Genesis 18:2) tells in detail just how strong this desire was.

It occurred that on the third day following his circumcision at the age of ninety-nine, when the physical pain of the operation was most intense, Abraham's wish to be kind forced him to ignore his own intense bodily discomfort and to sit by the openings of his tent during the severe desert heat. All this was done by our forefather in order to allow him the chance to perhaps spy a passerby with whom he could display his nature of kindness.

Yet, when God commanded him to act against his very nature and to bring his son (that he had so long awaited) as a burnt offering on Mount Moriah, Abraham was able to ignore his own prevailing attribute of kindness in order to more perfectly serve the will of his Master.

The Torah (Genesis 22:10-12) reports that just as Abraham picked up the knife in order to slay his son Isaac for the offering of which God had commanded him, God ordered him through an angel to not touch the lad. Abraham was told "...for now I know that you fear God..."

Following this declaration in which God praises Abraham for his service which has now been proven to be more than that of just one individual following his natural tendency (kindness), the Bible (Genesis 22:13) further relates—"Abraham then looked up and saw a ram caught by its horns in a thicket. He went and got the ram, sacrificing it as an all-burnt offering in his son's place."

◄§ Recalling the Akeidah

It is therefore as a remembrance of this incident of the *Akeidah*, that is symbolized by the ram's horn (shofar), which as stated before occurred on Rosh Hashanah, that we today on this festival also blow the shofar of a ram.

We recall the horn of the ram (a male sheep) which served as a replacement for the sacrifice of Isaac who at that moment represented the continuity of the Jewish nation through his yet unborn offspring.

By our blowing of the shofar, we are declaring to God that in a manner similar to Abraham who was willing to sacrifice his beloved son Isaac in order to serve God, so we too are willing to sacrifice our own lives for the sanctification of His holy name.

Therefore, we pray that just as God had mercifully spared

Abraham's son, likewise should He recall the merit of our forefather when we blow the shofar on Rosh Hashanah. We ask God to remember the loyalty of the patriarch and in turn demonstrate His mercy for Abraham's descendants today.

When we sound the shofar, we are begging God that in the same manner that Abraham overcame his nature of being kind in order to serve Him by bringing Isaac as an offering, so too God in turn should overcome His nature (of strict judgment) which is prevalent at this time (Tishrei) and demonstrate His Divine mercy by inscribing the offspring of Abraham into the Book of Life which is opened on Rosh Hashanah.

◄§ Sign of Nisan

To gain another insight into the importance of sounding the shofar on Rosh Hashanah, let us return to our review of astrology. What is the constellation of the Ram? The Ram is the astrological sign representing the Hebrew month of Nisan.

We can now understand that when we blow the ram's horn in Tishrei, we are in a sense transporting the attribute of Nisan's mercy into the month that is normally dominated by the quality of justice.

The shofar symbolizes the month of Nisan in which God completed Tishrei's Creation of the world by thought and in turn finalized this creation into action.

In the Midrash we find a reference to the two times that God Himself will blow the shofar. The first occurred at Mount Sinai, just preceding the awesome revelation of His holy Torah to the Jewish nation.

Although this first blast was sounded during the month of Sivan, this too is tied to the month of Nisan whose astrological sign is that of the ram. In truth, the entire purpose of the Exodus from Egypt was that the Jews should be liberated from their physical bondage and accept the responsibility of obeying God's Torah.

Thus, this sounding of the ram's horn by God in Sivan at Mount Sinai was the climax of a drama that unfolded initially in the month of Nisan.

◄§ Just before Mashiach

The Midrash declares that the second time God will sound the shofar will occur in the future, just before the coming of *Mashiach* (Messiah). According to some major opinions of the sages in the Talmud, the main month in which we can expect the Messiah to arrive is that of Nisan.

God will thus herald our liberation from the oppression of this last *Golus* (Exile) by sounding the shofar which represents the month of Nisan that is also symbolized by the Divine attribute of mercy.

That ram which Abraham sacrificed in the place of Isaac was caught by its horns in the thickets of Mount Moriah. Why does an animal have horns in the first place? The answer is that a creature has horns in order to assist it in attacking other animals.

The Talmud points out that this is one of the reasons that we blow the shofar on Rosh Hashanah. We blast the ram's horn in order to frighten and confound the Satan. Is it not ironic that in order to accomplish this task, we in turn resort to taking the weapon of an aggressive animal? Indeed, we grasp a weapon used primarily for goring other creatures and transform it into a vehicle that can now serve in the task of elevating ourselves to new and higher levels of holiness.

To further study the significance of our sounding the shofar on Rosh Hashanah, we can ask a second question. What is man's most potent weapon? It is the head, the part of the body which houses the mind from which an individual thinks.

◄§ Attacking the Satan

From where does the ram's horn grow? It develops from the animal's head. Our taking of the shofar on this festival indicates the desire of the Jew to utilize his own head (mind) in the fight against the Satan and the evil he represents.

It is interesting to consider that this test of the *Akeidah* in which God challenged Abraham by asking him to bring his son Isaac as a burnt offering was the tenth such test that He had subjected the patriarch to.

In the Midrash, we learn that as a reward for Abraham's overcoming those ten tests, God granted our forefather and his offspring, forever, ten especially auspicious days in which to do *tshuvah* (repentance). These days most appropriately begin on Rosh Hashanah and continue until Yom Kippur. This period in time is called the *Yomim Noraim* (Days of Awe).

We can conclude our present discussion of Rosh Hashanah by asking and answering one more question. Where is the first place in the Torah where Rosh Hashanah is mentioned as a holiday that we as Jews must observe?

It is very strange indeed that in the Chumash (Bible) all the other *Yomim Tovim* (festivals) are discussed before anything is ever said about Rosh Hashanah.

The very first reference to the day as a holiday to be commemorated is to be found in the weekly Torah section of *Emor*. It is discussed in Leviticus 23:23 following a report on how the *Mishkan* (Sanctuary) was completed. Once again, we must ask ourselves why Rosh Hashanah is not mentioned in the Torah until so late after all the other festivals have already been discussed. Passover, Shavuos, Succos and Shemini Atzeres have all been listed and described in the Torah section of *Ki Sisa* while Yom Kippur is to be found highlighted in the section of *Achrei Mos*.

~§ A Difficult Concept

To understand the reason, we must recognize that in truth, it was very difficult for the Jews to recognize the true significance of Rosh Hashanah when they had first left Egypt in Nisan.

Upon being liberated from their Egyptian bondage, the Jews lacked an intellectual connection with the Creator of the world. The Ibn Ezra asks a question—When God introduced Himself to the Jewish people at Mount Sinai, why did He say, "I am *Hashem*, your God, who brought you out of the land of Egypt?"

Would not it have been more impressive for Him to have declared—"I am *Hashem*, your God, who created you?" At first glance, this would definitely appear to be a more significant accomplishment than merely the taking of someone out of a degraded place (Egyptian bondage) in time.

Ibn Ezra answers his question by stating that this introduction of God as the Creator of the world would have simply been too abstract a philosophical concept for the Jewish nation (which was only then just about to begin receiving the Torah and to develop themselves on a spiritual plane) to grasp.

However with their own eyes, the Jews had witnessed their Exodus from Egypt and this was indeed a tangible action that they could comprehend with their minds and accept. At this point in time, they were only able to recognize God as Director of the world.

~§ Creating the Mishkan

At what moment were the Jews first able to visualize God as the Creator of the world? This only occurred following the construction of the *Mishkan* (Sanctuary) in the desert. Why? Because as stated in the Midrash, the *Mishkan* was a microcosm of God's creation of the world in that God commanded us not to work on the Sabbath Day, since after He had completed Creation, He too had rested on the Seventh Day.

The commandment to observe the Sabbath is the only one in all of the Torah that God instructed us to carry out in order that we (Jews) should emulate Him and His behavior. If one wants to follow *Hashem's* path and be Godly, the Torah instructs that individual to keep the Sabbath. Yet, in order to know what is permissible on this day and just what actions are forbidden, it is important for the Jew to know exactly which types of work are prohibited.

From whence does the Torah determine exactly which activities must not be performed on the Sabbath? The answer comes from analyzing the various functions which were necessary for the construction of the *Mishkan*. These thirty-nine types of work are forbidden to the Jew on the Sabbath Day. From this lesson, we can further conclude that the construction of the *Mishkan* was indeed a microcosm of God's Creation of the world.

Before the actual construction of the *Mishkan*, the Jewish nation did not accurately know how to rest on the Sabbath. But, even more importantly, we did not know just how to relate to God as the Creator of the world.

This point is clarified if we recall that just before the Jews began to actually construct the *Mishkan*, God demanded of them that they should keep the Sabbath day holy. The reason that this commandment for observing the Sabbath was reiterated at this time is that by their construction of the Sanctuary in the Wilderness, the Jews were, as we said before, imitating God's initial Creation of the world.

◄§ Emulating the Sabbath Rest

In the same manner that we as Jews emulated God's creation of the world by our construction of the *Mishkan*, likewise we have to emulate His resting on the Seventh Day by our observing the holiness of the Sabbath.

With the completion of the *Mishkan*, the Jews were at last able to intellectually comprehend God as the Creator of the world. It is therefore most appropriate that only at this time when the Torah has just completed discussing the construction of the *Mishkan* by the Jews in the Wilderness (in the Torah section of *Emor*), that then and only then can God speak to the Jews about the important *mitzvah* of observing the festival of Rosh Hashanah.

May we once again come to a deeper appreciation of God's role as the Creator of the world. By our careful observance of the *mitzvah* of hearing the shofar's blast on Rosh Hashanah, we should further merit to witness the manifestations of God's combined qualities of Divine mercy and strict judgment.

Together may they result in the speedy arrival of the righteous Messiah whose coming will once again herald another chapter in the world's history that can truly be defined by the words "very good" in practice as well as theory.

Yom Kippur Thoughts

A Good Day
for Repentance

CONCERNING THE HOLIDAY of Yom Kippur, we find an interesting statement in *Pirkei DeRabbi Eliezer*. This *sefer* (book) states that Yom Kippur is the birthday of the Jewish people. How were the Jewish people born? They were born with the covenant of circumcision—the *bris milah*. According to *Pirkei DeRabbi Eliezer*, our patriarch Abraham was circumcised on Yom Kippur. This act and day therefore constitute a very auspicious beginning for the Jewish people.

One might however ask what specifically does the circumcision of our forefather Abraham have to do with the day of Yom Kippur as we know it? What is its relationship with the concept of the atonement of sin that we associate with Yom Kippur? To understand this connection, let us analyze a few ideas connected to these particular actions. What does the *bris milah* represent? The Midrash says that when Adam (the first man) was created, he was born perfect, with the mark of circumcision.

Turning to the Talmud, we find it stated that Adam caused himself to lose the mark of circumcision. The *Maharsha* explains that this was a consequence of Adam's sin of eating the forbidden fruit. Therefore, when God told Abraham to circumcise himself, it was in a way a *tikun* or mending for the first sin of man. Now since this *tikun* of the first sin was done on Yom Kippur, this day has become a time set apart for the mending of all subsequent sins in all future generations.

This article was originally transcribed from Rabbi Kaplan's lecture notes, for publication in the Crown Heights Chronicle—September 1981.

◆§ Yom Kippur and the Golden Calf

Another question worth delving into is that of the connection between the day of Yom Kippur and the sin of the Golden Calf. Most readers, I am sure, are informed of the entire chronology of the giving of the Torah.

The Jews left Egypt on Passover. Seven weeks later they completed the *sefirah*, and on Shavuos, the Jewish nation received the Torah.

Moses then went up to Mount Sinai to get the *Luchos* (the Tablets containing the Ten Commandments). During this forty-day period, Moses remained atop Mount Sinai and received instruction in the Torah from God. He came down from Mount Sinai on the seventeenth of Tammuz. He then saw the sin of the Golden Calf, where some of the Jews were dancing and celebrating around a graven image.

At this point Moses broke the original Tablets. He went up again to the top of Mount Sinai and remained for an additional forty days. There he asked God to forgive the Jews. He came down a second time on Rosh Chodesh Elul. That same day, God told Moses to go up to Mount Sinai and receive the second set of Tablets. We learn further, from the Talmud, that he came down with this second pair of Tablets and arrived in the camp of the Israelites on the day that was Yom Kippur. This was a Divine sign that God had forgiven the Jews for their earlier sin of the Golden Calf.

◆§ A Similarity in Sins

We can find a very strong similarity between the sin of the Golden Calf and that of the original sin of Adam. The Talmud says, in tractate *Avodah Zarah*, that the writing on the Tablets was free. The writing was engraved on the Tablets. The sages of blessed memory say that one should not read *charus*, engraved, but rather *cheirus*, which means free.

The Tablets constituted freedom for the Jews—freedom from subjugation to foreign governments and freedom from the Angel of Death. After the giving of the Torah, the Jewish people were on the same level as was Adam before the first sin.

When the Jews sinned with the Golden Calf, they had to suffer the same loss that Adam suffered because of his sin. Therefore, the Yom Kippur in which Moses came down with the second pair of Tablets was an atonement for their sin, in the same way that Abraham's circumcision on an earlier Yom Kippur day had served as an atonement for the first sin of Adam.

◆§ Atoning for Sins

We can now investigate the method in which the day of Yom Kippur and fulfilling the requirements established on that day help the Jew to atone for his sins. Regarding the atonement of sins, we find in the Talmud that there are four types of atonements listed for various sins.

The Rambam also recites this list in the beginning of *Hilchos Tshuvah*.

(1) A person who violates a positive commandment does not even have to pause to gain atonement. He is forgiven immediately.

(2) A person who violates a negative commandment has his repentance held in abeyance until Yom Kippur. After observing the requirements of that day, he obtains complete atonement.

(3) The Talmud states another case whereby a person violates a negative commandment which has the penalty of *korais* (excision from the Jewish people or a death decree from the Heavenly tribunal). In this situation even repentance and Yom Kippur do not suffice to cleanse the sin. In addition, suffering is required to atone for the transgression of a negative commandment that carries the penalty of *korais*.

(4) The final case brought up by both the Talmud and the Rambam is the worst possible sin of all—*Chilul Hashem* or the desecration of God's name. In this case even repentance, Yom Kippur and suffering can only hold in abeyance. The sin cannot be totally atoned for until the person who commits it dies.

✑ Desecrating God's Name

We can learn from the above that the desecration of God's name is a very serious act. In truth, it is very frightening to read what the Talmud says about this transgression. Among the things it defines as constituting a desecration of God's name include the case of someone who is not scrupulously honest in his business dealings with both Jews and gentiles. Further, even someone who does not speak nicely to people is considered to have committed this serious sin.

Let us imagine that a non-religious person walks into a store and the religious shopkeeper is brusque to him. Thereafter the customer walks away and says, "These religious Jews are rude and don't have any manners." According to what the Talmud has defined, our shopkeeper has committed a desecration of God's name.

It goes without saying, that if an individual can point to another individual and say "There goes a religious person. He has a beard, *payos* and even wears Chassidic garb. Yet he cheated me," this incident is a desecration of God's name.

In commenting on the Tractate *Yoma*, Rashi describes this very serious transgression (the desecration of God's name) as being the act which brings others to do sins. What does he mean? It is really quite obvious. For example, when people see religious Jews not behaving properly in business or in just talking properly, they can say, "What is the use in being religious if a person isn't honest or cannot talk nicely?"

✑ How to Make Atonement

Now the reader might just wonder what he can do to atone for the acts described above which constitute a desecration of God's name. Earlier we learned that for this transgression not even repentance, Yom Kippur and suffering combined can atone during the life of the person. Only death can bring atonement. However let us study in further detail the types of repentance available and how we can even rectify this most serious sin of the desecration of God's name in our own lifetimes.

The Talmud states that repentance is great because purposeful sins become like accidental sins. The Talmud also states that purposeful sins can, through repentance, become like good deeds. At first glance there appears to be a contradiction. The Talmud however reconciles the two statements.

The first statement speaks of a person who repents out of a fear of God, while the second refers to an individual who repents out of a love for God.

When a person repents out of fear, his sins become like accidents, whereas the person who repents out of love, finds that his sins have been transformed into good deeds.

✑ Repenting out of Love

A person who commits an accidental sin, by doing something inadvertently, still needs further atonement. During the time of the *Beis HaMikdash* (Holy Temple), the individual had to bring a sin offering to atone for his accidental transgression. Today when we are without the *Beis HaMikdash*, one must make atonement by arousing in his heart a sense of repentance. Therefore the Talmud says that if a person does repentance out of fear, he requires further atonement. This additional atonement can only be obtained by elevating his repentance to that of the level of having been generated by a love of God.

Should a person accomplish his repentance out of a love for God, as the Talmud states, every transgression he ever committed becomes like a *mitzvah*. These are now judged in his merit.

To reiterate this point, both the books *Chareidim* and *Minchas Chinuch* say that the four categories of atonement listed earlier apply only if a person repents out of fear of punishment. But should the individual repent out of his love for God, he is immediately forgiven all sins. So therefore it behooves us to all learn to repent out of a love for God.

Many individuals today claim that it is hard to reach this lofty level when there are so many distractions facing us. They argue that we have more ideological and spiritual diversions than did our grandparents who lived in simpler times. I however believe just the contrary. People today are better equipped to have a love for God than were people living in previous generations. This is especially true as we are living in the times that are so close to the coming of *Mashiach* (the Messiah).

Most *baalei tshuvah* (individuals who return to religious observance) do not have images of *Gehinnom* (Hell) before their eyes. Usually they become religious because of a special love they possess for both

Judaism and God. Therefore the idea of generating a repentance out of love for God is not such a far-fetched idea in our times.

✥ How to Love God

A suggestion for the many people who want to exercise their inherent love for God, is perhaps as Rambam writes, to meditate on "the greatness of God." The individual should think of His greatness, think of all that God has done for us and about the greatness of God's deeds. Try and meditate about what God is. One should set aside fifteen minutes at the beginning of Yom Kippur to sit down and ponder over the greatness and wonders of God. This will bring the person to a love of God and facilitate repentance on this level.

Another important thing for people to do is to recite the *Shemoneh Esrei* (*Amidah*) with strong *kavanah* (concentration) on Yom Kippur, especially the first blessing which is called the *Avos* (forefathers). But if you really analyze this blessing, you will discover that it is an introduction and serves as a method of defining God to ourselves.

That blessing uses terms such as "the great, mighty, awesome God." The person who truly says this blessing and all its words with concentration, carefully, slowly and thinking about the meaning of every word, will at that moment come to a tremendous love for God. He will think that "I love God so much. I want to be so close to Him. How could I have possibly sinned?" This will inevitably bring a person to repentance with love.

✥ A Day of Fasting

Perhaps the aspect of Yom Kippur which attracts the attention of most individuals is that of fasting. Even the majority of non-religious Jews fast on this day. While fasting is important, we must not forget that the main aspect of Yom Kippur is bringing ourselves to a level of repentance for our past sins. Of course, fasting is very significant because it is one of the commandments of the Torah and helps lead one to repentance. One who eats on Yom Kippur commits an extremely severe transgression. Yet God tells the Prophets that fasting alone will not do the whole job. It must be accompanied by repentance.

Repentance does not mean just saying, "I am sorry." It signifies a major change in one's lifestyle. It represents a commitment to change for the better. According to some authorities if a person does not fulfill his promises on Yom Kippur to change, there is a serious question as to whether his repentance of Yom Kippur was valid.

✥ Atoning for Adam

A person might wonder why, of all things, the Jewish law requires one to fast on Yom Kippur. We find a model of how the main method by which Yom Kippur leads the individual to seek forgiveness of sins is that of fasting. What does fasting have to do with atonement?

The very first sin involved eating. Sin in a sense came to the world as a result of eating (when Adam ate the forbidden fruit) and therefore the atonement of sin is rendered by refraining from eating on Yom Kippur.

Uniting with God
Via the Torah

O NE CAN ASK THE QUESTION, "Why do we celebrate Purim as a holiday?" At first glance, an individual answer might arise that Purim commemorates the events in Shushan, Persia where the entire Jewish community was saved from a Divine decree ordaining their death. This threat arose because they participated in the festive meal celebrations of King Ahasuerus who employed the sacred vessels that Nebuchadnezzar had plundered after destroying the first Holy Temple in Jerusalem.

These events are fully recorded in the *Megillah*, or Book of Esther, which also tells of how the Jews repented of their serious sin. Even though the name of God is never directly mentioned in the *Megillah*, commentators point out how the text clearly reveals the hand of God as it appeared in what might otherwise be regarded as the natural turn of events.

Because the Jews fasted and repented, God reversed the death decree and instead it was their enemies, led by the wicked Haman, a descendant of Amalek, who were destroyed. A simple interpretation of the Purim story would seem to indicate that this is the reason that we celebrate the holiday today.

⊷§ From Death to Life

Nevertheless, the question as to why we observe the festivities of Purim still remains unanswered. It is not just a simple thing to add a new holi-

---

This article was originally transcribed from Rabbi Kaplan's lecture notes, for publication in the Crown Heights Chronicle—March 1982.

day to the Jewish calendar. When Esther and Mordechai made the suggestion, they were immediately challenged by the other Torah scholars of their day—the *Anshei Knesses HaGedolah* (Members of the Great Assembly).

Esther and Mordechai argued that if, when the Jews departed from Egyptian slavery and entered freedom, a holiday (Passover) was ordained by the Torah, then certainly the Torah should make a provision for instituting a holiday (Purim) to denote our transition from apparent death (Haman's scheme) to life. While the Torah sages accepted the request of Esther and Mordechai to add the holiday of Purim, we must realize that this decision of the *Anshei Knesses HaGedolah* was based on more than just the desire to publicize the miracle which occurred to the Jews of those days in Shushan, Persia.

✑§ Accepting the Oral Torah

To recognize the deeper significance behind the festival of Purim, we should understand that the Purim miracle did not constitute the first nor the last time that Jews were rescued miraculously from an apparent major calamity. Yet, we do not find that these other numerous joyous events were transformed into important religious holidays that all Jews in subsequent generations are required to observe.

Indeed, if one desires to truly understand the deeper meaning of why Purim was added to the Jewish calendar, the individual should realize that the events of Purim led into the construction of the second Holy Temple in Jerusalem. What is the whole idea of Purim? The underlying reason that we celebrate this holiday is that it marks the final acceptance of the Torah by the Jewish people.

The Talmud in tractate *Shabbos* (88a) states that after their miraculous redemption from Haman's horrible scheme to annihilate them, the Jews of their own free will chose to accept the Oral Torah, thus completing the process begun at Mount Sinai some nine hundred years before. The *Megillah* (9:27) declares that "they (the Jews) sustained and they accepted," i.e., the complete Torah—both the Written Torah (Scripture) and Oral Torah (Talmud).

It was only following the events of Purim that the Jews eagerly accepted the entire Torah. We learn that when the Jews were gathered at Mount Sinai to receive the Torah some fifty days following their liberation from Egyptian bondage, God picked up the mountain and held it over their heads, declaring, "If you do not take My Torah, there (under the mountain) shall you be buried." The Talmudic passage which recounts this episode indicates that the Jews apparently accepted the Torah because of coercion. Had they chosen to refuse, Mount Sinai would have fallen upon them and become their communal grave.

The Midrash (*Tanchuma, Noach*) teaches a very interesting point in connection with the two occasions when the Jews accepted the Torah, at Mount Sinai and on Purim. When God offered the Torah to the Jewish people at Mount Sinai, they eagerly said, *"Na'aseh v'nishma"* ("We will do and we will listen"). This declaration is recorded in the Bible. How can anyone therefore argue that the Jews at Mount Sinai were coerced into accepting the Torah? The Midrash explains that what the Jews happily accepted at Mount Sinai was the Written Torah. Yet at Mount Sinai, they were initially repelled by the prospects of accepting the Oral Torah.

Moses read *Sefer HaBris* (the *Book of the Covenant*) and the Jews happily accepted the Written Torah, declaring, *"Na'aseh v'nishma."* This *Sefer HaBris* was the Written Torah. It was only after they had accepted the Written Torah based on what Moses had read to them that the Jews were informed of the Oral Torah. Upon learning of its contents, they became afraid and were hesitant to accept this part of the overall Torah. It was because of this reaction that God was forced to pick up Mount Sinai and hold it over the heads of the Jewish nation, pressuring them into reluctantly accepting the entire Torah.

✑ Intimidation at Mount Sinai

The concepts enumerated in the Written Torah at first glance appear easy and even enjoyable. For example, one should observe the *Shabbos*, and each man should don *tefillin* every weekday. Yet after glancing at the general terms which are mentioned in the Written Torah, the Jew is told that he must study all the varied rules applying to these *mitzvos* (commandments) as they are enumerated in great detail in the Oral Torah. It is not surprising that the Jews at Mount Sinai were intimidated by what they at first perceived to be burdensome regulations.

It came to be that only on Purim after their miraculous redemption from death, that the Jews accepted the Oral Torah of their own free will, with no coercion applied. Therefore, the holiday of Purim has come to signify something more that just a simple miracle—it marks the final completion of the Jew's acceptance of God's Holy Torah. With this act, our nation truly became God's chosen people.

✑ Oath and Covenant

There were two actions which symbolized the fact that the Jews had become God's chosen people. The first consisted of a *sh'vuah* (oath) and the second was that of a *bris* (covenant). When the Jewish people accepted the Torah, they in a sense became married to God. This marriage required two actions, an oath and a covenant. Whenever a man marries, his status automatically changes. Similarly, when our forefathers accepted the Torah, their status changed from that of gentiles to that of Jews.

The Torah which symbolizes the union between God and the Jewish nation was given over to the Jews by God with both an oath and a covenant. The oath was uttered when we said at Mount Sinai.

"Na'aseh v'nishma." The covenant is however much more than just a promise. Rather it is the act of making a covenant which constitutes a major change in the status of the individual and finalizes the union. That is why a male convert to Judaism must undergo both a circumcision and *mikveh* immersion. These acts make up the covenant and symbolically change the status of a convert from that of a gentile to that of a Jew.

If the words *Na'aseh v'nishma* at Mount Sinai represented the Jews' oath, what action represented their covenant with God? The Talmud in tractate *Gittin* states the covenant between God and the Jewish people was sealed only with their acceptance of the Oral Torah on Purim joyously and without coercion. It therefore follows that Purim became the time when the Jews finalized the covenant with God.

The entire wedding ceremony between the Jews and God which began at Mount Sinai with the oath *Na'aseh v'nishma* was concluded successfully with the covenant on Purim when all Jews accepted the Oral Torah. This reason therefore dictates why the *Anshei Knesses HaGedolah* agreed to the request of Esther and Mordechai making Purim a holiday that subsequent Jewish generations would celebrate.

ᴥᔍ A New Era Dawns in Torah Learning

It is worth noting that after this act of acceptance by the Jews immediately following the miracle of Purim, a new era was initiated during which the learning of the Oral Torah reached incredible heights never before or again surpassed. It was only after this unanimous declaration of the Jewish nation that the *Mishnah* began to develop. From this point onwards the Jews devoted more energies to the study of the Talmud—the *Mishnah* and the *Gemara*—which is the major component of the Oral Torah.

Furthermore one discovers that shortly following the events of Purim, the Written Torah or Bible was closed by the *Anshei Knesses HaGedolah*. The destruction of the first Temple a few decades before Purim ushered in the closing of the era of prophecy. The Membership of the *Anshei Knesses HaGedolah* included the last prophets of Israel, having been exiled following the destruction of the Temple in Jerusalem.

We learn from the Talmud that a major requirement for prophecy is that the majority of Jews must live in the Land of Israel. Even with the construction of the second Temple which commenced almost immediately following the Purim events, the majority of Jews never again lived in Israel. Therefore prophecy was lost and the Written Torah sealed.

Symbolic of Purim representing the final chapter in the era of the Written Torah is the fact that the Psalmist refers to Esther, the heroine of the Purim *Megillah*, as "the morning dawn." Just as the dawn marks the end of night, so too did Esther signify the end of all prophetic-style miracles.

✧§ Understanding Supersedes the Sefirah of Wisdom

In the aftermath of Purim, a tremendous new interest in the study of the Oral Torah developed among the Jewish people. Since one does not usually exhibit much enthusiasm or enjoyment for an activity in which one participates under duress, it is easy to understand why, prior to their acceptance of the Oral Torah on Purim, the Jews failed to distinguish themselves in this area of learning.

A major transformation in the service of the Jew developed during the time between the First and Second Temples. The main focus during the period of the First Temple was mystical, while that of the Second Temple was of a more intellectual nature. The first Temple was dominated by the *sefirah* of *chochmah* (wisdom) which is a mystical quality. The Second Temple was influenced by *binah* (understanding) which is basically an intellectual characteristic.

It makes sense that the Second Temple was dominated by *binah*, an intellectual aspect, as it was during this time that the study of the Oral Torah blossomed. The Written Torah flourished during the First Temple when the quality of mysticism reigned supreme.

A question may be asked concerning the arrival of *Mashiach* (the Messiah) and the construction of the Third (the final and eternal) Temple in Jerusalem. What will be the important aspect governing Jewish awareness during the Messianic era? Will Jews be influenced by the *sefirah* of *daas* (knowledge)? We do find the verse in the prophetic Book of Isaiah (11:9) which predicts that in the future, "The world will be filled with *daas* (knowledge) of the Lord, as the waters cover the sea."

✧§ The Cause of Man's Downfall and Its Rectification

There is an additional lesson regarding Purim that we can learn from Purim. It concerns details that the Talmud mentions in connection with the coming of *Mashiach*. To better understand this, let us ask the question, "What was the cause of the original downfall of man?" It came through *daas* (knowledge) or more specifically through the act of Adam's eating from the *Etz Hadaas* (the Tree of Knowledge) concerning good and bad. The Talmud teaches that when *Mashiach* arrives, the world order will be rectified. This means that *daas* (knowledge) which was corrupted on the sixth day by Adam will also be corrected and elevated to its original position during the creation of the world.

Purim has a very direct connection with *daas*. There are three stated opinions regarding the identity of the forbidden fruit. One opinion, and this is the view we will pursue, is that the *Etz Hadaas* was a grapevine. After the flood, Noah tried to go back to this source of

Adam's downfall and rectify it. Unfortunately, he too got careless, became drunk, and the end result was quite disastrous for him and the rest of mankind.

Nevertheless, the Jew realizes that the Torah always includes a *tikun* (method of mending) for all past mistakes, including the original sin of Adam. According to the opinion we have adopted, this sin consisted of drinking wine. If so, we may seek a *mitzvah* in the Torah which is a *tikun* for Adam's sin.

One way to rectify Adam's sin is to abstain from drinking wine or eating the fruit of the vine in any form. A person who undertakes such abstention by means of a vow is called a *Nazir* (Nazirite). The *Nazir* takes it upon himself not to drink wine because he wants to put himself in the state of Adam before the sin of eating from the Tree of Knowledge. It was from this act of eating (i.e., drinking) the forbidden fruit (i.e., wine) that the quality of knowledge was blemished for all generations. And it is the *Nazir's* abstention that rectifies this act.

◄§ Purim Offers another Solution

Another way to rectify Adam's sin is with the celebration of the holiday of Purim. The Talmud teaches that one must drink wine until he is devoid of knowledge and is unable to distinguish between blessing Mordechai and cursing Haman. The key words are however that one must drink until he is devoid of "knowledge." This knowledge of which we must rid ourselves is that which Adam corrupted when he sinned by eating from the Tree of Knowledge.

Therefore in the days prior to *Mashiach* who will soon redeem the world, including the blemished quality of *daas* (knowledge), and the verse of Isaiah (11:9), "The world will be filled with *daas* of the Lord, as the waters cover the sea," will be fulfilled, the Jew has his own opportunity to make amends for the initial misdeed of the first man. This correction can best be carried out when all Jews fully observe the commandment of Purim to celebrate this joyous and important holiday by drinking in a proper and holy manner.

The Rectification
of Adam's Sin

WHAT IS THE SIGNIFICANCE of Passover? To grasp the answer to this very important question, we must recognize that Passover was and continues to be the gateway to God's giving of the Torah to the Jewish people on the day that we today celebrate as the festival of Shavuos.

The Talmud states that with the giving of the Torah all the negative effects of Adam's sin were annulled with respect to the Jewish nation. In particular, the Jews were freed from the power of the Angel of Death.

It was only later, some forty days following the Sinai experience when the Jews tragically transgressed by worshiping the Golden Calf, that we as a people reverted back to the unrectified state that was introduced to mankind by the initial sin of Adam.

The *Arizal* (Rabbi Yitzchak Luria, of blessed memory) teaches that the whole concept of Passover provides the Jews with a method of rectifying Adam's sin. One can learn many valuable lessons from this point.

First of all, let us ask ourselves the question, "What is the historical background of Passover?" At first glance, Passover is merely a memorial to the fact that the Jews had been enslaved in Egypt and that God had liberated them from there. But then we may ask, "Why were the Jews in Egypt in the first place?" The answer is that they were there as the result of a question that their forefather, Abraham, had asked of God after He had promised to give Abraham and his descendants the Land of Israel as an eternal inheritance (Genesis 15:8).

This article was originally transcribed from Rabbi Kaplan's lecture notes, for publication in the Crown Heights Chronicle—April 1982.

❧ Abraham's Question

Abraham had asked of God, "How will I *know?*" The Talmudic sages teach that the entire Egyptian slavery came about because of this one question asked by Abraham. This question constituted a seeming lack of faith on Abraham's part to a direct promise uttered to him by God. The mistake in this question can be identified by focusing on the word "know." Abraham's error indicated that he had not completely refined the quality of *daas* (knowledge) that had been blemished by Adam's sin.

In answer to Abraham's question, God appeared to the patriarch in a vision and said, "Abram, know for a surety that your seed shall be strangers in a land that is not theirs and they shall serve them..." (Genesis 15:13).

To better understand Abraham's failing and God's purpose, let us study the exact nature of Adam's first sin which resulted in all mankind being plagued with various curses, including that of death.

Adam's sin consisted in having violated God's prohibition against eating from *Etz Hadaas* (the Tree of Knowledge) of good and bad.

The challenge that God had posed before Abraham was that he try to rectify the blemished state of knowledge that was created when Adam had eaten from the Tree of Knowledge.

There were many ways that Abraham could have redeemed knowledge from the stain imposed upon it by Adam's sin. To some degree, Abraham had made major progress in elevating the quality of knowledge. Unfortunately, his question to God gave proof that Abraham had not completely mastered the assignment.

❧ The Bris Milah

To better illustrate just how Abraham was given the opportunity by God to atone for the sin of Adam, we can further study the concept of the *bris milah* (circumcision) as it applied to each of them individually.

We learn in the Talmud that immediately after Adam ate from the forbidden fruit of the Tree of Knowledge, his body lost the mark of circumcision which he had possessed when he was created by God on the sixth day. The mark of circumcision symbolizes a perfection in the body and Adam was therefore incapable of bearing this privileged sign after his sin.

The generations succeeding Adam were also denied the right of circumcision until the time that God specifically commanded Abraham to circumcise himself and all of his offspring. This command indicated God's desire that Abraham begin to rectify the effects brought upon the world by Adam's sin.

Although Abraham had made significant progress in elevating the quality of knowledge, his question, "How will I know?" indicated that he had not completely mastered the challenge. Therefore God ordained that Abraham's descendaents, the Jewish people, would have to go down to Egypt where they would be enslaved by a strange people in order to complete the rectification of knowledge.

⊷§ "You have been Shown to Know"

Immediately following their liberation from this bondage on Passover, God said to them, "You have been shown to know that the Lord is God; there is none else aside from Him" (Deuteronomy 4:35). With this statement, the Jews were taught that they had successfully rectified the sin of Adam, particularly regarding the damage that had been inflicted on the quality of knowledge.

The Talmud comments that Adam had only been prohibited from eating the fruit of the Tree of Knowledge for just a few hours. Man had been created on the sixth day of Creation which was a Friday, and God merely wanted Adam to refrain from eating from the fruit of the Tree of Knowledge, which according to one opinion was a grapevine, until the start of the Sabbath on Friday night. Just before that time, Adam would have been encouraged to take the fruit of the Tree of Knowledge (the grapevine) and to make wine with which to sanctify the Sabbath. Had he only waited until the proper time, Adam could have eaten from the Tree of Knowledge and then succeeded in truly elevating the quality of knowledge.

⊷§ The Sabbath and the Manna

It is interesting to reflect that the Jewish nation was not given the commandment to observe the Sabbath until shortly after the Exodus. God manifestly bestowed the Sabbath on the Jews following the Passover liberation from Egyptian slavery at the same time that He also gave them the heavenly manna for a food.

One should notice that it is no coincidence that the Jews were given the Sabbath and the manna at the same time. And once again, two seemingly unrelated incidents point back to Adam's sin, his act of eating that which was forbidden. The relationship between the Sabbath and the manna becomes more apparent when we reflect upon the curse with which God punished Adam.

What was the nature of this curse? The curse forced Adam to gain his bread (food) through the sweat of his brow (hard work). Moreover, the ground was cursed thereby making it harder for Adam to obtain the food his body needed.

Through their liberation from Egyptian slavery, the Jews rose to a level of Adam before the sin, that is, the difficult, backbreaking labor of the Egyptian bondage rectified Adam's sin. To indicate this enhanced status God granted the Jews a special source of divine food (the manna) in a manner that completely contradicted that which He had imposed on Adam. The Jews would no longer have to gain their bread by the sweat of their brow. It would come down to them as a direct gift from God. Furthermore, they were given the Sabbath. The very concept of the Sabbath emphasizes the rest and relaxation from the normal need to work and exert oneself in the goal of obtaining one's bread or sustenance. By granting the Jews both the Sabbath and the manna simultaneously, God indicated that the Jews had rectified Adam's sin of eating improperly from the Tree of Knowledge.

Eating Bread

During the festival of Passover there are certain foods which we must eat and others which we are prohibited from consuming. Let us examine the case of bread.

What kind of bread is a Jew permitted to eat during Passover? We are permitted to eat only *matzah* (unleavened bread). With the exception of these days of Passover, the Jew may eat *chametz* (leavened bread) anytime he desires with, except, of course, on fast days.

It is appropriate for us to reflect on the nature of leavened bread. To create leavened bread, one must put down the dough to rot, or as we say chemically, to "ferment." Although dough is allowed to rot, with a controlled amount of fermentation, the dough is transformed into bread that is actually quite tasty. Obviously in an uncontrolled state where the dough is allowed to rot for too long a period of time, the end result would not be a food product that one could safely eat or even enjoy the taste of.

Nevertheless, we do have to put a "little" decay (fermentation) into our dough. Leavened bread is not perfect in its initial state. Rather to reach this desired level, where it is tasty and enjoyable, it must be permitted to decay just a little.

Symbolic of the Yetzer Hara

The Talmud says of this decay in the leavened bread, that it is representative of the *Yetzer Hara* (the inclination towards evil). This is illustrated by the argument of the Jewish sages to Hashem: "Master of the universe, we want to do Your will. But what prevents us? The leaven in the dough." This "leaven in the dough" refers to the *Yetzer Hara*. Just as we have this spiritual decay (the *Yetzer Hara*) in our physical body, so too the leavened bread which sustains our physical body during the majority of the year must also have a little decay.

Therefore, since the leavened bread possesses this decay or fermentation which is symbolic of the *Yetzer Hara*, the Jew is not allowed to eat leavened bread on Passover. The idea of Passover is for one to get as far away as possible from leavened bread. We want to symbolically distance ourselves as much as possible from the sin of Adam. We therefore eat only *matzah* which does not have any leaven at all.

THE RECTIFICATION OF ADAM'S SIN   115

Thus when the Jews came out of Egypt and were on their way to conquer the Holy Land which at that time was inhabited by the Canaanites, God specifically warned them to avoid behaving in the grossly immoral ways of both the Egyptians and the Canaanites, who were the descendants of Ham.

Fulfilling the Curse

The ultimate curse against Canaan was fulfilled when his offspring lost their land to the Jews following the Exodus from Egypt. While the Egyptians were not actually displaced from their land for their mistreatment of the Jews, we can easily recognize how Noah's curse against the Hamites was fulfilled. They suffered severely from the degrading manner in which God punished them during the course of inflicting upon them the Ten Plagues.

Therefore, when the Jew drinks his wine in a truly holy manner at the Passover seder, this act represents a concerted effort to elevate the essence of the wine from the degradations inflicted upon it during the two instances where Adam and Noah failed to utilize it (wine) for sacred purposes.

An interesting point can also be learned when making a comparison of how Jews observe Passover and Shavuos. On Passover, as already mentioned, we avoid any contact whatsoever with leavened bread that symbolizes, through its process of decay (fermentation), the concept of the Yetzer Hara (the Power of Evil).

However, on Shavuos, God especially commanded that the Jews should make a unique offering in the Temple of two loaves of leavened bread. Why, if the Jews must avoid leavened bread with its implication of the Yetzer Hara on Passover, are they commanded by Hashem to utilize leavened bread during the service of Shavuos which commemorates our receiving of the Holy Torah?

Like a Very Sick Person

To understand the reason, we must realize that on Passover, shortly after the Jews were saved from Egyptian slavery, they were similar in nature to a very sick person who was only just beginning to display the first indications of recovering from a disease that all the doctors had diagnosed as being both fatal and incurable.

Even though he is beginning to recover, the man is still very sick and must take great efforts to protect himself. That is why on Passover the Jew avoids any contact with leavened bread because of its symbolic relationship to the Yetzer Hara.

For forty-nine days following the first day of Passover, the Jews count the sefirah. Each sefirah relates to a specific moral quality such as mercy. On each day that they count sefirah, the Jews concentrate their energies on improving their own personal performance of that particular quality.

When the Jews left Egypt, they had already fallen into the forty-ninth level of moral impurity. Our Sages of Blessed Memory state that had God not taken the Jews out at precisely the moment that He did, the Jews would have fallen into the fiftieth level of impurity. This would have constituted a descent from which it would have been physically impossible for them to have been purified and healed of the moral disease that they had contracted while slaves in Egypt.

Regaining Strength for the Torah

Furthermore, considering that the Jews were still very spiritually sick, they were in no position to receive the Torah. God allowed them time with which to build up their strength in order to be able to receive this great holy gift.

This is the concept behind our counting the forty-nine days of Sefirah. Each day constituted an opportunity that the Jews took in perfecting a quality that helped to lift them up from the levels of impurity that they had fallen into while enslaved in Egypt.

After forty-nine days, the Jews had completely recovered from the descent to the forty-ninth level of Egyptian moral impurity. The very next day as pure and healthy individuals, they were capable of receiving the Torah. God did not then waste one second and He promptly bestowed His precious gift onto the Jewish nation.

On Shavuos day, the Jews were spiritually in the best of health. They no longer had to fear the power of the Yetzer Hara, as they had eliminated all the spiritual impurities of Egypt.

The Human Challah

The Midrash declares that Adam was himself made in a manner similar to dough. Dough is made by mixing flour and water. Likewise, Adam was made from a kneaded mixture of dust and water. The Book of Genesis records how the mist came up from the ground and watered the earth. At that point God made man from the dust of the earth. Moreover, just as a portion of each batch of dough must be set aside and consecrated (the mitzvah of challah), so was Adam set aside as the challah of mankind. The Jerusalem Talmud explains why the woman is given the special commandment regarding the separation of challah. The answer given is that this separation is an act of atonement, for she (Eve) destroyed (by bringing death to) the human challah of the world, which was Adam.

On Passover, the Jew is commanded to drink four cups of wine. What is the significance of the wine? According to the opinion which holds that the Tree of Knowledge was a grapevine, it would be understandable that our drinking of the four cups during the Passover seder is intricately connected to our task in rectifying the blemish brought on mankind by Adam's sin of eating (i.e., drinking) the forbidden fruit (i.e., wine).

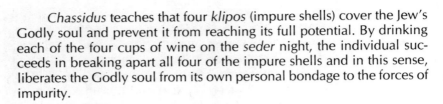

Chassidus teaches that four *klipos* (impure shells) cover the Jew's Godly soul and prevent it from reaching its full potential. By drinking each of the four cups of wine on the *seder* night, the individual succeeds in breaking apart all four of the impure shells and in this sense, liberates the Godly soul from its own personal bondage to the forces of impurity.

ᴥᔆ Why Egypt?

It is interesting to consider just why the Jews were sent to Egypt to be enslaved. God had merely told Abraham that his descendants would be "strangers in a land that is not theirs." Of all the possible lands where they could have enacted out their period of slavery until such time as *Hashem* would have liberated them, why did God choose to send the Jews to Egypt?

A second question which might shed some additional light on this topic is with whom is the land of Egypt associated? The Bible tells us that the descendants of Ham were the people inhabiting Egypt during the times that the Jews were enslaved there.

Ham is connected to a second instance where the Bible records how an individual failed in an attempt to eat from the grapevine (drink wine) in a manner that would serve the cause of holiness.

After the Flood which wiped out all human and animal life on earth with the exception of those aboard Noah's Ark, God promised Noah a blessing in whatever was the first activity that he performed upon disembarking from the Ark.

The first act of Noah was the planting of a vineyard. He then produced and drank wine. His desire was to rectify Adam's initial sin which came about through the drinking of wine. However, Noah was careless and instead got drunk.

The Book of Genesis tells how Noah's son Ham came to see his father naked when in a drunken stupor following this unfortunate drinking of the wine.

ᴥᔆ The Curse of Ham

As a result of this act of disrespect which he displayed to his father, Ham and all his descendants were cursed. This all came about because Noah had drunk wine. The curse of the Hamites and the concept of Egypt representing a source of evil can be traced to Noah's drinking of the wine.

Egypt, because of the curse that Noah inflicted on his son Ham, became even further enmeshed into the concepts of Adam's sin that Noah had tried in vain to rectify. It had become the most immoral place in the world and our Sages of Blessed Memory termed it the *ervas haaretz* (the immorality of the earth).

Just as when Adam first ate (drank wine) the fruit from the Tree of

Knowledge, Noah's drinking of wine also set the stage for the increase of immorality among mankind with the strengthening of the *Yetzer Hara* into the body of man.

Not only did Ham sin by dishonoring his father when Noah was drunk, but also Ham's son Canaan transgressed against the dignity of his grandfather.

Biblical commentators point out that Canaan was jealous that Noah might beget additional offspring and that this would result in his share of the inheritance of the world being diminished. To prevent such a material loss, Canaan castrated his drunken grandfather. The curse that the Bible records Noah uttering against his son Ham also mentioned his grandson Canaan.

✒§ Transforming Evil into Holiness

Indeed, they could grasp the very essence of the leavened bread, despite its symbolic relationship to the *Yetzer Hara* (Evil) and successfully transform it into holiness. This is the meaning of why on Shavuos God commanded the Jews to make a special offering of two loaves of leavened bread.

May we too be like that generation of Jews who were worthy to be redeemed from Egyptian slavery, purified of their spiritual defilements and rewarded with the gift of the Torah. God should grant us the power to overcome the pulls of any contemporary temptations similar to the sin of the Golden Calf. In this way, we will truly complete the rectification of Adam's sin and merit to witness the speedy arrival of our Righteous Mashiach who will herald the final elimination of the plague of death, when all Jews will truly be able to eat bread and drink wine in a most holy manner.

God, Israel and Torah

The God of Israel — '72

'Do you not know? Have you not heard?
Has it not been told to you from the
beginning? Have you not understood the
foundations of the earth?' (Isaiah 40:21).

A PHILOSOPHER ONCE CAME to Rabbi Meir and told him, "I don't believe in God. I believe that the universe came into being by itself, of its own accord, without any outside help."

Rabbi Meir did not reply. A few days later, Rabbi Meir came to the philosopher, and showed him a beautiful piece of poetry, written in a fine hand, on smooth white parchment.

The philosopher looked at the parchment and admired it. He asked, "Who is the fine poet who wrote this lovely poem? Who was the talented scribe who copied it?"

Rabbi Meir shook his head and answered. "You're completely wrong. There was no poet. There was no scribe. This is what really happened. The parchment was sitting on my desk right next to a bottle of ink. I accidentally knocked over the bottle and spilled the ink all over the parchment. This poem was the result."

Intercom—February 1972

The philosopher looked at Rabbi Meir in amazement. He said, "But that is impossible. Such a lovely poem! Such a perfect script! Such things do not come into being by themselves. There must be an author! There must be a scribe!"

Rabbi Meir smiled. He answered the philosopher, "You yourself have said it! And how could the universe, which is much more beautiful and complex than any poem, come into being by itself? There must be an Author. There must be a Creator."

Some of the most fascinating scientific studies in recent years have been in the field of molecular biology, the study of the tremendously complex chemical reactions that take place within living creatures. And when we think about it, it is really amazing that these reactions can work at all. What perfection of natural law to make all these reactions possible! We know that all chemical properties of matter are ultimately derived from the properties of the electron. Therefore, even though the electron is the simplest possible element of matter, it contains the potential of something as wonderfully complex as the human brain.

And here we have the opportunity to ask some very important "why" questions. Why does the electron have just these properties? Why are the complex chemical reactions of life possible at all? And when we try to answer these questions and really think about it, the hand of God is almost visible. And this is how we must look at Rabbi Meir's argument in the 1970's.

One of the great classics of systematic Jewish theology is Rabbi Moshe Chaim Luzzatto's book, *Derech HaShem*, or *The Way of God*. Luzzatto writes that he has carefully examined everything in Jewish literature that has been written about God, and has come to the conclusion that there are six basic things that we can say about God. The six things are:

1. God exists.
2. God is absolutely perfect.
3. God's existence is absolutely necessary.
4. God is absolutely independent.
5. God is absolutely simple.
6. God is absolutely one.

If we look into these six things even more deeply, we see that only two of them are really basic, and the other four can be derived from them in a formal and systematic way. If we look very deeply into it, the two most basic things that we can say about God are:

God is absolutely perfect.
God is absolutely simple.

We can take these two most basic statements about God as axioms, and from these we can derive the rest.

Let us begin by defining God as a perfect and simple being. We can develop the concept of a perfect and simple being in a highly systematic and formal way, just as we do in Euclidian geometry or in Axiomatic Quantum Field Theory, and in this manner, we can derive the classical concepts of God. I will not go into the entire development here, but there is one very fascinating concept that comes out of this.

It can be proven that a perfect being must be active, and that a passive being cannot be perfect. On the other hand, it can also be proven that a simple being cannot be changed. Therefore, if we are speaking about a being who is both simple and perfect, such a being must be active, and must have something to act upon. However, since this being is simple and cannot be changed, it cannot act upon itself. Therefore, it must create something other than itself to act upon.

And this explains why God, the perfect and simple being, created the universe.

This also gives us a good beginning to define God in a much simpler manner. We can define God as the Creator of the universe. This is a good working definition, a fruitful definition, and it is also a very traditional definition. If we look in the opening verse of the Bible, we actually find this definition of God: "In the beginning God created the heaven and the earth."

It does not make any difference here when God created the universe, or at what stage He created it. But if we go back far enough, we find that science stops, and it cannot answer the question, "How did the universe get there to begin with?" And therefore, it is not at all unscientific to assume that God created the universe at some point in the past.

In many places in the Bible, we see that God was considered the Creator. A particularly clear statement of this is found in the Book of Isaiah (44:24), where the Prophet says in God's name, "I am the Lord, I make all things..."

Now that we have defined God as the purposeful Creator of the universe, we can say some very important things about God.

First of all, God becomes very real. He becomes as real, or even more real, than we ourselves are. Therefore, we cannot speak of God as some abstract ethical force or as some social convention. As Creator, God stands on a higher plane of existence than any of His creatures, and it is for this reason that we call him the Supreme Being.

When we define God as Creator of the universe, we learn a second very important thing. If God is Creator of the universe, then He is also the Creator of all matter, and if we make use of Einstein's Relativity, we can come to a most interesting conclusion. Even though Relativity may sound very esoteric and difficult, the one aspect of it that I will make use of is really very simple.

Relativity teaches us that both space and time are attributes of matter.

Therefore, if we define God as Creator of the universe, and hence the Creator of all matter, it is obvious that God is also the Creator of space and time. But this leads to a very interesting and important conclusion. If God is Creator of space and time, then space and time cannot contain (confine) God. God cannot be constrained within space and time. He is independent of it; He exists outside of it. This result can also be formally derived from the assumption we have made earlier that God is absolutely simple, and, indeed, the two concepts are very closely related.

This is really a very deep concept and it is quite surprising that it was first mentioned in a Midrash almost 2,000 years ago. The Midrash notes that, in Hebrew, God is often called "*Makom,*" the Hebrew word for "place." The Midrash asks why God is given such a strange name, and it answers that the reason is because God is the "place of the world," and "this world is not His place." The universe of space, time and matter is a creation of God and therefore it cannot confine Him.

Of course, this line of reasoning can lead us even farther. If God does not exist in space, then it is obvious that He does not have any body, or for that matter, any shape or form at all, since all of these are attributes of space. Like so many other things regarding God, this is also mentioned in the Bible, in the Book of Deuteronomy (4:15), "Take good heed of yourselves, for you saw no manner of form on the day that the Lord spoke to you at Horeb."

In many places the Bible speaks of God as if he had a human body. We call this anthropomorphism. We find such expressions as, "the eyes of God," "the hand of God," and many others. However, it is important to understand that the Bible does not mean to say that God has a body like you or I have. The great Jewish theologians write that the Bible merely borrows terms usually applied to man, and uses them to express God's relationship with the world.

This also explains what the Bible means when it says that God created man in His image. This does not mean that man looks like God, or that God looks like a man. This is merely an allegorical expression, and it means that man has intellectual powers like God, and that man has free will, and like God Himself, is not completely bound by the laws of nature.

We have said that God exists outside of the realm of space. We have also said that He exists outside of the realm of time. When we say that God exists outside of time, we are also led to some very interesting conclusions. If we think about it for just a moment, we see that such concepts as age, beginning, and end, all take place in time. Therefore, if we say that God exists outside of time, we cannot apply any of these concepts to God.

There is a question that children often ask: If God created the world, then who created God?

But let us think of it for a moment. If we ask, "Who created God?" we are really asking how and when did God begin. But if we speak of God having a beginning and ask how and when He was created, then we are also asking how old is God, and by our very question, we are assuming that God exists in time. But this is a false premise, and therefore, the question has no meaning. The very concept of time—or age—or beginning—does not apply to God at all.

At this point, some of us might be quite puzzled. We might be saying to ourselves, "But everything must have a beginning! Isn't this a rule of nature? Isn't this an axiom?"

But the answer to this should be obvious:

God is not bound by nature.

God is not restricted by rules.

The fact is that God is the exception to every rule.

Hence the correct statement might be, "Everything must have a beginning, with the exception of God."

When we say that God exists outside of time, we arrive at another very important and obvious consequence. All change must take place in time, and therefore, if God exists outside of time, He must be unchanging and unchangeable. This concept is also found in the Bible, expressed quite explicitly in the Book of Malachi (3:6), "I am the Lord, I do not change." And if we remember that God is the Creator of time, then it is not very difficult to understand how He can cause change in the world without changing Himself.

At this point, some of us might be asking another question: If God does not change, then how can the Bible, which, after all, is our primary source of information regarding God, speak of God as becoming angry, or happy, or sad? But the answer is that here again the Bible is speaking in allegory, and merely describing God's actions, and describing them in terms of the same emotions that we humans would feel when performing such actions.

When we speak of God as being the Creator, a third thing also becomes obvious.

If God is Creator of the world, then He must be able to do everything in the world, and therefore His power in the world must be unlimited. Of course, this is also required by our previous statement that God is perfect. This is the reason why we speak of God as being all-powerful or omnipotent. It is also the reason why in many prayers, we call God "King of the universe." We also find this thought expressed very clearly in the Bible, in the Book of Psalms (135:6), "All that God wishes, He does, in the heaven and earth, in the seas, and in all the deeps."

One of my students once asked me this question, and it really is quite tricky: "Can God create a stone that He cannot lift?"

This question is a very intriguing one, and is actually very similar to some questions raised by Maimonides. In his *Guide to the Perplexed* (3:15) Maimonides asks such questions as:

Can God produce another being like Himself?

Can God destroy Himself?

Can God change Himself?

Can God create a body for Himself?

Maimonides answers "no" to all these questions, stating that "we do not ascribe to God the power to do what is categorically impossible," and of course all these things mentioned above are categorically impossible.

We can understand this a bit more deeply. According to what we have said earlier, God exists outside of time, and for this reason, cannot change. One important consequence of this is that God does not change His mind. God does not suddenly decide that He would like a companion God, or that He wants a body, or that He wants to commit suicide. So the answer to these questions, to some extent at least, is included in the concept that God exists outside of time.

We can also explain this in terms of a concept mentioned earlier, namely that God is a Perfect Being. As a Perfect Being, God must be omnipotent, that is, able to do every possible thing. However, perfection only requires God to be able to do the possible—it does not require Him to be able to do the impossible. And one thing that is categorically impossible by the very definition of God as an absolutely perfect Being is for God to become any less perfect. But any of the abovementioned things such as the creation of another God, His self-destruction, or His making Himself a body, would make God less perfect, and this can be proven formally from the concept of perfection. If a stone existed that could not be lifted by God, then something other than God would exist over which He had no control. Since this would make God less perfect, this is also categorically impossible.

Therefore, we do not ascribe to God the ability to create a stone that He cannot lift.

All that we have discussed so far, including God's perfection, is really a consequence of our definition of God as Creator of the universe, and is therefore all implied in the first verse of the Bible, "In the beginning, God created the heaven and the earth."

Now let us discuss another concept regarding God. This concept is contained in the *Shema*, the declaration of faith that is recited at both morning and evening services, taken from the Book of Deuteronomy (6:4): "Hear, O Israel, the Lord is our God, the Lord is one."

This is a very simple sentence, but it also contains some very important implications: One God, over the entire universe, and over any other universe that might exist. One God, over all the planets, all the stars, and all the galaxies. Just one God over all.

But this raises an important question and one that is frequently asked: If God is King over the entire universe—a universe containing at least hundreds of billions of galaxies and quadrillions of suns—a universe at least billions of light years in diameter—how can such a God care about man? How can He even care about this little speck of cosmic dust that we call our planet earth?

But we have said earlier that God exists independent of space, and therefore it is not too difficult to imagine that size alone is of little consequence to God.

However, we do know that we are among the most complex things in the universe. Indeed, the most complex thing known to us is nothing other than the human brain. It is infinitely more complex than even the largest galaxy. And not only are we the most complex things in the universe, but we are also the most aware, the most perceptive, and the most introspective. No other form of matter that we know of has these properties.

Therefore, when we think about it, it is not too surprising that God thinks about us after all. Because, really, these are the things that should really matter to God.

Actually, this very question is posed in the Bible, in the 8th Psalm:

> When I behold Your heavens,
>   the work of Your fingers,
> The moon and the stars,
>   that You have established;
> What is man that You consider him?
>   Or the son of man, that You think of him?
> Yet, You have made him but a little lower than the angels,
>   You have crowned him with glory and honor.

People also ask a similar question: "If God rules the entire universe, how can He pay attention to me? How can He pay attention to each and every single individual?"

The answer to this question is not too difficult. Just as God Himself is infinite, so is His wisdom. The Psalmist says just this (147:5), "His understanding is infinite." Therefore, God literally knows everything. He knows exactly what is happening to every one of the three billion people on earth at every single instant. Indeed, God knows what is happening in the entire universe, to every single atom in all creation.

This may seem difficult to comprehend, but let us think of it this way: God's intelligence is infinite, and no matter how large a number may be, it is still very small when compared to infinity.

But we may ask: "How does God know everything? Just how does He receive all this information?"

The answer is that God fills all existence. Therefore, since He is in proximity with everything, He is aware of all that is happening. The Bible expresses this concept very exactly in the Book of Jeremiah (23:24): " 'Can a man hide himself in secret places, that I shall not see him?' says the Lord. 'Do I not fill heaven and earth?' "

Another thing that we know about God's knowledge is that He knows the future. This might seem difficult to imagine at first, and might appear to present many paradoxes, but if we remember our earlier discussion, we can begin to understand it.

God exists outside of time, and therefore, to Him the future is exactly the same as the past. Therefore, God knows the future exactly in the same manner as He knows the past. This precise idea is also found in the Bible, in the Book of Isaiah (41:4): "I call the generations from the beginning, I, the Lord, I am the first, and with the last, I am the same." If we look into this passage, we not only see that God knows the future, but we also find the reason. First the Prophet says, "I call the generations from the beginning," telling us that God knows the future. Then the Prophet gives us the reason, "I am the first, and with the last, I am the same," telling us that the reason for this is because God is unchanging and exists outside of time.

The final question that I will discuss is one that children especially frequently ask: "Why can't we see God?"

In brief, the reason why we cannot see God is not because He is too far from us, but because He is too near. God fills all creation, and therefore, there is no place empty of Him, so that we have no comparison which we can use to detect His presence.

If we think about it, this is also the reason why we cannot see the air around us. The only time that we are aware of the air is when we feel it, such as when the wind blows. Similarly, the only time that we are aware of God is when He acts to reveal His presence. This may indeed be the reason why the Hebrew language has the same word *ruach* for both wind and spirit.

Almost everything that we can say about God is included in the two most important statements about Him in the Bible. They are very easy to remember:

In the beginning, God created the heaven and the earth.
Hear, O Israel, the Lord is our God, the Lord is one.

Paragraphs

Paradoxes

A FAVORITE QUESTION raised by bright youngsters when they want to catch their teacher is: "Can God create a rock that He cannot lift?" At first thought the question seems unanswerable, and the paradox is obvious. Since we say God is the omnipotent Creator, we cannot say that it is impossible for Him to create such a rock. Yet, on the other hand, we also say that God is absolutely omnipotent, and therefore, a "rock which He cannot lift" simply cannot exist.

Any serious student of Jewish thought quickly becomes aware that there are a number of paradoxes that seem to be built into the very structure of Jewish philosophy. In general, it is recognized that most of these paradoxes result from the inability of human intellect to ultimately grasp the true nature of God, even on a plane beyond our understanding. Although the existence of unresolved paradoxes does not in any way diminish our faith, a deeper understanding of why such paradoxes must exist can give us deeper insight into this entire area of thought.

⋖ Omniscience and Free Will

Probably the most famous of these paradoxes involves God's omniscient knowledge of the future and man's free will. Briefly stated, it is a fundamental belief of Judaism that God has absolute knowledge of the future, and we cannot ascribe any ignorance to Him. At the same time, however, it is also a basic belief that man has absolute free will, and God in no way determines whether he will do good or evil. The paradox is most succinctly presented in the words of the Rambam (Maimonides):[1]

A very legitimate question may then be asked. We must either say that God knows the future, and therefore knows whether an individual will be good or wicked, or else we must say that He does not know. If we say that God knows that a person will be good, then it is impossible for that person to be otherwise. If, on the other hand, we say that God knows that this person will be good, and it is still possible for him to be evil, then we must say that God's knowledge is not absolute.

What the Rambam is saying here is that if God's knowledge is absolute, then we cannot logically say that man has free will, and if man has free will, then we cannot logically say that God's knowledge is absolute. The essence of the Rambam's answer to this is that man's logic cannot apply to a domain that includes God's knowledge, and that even though man's intellect cannot resolve this paradox, it is, in fact, resolvable.[2]

This paradox is discussed in virtually every major work on Jewish philosophy. Although most authorities do not express it as clearly as the Rambam, they are essentially expressing the same thought when they say that even though we do not understand how, God's knowledge of the future in no way deprives the individual of his own free choice.[3]

Particularly ingenious is the approach of Rabbi Moshe Almosnino.[4] He explains that God is the Creator of time, and is therefore not in any way bound by it. Since God exists outside of time, His knowledge of the future is *exactly the same* as His knowledge of the past and present.[5] Therefore, just as His knowledge of the past and present does not interfere with man's free will, neither does His knowledge of the future.

Of course, all that Almosnino is doing here is demonstrating that God's omniscience does not interfere with free will. With a little thought, however, it becomes obvious that the paradox itself is not resolved by his approach. The paradox, as first expressed by Rabbi Akiba, still remains, "All is foreseen, yet free will is granted."[6]

≈§ Immutability and Creation

Another important paradox involves God's immutability and creation, and, as we shall soon see, this is actually related to the previous paradox. Briefly stated, one of our fundamental concepts of God is that He is absolutely immutable and unchanging, as He declares to His Prophet (Malachi 3:6), "I am the Lord, I do not change."[7] On the other hand, we also know that God created the universe, and it is very difficult to imagine how He did so without some change on His part. At the very least, with the advent of creation, it would seem that He gained the attributes of Creator and Ruler of the universe.

Most authorities who discuss this do not present it as a paradox, but simply that the act of creation did not in any way change God.[8] Some try to resolve the difficulty by stating that God is the Creator of time itself, and therefore, the very concept of change was created by Him.[9] This is true, but it still does not resolve the paradox completely, since we can still speak of the state of "before creation" and that of "after creation."

This entire question is actually very closely related to the concept of the Constriction or *Tzimtzum*, widely discussed by the Kabbalists. What this concept essentially says is that God's essence originally filled all "space," and that in order to make a "place" in which to create the universe, God constricted His essence out of a certain "area," bringing into being a "Vacated Space." It was then in this "Vacated Space" that He created all worlds.[10]

The reason why "space" and "place" were placed in quotation marks is because most authorities agree that the reference is to conceptual, rather than to physical, space. This Constriction took place on a nonspatial spiritual level, where God's essence included every possible concept as part of His absolutely simple essential nature. The Constriction was necessary in order to allow a "place" for the concepts that exist in creation, that is, to allow them to have a measure of independent existence.[11]

One thing that we immediately see is that the concept of Constriction apparently contradicts that of God's immutability. How can we say that God constricts Himself, and at the same time say that He does not change? Actually, this is merely a reflection of the immutability-creation paradox, and to some extent, it elevates it to a higher plane. God creates within the Vacated Space, and therefore, creation itself does not in any way affect His essence. The paradox is therefore transformed from creation itself to the concept of Constriction.

◄§ Rabbi Nachman's Paradox

The concept of Constriction itself, however, also contains its own paradox. This was first formulated, and is best expressed by Rabbi Nachman of Breslov.[12]

This Constriction, which resulted in the Vacated Space, cannot be understood or comprehended at all. (The only time that it will be understood will be in the Ultimate Future.) This is because we must say two contradictory things about the Vacated Space, namely the presence and absence of God's essence. The Vacated Space came into being as a result of the Constriction, when God (to the extent that we can express it) constricted His own essence. God's essence therefore does not exist in this Space. If His essence were there, this Space would not be vacated, and there would be nothing other than the Infinite

Essence. If this were true, however, there would also be no place whatsoever for the creation of the universe.

The actual truth, however, is that God's essence must be in this Space. For we know for certain that nothing can exist without His Life Force. Since this contradiction exists it is impossible to understand the concept of the Vacated Space at all, except in the Ultimate Future.

The paradox, as elucidated by Rabbi Nachman, is actually very basic. Since God created all things in this Vacated Space, we must say that His creative power exists there. Since God is an absolute Unity, He cannot be separated from His creative power, and therefore, we must also say that He exists within the Vacated Space. This, however, contradicts the basic concept that this Space is *vacated*, and that by definition, God constricted His essence from it.

✌ Double Vision

If we look a bit deeper, we find that the Ramchal's dichotomy, and hence, all our other paradoxes, are rooted in the fact that we actually perceive God with a sort of double vision. This stems from the obvious fact that we cannot understand God directly, nor can we make any direct statements about His essence.

Since we cannot make any direct statements about God, we can only speak of His attributes. As a number of major Jewish philosophers point out, however, God's attributes are divided into two basic categories, namely, negative attributes and attributes of action.

The negative attributes relate to God Himself, and tell us what He is not. Included in this category are such attributes as His unity (non-plurality), eternity (non-temporality), incorporeality, omnipotence (non-impotence), and omniscience (non-ignorance). The attributes of action, on the other hand, do not tell us anything directly about God Himself, but do tell us how He relates to His creation. Examples of this second category are the attributes of God as Creator, Revealer, Redeemer, Mighty and Merciful. The concept of these two categories is discussed at length by the Jewish philosophers.[19]

If we think about this somewhat more deeply, however, we see that the fact that we perceive God by means of two types of attributes—negative attributes and attributes of action—actually causes us to see Him with a sort of double vision. It is very much like looking at a single object through two different lenses—there may only be one object, but we might see two distinct and very different images. In a similar manner, the two categories of attributes are like two lenses, through which we peer at God.

A very good analogy would be trick glasses in which the right lens is red and the left is green. Therefore, if a person wearing such glasses looks at a white paper, he sees it as red with his right eye, and as green with his left. If he looks at it through both eyes, he sees some psychedelic mixture of red and green, but under no condition can he perceive the color white. All perception of color is similarly distorted. The same is very much true of our perception of God through two different categories of attributes. Another good analogy would be the wave-particle duality of our perception of the fundamental particles of matter.

In many cases, the two images converge and there is no problem. Indeed, as the *Ikkarim* points out, there are a number of attributes that come under both categories simultaneously.[20] Nevertheless, there are a number of important instances where the two images do not converge, and this is responsible for the paradoxes that we encounter when we speak about God. These paradoxes are built into the system as a result of our double, incomplete vision.

We can immediately see how this is responsible for the Ramchal's dichotomy, and since this encompasses other important paradoxes, we can also perceive how it gives rise to them. One of the most important negative statements that we can make about God is that He does not partake of any plurality whatsoever, and must therefore be absolutely simple. God's simplicity is therefore a basic negative attribute.

When we speak of God's perfection, however, we are basically speaking in terms of His attributes of action.[21] Since we see God's perfection through the lens of "attributes of action," while we see His simplicity through that of "negative attributes," the apparent dichotomy is merely a result of our double vision.

The same is also true of Rabbi Nachman's paradox. When we look at God through the filter of "attributes of action," we see Him as Creator, and therefore, we must say that He constricted Himself from the Vacated Space in order to create the world. This is also implied by the attributes of action which state that God is invisible and undetectable. On the other hand, when we look at God's utter simplicity through the filter of "negative attributes," we see that He cannot have constricted Himself from the Vacated Space, and hence the paradox. Looking at Rabbi Meir Simcha's presentation of the omniscience-free will paradox, we see that this results from similar double vision.

The Stone Dilemma

This brings us back to the tricky question asked by our clever student: "Can God create a stone that He cannot lift?" Here too, we look at both sides of the question through different lenses. Looking at it through the lens of "attributes of action," we say that God is omnipotent and can do all things, and therefore, He must be able to create such a stone. But then, we also look at this question through the lens of "negative attributes" which tells us that God cannot be impotent in any way, and therefore, that a "rock that He cannot lift" simply cannot exist. Looking through this lens, we would say that He could not create such a stone. If we can only see red and green, we cannot answer a question in terms of black and white.

Actually, Rabbi Nachman's paradox is directly related to the immutability-creation paradox. For if we say that God's essence is in the Vacated Space, then nothing has changed, and we have no problems involving God's immutability. It is only when we look at the other side of the coin and say that the space is actually vacated that we find it contradicting immutability. As such, the resolution of Rabbi Nachman's paradox would also most probably involve the resolution of the immutability-creation paradox.

❧ Immanence and Transcendence

Closely related to this is another important dichotomy, namely that of immanence and transcendence. On one hand, we say that God is transcendental and ultimately removed and distant from all wordly concepts. On the other hand, however, we also say that God is immanent, and ultimately near and involved with His world.[13] These two concepts are obviously contradictory, and they involve an important dichotomy and tension in our understanding of God.

This dichotomy, however, is very closely related to Rabbi Nachman's paradox. If we say that God is absent in the Vacated Space (which contains all creation), then we must say that He is absent from creation itself, and as such, is ultimately distant and transcendental. If, on the other hand, we say that God exists in the Vacated Space, then we can also say that He is immanent.[14] Rabbi Nachman's paradox therefore gives us additional insight into his well-known dichotomy.

Upon further examination, we find that Rabbi Nachman's paradox also includes that of free will and God's omniscience. As Rabbi Meir Simcha explains, the reason why man can have free will is because God constricts His knowledge from the future.[15] He therefore acts as if He were indeed ignorant of our future free choice.

In many ways, the constriction of God's knowledge from the future is very much like the constriction of His essence from the Vacated Space, and Rabbi Nachman's paradox applies equally well to this case. On one side, we cannot say that God is really ignorant of the future, and we must therefore say that His knowledge actually does exist there. On the other hand, however, the fact that we have free will implies that His knowledge does not exist in the future. Just as in the case of the Vacated Space, we must say that God's knowledge (which, as the Rambam points out, is equivalent to His essence)[16] both does and does not exist in the future. This, however, is a precise temporal parallel of Rabbi Nachman's paradox.

❧ The Ramchal's Dichotomy

There is another important dichotomy, namely between God's simplicity and His perfection. Briefly stated, we say that God's essence contains every possible element of perfection imaginable. On the other hand, however, we also say that He is absolutely simple, containing no element of form, structure or plurality. This being true, then, how can we say that He contains every element of perfection?

This dichotomy is expressed most clearly by the Ramchal (Rabbi Moshe Chaim Luzzatto):[17]

There exist in God qualities that in a human being would be different, since He has will, wisdom and ability, and is perfect in every conceivable way. Nevertheless, the true nature of His essence is a single attribute—one that intrinsically contains and encompasses everything that could be considered perfection. All perfection therefore exists in God, not as something added on to His existence, but as an integral part of His intrinsic identity, whose essence includes all types of perfection. By virtue of its intrinsic nature, it is impossible that His essence not include all perfection.

Admittedly, this is something that is far beyond our understanding and imagination, and there hardly exists a way to express it and put it into words...

The Ramchal's dichotomy actually includes Rabbi Nachman's paradox as a special case. On one hand, God's perfection implies that He has the power to create, and as a corollary, He can constrict His own essence in order to allow a "place" for creation. It furthermore allows us to speak of different concepts in relation to God, which in our case would be His essence and His power of constriction. Since we cannot say that any outside power constricted His essence, constriction must also be one of God's attributes and an element of His perfection.

God's simplicity, on the other hand, does not allow for any structure whatsoever in His being, even conceptually, and therefore, we cannot say that the Vacated Space is devoid of his essence. By the same token, according to this side of the coin, we can also not say that His power of constriction is any different than His essence.[18]

The Ramchal's dichotomy thus encompasses Rabbi Nachman's paradox. Since, as we have seen, Rabbi Nachman's paradox includes the other ones under consideration, they are also included in the Ramchal's dichotomy. We therefore see that most of the difficult paradoxes of Judaism are actually rooted in a single basic dilemma.

Of course, there are a number of more sophisticated questions very closely related to this. Thus, for example, we can ask questions such as:

Can God produce another being like Himself?
Can God destroy Himself?
Can God change Himself?
Can God corpify Himself?

Also closely related to this question is the entire subject of Constriction.

These questions are actually raised by the Rambam, who states that "we do not ascribe to God the power to do what is categorically impossible."[22] Nevertheless, as Rabbi Aaron Marcus points out, this is not a definitive statement, since we cannot ascribe any impotence to God.[23] The Ramchal echoes this when he categorically states that God's omnipotence is absolute, even with regard to things that we would consider impossible.[24]

If we look carefully at these questions, however, we see that they all would involve a violation of God's negative attributes. Therefore, through the "negative attributes" lens, we see them as being categorically impossible, and perhaps the Rambam is taking this viewpoint. Looking through the lens of "attributes of action," however, we must take the Ramchal's side, and say that God's omnipotence is absolute. Here again, the apparent paradox is merely a result of our double vision.

It is interesting to note that in presenting his paradox, Rabbi Nachman states that we will only learn the answer to it in the Ultimate Future. In another place, he also makes the same statement with regard to the paradox of omniscience and free will.[25] Regarding the Future World, it is written (Isaiah 30:20), "Your eyes shall behold your Master." We will no longer have to look at God through lenses, and therefore, all dichotomies and paradoxes will be resolved.

NOTES

1. Yad, Tshuvah 5:5
2. Cf. Moreh Nevuchim 3:20 Shemonah Perakim no. 8.
3. Emunos VeDeyos 4:4 (65b), Kuzari 5:20 (47b), Chovos HaLevavos 3:8, Milchamos HaShem 3:106, Or HaShem 2:4, Ikkarim 4:3, 7-10, Akeidas Yitzchak 21 (151a), Bais Elokim 3:411, Tshuvos Rivash 119, Shnei Luchos HaBris "Bais HaBechirah" (1:43a), Pardes Rimonim 4:9; Asarah Maamaros, "Chokar Din" 4:9 (122a), "Maamar HaMidos" 4 (160a), Gevuras HaShem 2, Rabbeinu Bachya on Exodus 15:118. Cf. Tosafos, Niddah 16b "HaKol."
4. Quoted in Yesod HaEmunah (Rabbi Baruch Kasover), chapter 2, Midrash Sh'muel, Tosefos Yom Tov, on Avos 3:15, Sh'vil Emunah (on Emunos VeDeyos) 4:4:11 Cf. Tanna DeBei Eliahu Rabbah 1. Ramasyim Tzofim ad loc. 1:18; Kol Yehudah (on Kuzari) 5:20 (847b) "Ki," Otzar Nechemad (on Kuzari) 1:1 (11b) "Kol." Also see Tanchuma, VaYeshev 4.
5. Ikkarim 2:19.
6. Avos, 3:15, according to interpretation of Rambam, Rabbeinu Yonah, Bertenero, Tosefos Yom Tov, and Tiferes Yisrael. Rashi and Machzor Vitri, however, interpret this Mishnah somewhat differently. We find that the word Tzafuy is used to indicate the future in Pirkei DeRabbi Eliezer 26 (61b), 36(883a), 38(88a), and 48(114b). For further discussion, see the essay, Free Will and the Purpose of Creation, elsewhere in this volume.
7. Yad, Yesodei HaTorah 11:12, Moreh Nevuchim 1:11.
8. Shnei Luchos HaBris 1:6a (note), Cheredim no. 5 (p. 40). Cf. Pirkei DeRabbi Eliezer 3.
9. See Shomrei Emunim (HaKadmon) 2:16, 17.
10 Etz Chaim, Drush Egolim VeYosher 2, Movo Shaarim 1:1:1, (Likutei Moharan 49, 64. Cf. Pardes Rimonim 4:9, 6:3, Shefa Tal 6:1 (89b, 90d), 6:8 (101a), Bahir 14, Zohar HaRakia on Zohar 1:116a. The Constriction was in God's light and not in His essence, see Shaarei Gan Eden, "Orach Tzadikim" 2:1, Pelach Rimon 4:3, Derech Mitzvosecha (Chabad), "Emunas Elokus" 6 (51a), "Shoresh Mitzvas HaTefillah" 34 (136a).
11. Shomrei Emunim (HaKadom) 2:49, KaLaCh Pischei Chochmah 24, Likutei Amarim (Tanya), Shaar HaYichud VeHeEmunah 7.

12. Likutei Moharan 64. For attempted resolutions, see Nefesh HaChaim 3:7,8, Likutei Amarim ibid.
13. Cf. Megillah 31a, Ibn Ezra on Psalms 113:5. See next note.
14. Rabbi Nachman himself recognized this relationship, speaking of God as both filling and encompassing the world, and of the Vacated Space differentiating the two concepts. (Likutei Moharan 64:2). Kabbalistic terminology expressed God's immanence and transcendence respectively by saying that He "fills and surrounds all worlds." Cf. Zohar 3:225a, Nefesh HaChaim 3:4, Reshis Chochmah, "Shaar HaYirah" 1 (9a).
15. Meshech Chochmah, Berashis "Naaseh" (p. 3). Cf. Or Someach on Yad, Tshuvah 5:5. Also see Or HaChaim on Genesis 6:2, Elemah Rabosai (RaMaK) "Eyin Kol" 2:18. This is apparently also the meaning of Rabbi ben Korcha's answer to the Roman, Bereshis Rabbah 27:7. Also see Yerushalmi, Rosh Hashanah 1:3 (7b).
16. Yad, Yesodei HaTorah 2:10.
17. Derech HaShem 1:15.
18. See Pardes Rimonim 4:9. This also raises difficulties with the attempt of Nefesh HaChaim, op. cit., to resolve Rabbi Nachman's paradox by stating that Constriction (Tzimtzum) actually refers to "hiding" and not to "withdrawing." The barrier behind which God hides, however, cannot be differentiated from His essence, and the paradox therefore remains.
19. See Moreh Nevuchim 1:58, Ikkarim 2:22, Chovos HaLevavos 1:10.
20. Ikkarim 2:24.
21. Even though we can speak of God's perfection as a negative attribute, namely, the fact that He is devoid of imperfection, even imperfection is basically related to His attributes of action. Furthermore, both perfection and its absence are actually undefinable in relation to God's essence.
22. Moreh Nevuchim 3:15. Cf. Shefa Tal 1:3, Pardes Rimonim 2:7. Also see Yerushalmi, Taanis 2:1 (9a), from Numbers 23:19.
23. Keses HaSofer 9a.
24. KaLaCh Pischei Chochmah 30 (22b).
25. Likutei Moharan 21:4.

Belief in God

◆§ Life Has Purpose

THE FOUNDATION OF JUDAISM is the realization that life has purpose. This, of course, is true of every major religion, but in the case of Judaism, it is absolutely central. Insofar as we can say that Judaism has one central teaching, it is that man has purpose in life. The universe was created for a reason, and somehow, man partakes of it.[1]

But to merely say that the universe exists for a purpose is not enough. Judaism goes a step further and states that both man and nature have purpose because they were created by a purposeful being. We call this being God.

Without the concept of a Creator, we would view the universe as nothing more than a meaningless accident. Without belief in God, human existence is ultimately pointless, and life is devoid of meaning and hope. The Psalmist alludes to this when he says (127:1), "If the Lord does not build the house, they who build it labor in vain. If the Lord does not guard the city, the sentries watch it in vain."

The arguments for the existence of God are many, but in general are beyond the scope of this work.[2] We can say, however, that Judaism has recognized that the universe does indeed appear to have been designed by an intelligent being. If one confines the discussion to the planet Earth alone, it may be argued that life is due merely to some chance process. But when we take the universe as a whole, such glibness is no longer possible. The fact that the inorganic universe contains everything needed to make organic life possible at least indicates, if it does not prove, that it was conceived by a purposeful Creator. We find

Collegiate Hashkafa Series—1973

the universe prepared as an arena of life, and the probability that this should be entirely due to chance is infinitesimally small.

We find this concept expressed in any number of places in our classical literature. The earliest expression of this, is found in the words of the Psalmist, who said (139:14), "I will give thanks [to God], for I am fearfully and wonderfully made."[3] According to many commentators, this is also the meaning of Job's words (19:26) when he said, "From my flesh, I will see God."[4] What Job is saying is that the very fact that something as wonderful as his body could exist demonstrates the work of God.

According to Maimonides (Rambam), this is also the meaning of such passages as (Psalms 19:2), "The heavens declare the glory of God, the firmament shows His handiwork." When we say that inanimate things praise God, we mean that their very existence is a hymn, demonstrating God and His handiwork.[5]

Another major Jewish writer puts it in very simple terms. He states that it is as unthinkable to conceive of the universe as arising by chance without a purposeful Creator, as it would be to conceive of a beautiful poem written with a random splash of ink.[6]

Although our sacred literature abounds with discussions regarding God, the Torah provides us with three most basic statements:

First of all, the Torah speaks of God as Creator. We find this in the very opening words of the Torah: "In the beginning, God created the heavens and the earth."

Secondly, we have the statement of God's unity (Deuteronomy 6:4): "Hear O Israel, the Lord is our God, the Lord is One." This is the *Shema*, the basic declaration of faith recited twice daily by every faithful Jew. It is also the major statement contained in the parchment in the *Mezuzah* and *Tefillin*.

We will discuss the implications of these two statements in depth in the second section.

The third major statement is contained in the opening words of the Ten Commandments (Exodus 20:2): "I am the Lord your God, Who has brought you up out of the land of Egypt, from the house of bondage."

This statement tells us that God is intimately concerned with our affairs, even to the point of hearing our cries and delivering us from the Egyptian slavery. It tells us that we conceive the Supreme Being as not only the God of creation, but also as the God of history.[7] It is a statement rejecting the deistic concept that God created the universe, and then abandoned it with neither ruler, guide nor judge.[8]

Judaism has always seen the existence of a Supreme Judge and Master of human affairs as being self-evident. We have ample evidence for this in the experience of men and nations where only the good is stable, while evil tends to destroy itself.[9] This may well be the meaning of the wise words which state (Proverbs 19:21), "There are many thoughts in man's heart, but God's counsel, that is what shall stand."

◁§ God, Creator of All Things

The very first statement that we find concerning God is the opening verse of the Torah, "In the beginning, God created the heavens and the earth." This provides us with a basic definition of God as Creator of all things. We find this concept repeated many times in such passages as (Isaiah 44:24), "I am the Lord, I make all things."[10]

This definition of God can immediately teach us many things about Him. Although we might say that God fills all creation, we cannot take the pantheistic view that God is synonymous with the universe as a whole. As Creator, God must be more than the sum total of His creation.

There are others who speak of God as some abstract ethical force or social convention. Thus, we have statements claiming that God is love, truth, justice or goodness. All these may be attributes of God, but we must say that He is more than the sum total of these things. Even such lofty things as love and truth are ultimately created concepts, which cannot exist except within the context of a society such as that of man. When we look to God, however, we see Him on a much higher plane than any of these things.

When we look to God as Creator of all things, then we must say that He stands apart from everything else. All other things are created, while only God is Creator. It is for this reason that we speak of God as the Supreme Being.

God Himself, of course, is absolutely and ultimately unknowable. There is absolutely nothing in our experience that can be used as a means of comparison. There is nothing in human or any other language that can be used when speaking of God Himself.

Nevertheless, there are some statements that we can and do make about God. Our great philosophers divide these statements into two categories:[11]

1. Statements speaking of God's relationship to the universe. These are statements of how we experience God and how He affects our lives.

2. Negative statements. Although we cannot know what God *is*, we can learn much by knowing what He *is not*.

The most important statement regarding God's relationship to the world is that He is its Creator. Most other statements in this category stem from this.

The primary negative statement that we can make about God is that He does not contain any element of plurality. This is usually stated in a positive sense, namely God is One. The belief that God is the most perfect and absolute unity is one of the main foundations of our faith.[12] As mentioned earlier, this is the main affirmation of our faith: Hear O Israel, the Lord is our God, the Lord is One.[13]

If we speak of God as Creator of all things, then it logically follows that He is one and unique. It is self-evident that there can be only one Creator of all things.[14]

Although the universe contains many galaxies, each containing numerous stars and planets, there is but one Creator and one God over all. Moreover, even if there were other universes, whether material or spiritual, God would still be one over all. This may well be what the Psalmist means when he says (145:13), "Your dominion is a kingdom of all worlds."[15]

An important corollary of God's unity is the concept of His absolute simplicity. The logic behind this is that any additional quality that we would ascribe to God would add an element of plurality to His being. Thus, for example, let us assume that we wish to speak of God's intellect as an entity in itself. We would then have to speak of two concepts, namely God's essence and His intellect. Since this would imply an element of plurality within God, it must be rejected. This is true of any other attribute which we may wish to ascribe to God, and therefore we must say that no such independent attributes exist. But if we cannot ascribe any attribute at all to God, then we must conceive Him as being absolutely simple. This indeed is the consensus of opinion among our great thinkers.[16] Nevertheless, His very simple essence implies every attribute with which God rules the universe.[17]

As Creator of all things, God's power over His creation is unlimited. We therefore speak of Him as Omnipotent, and call Him the "King of the universe." The Psalmist speaks of this when he says (135:6), "All that the Lord wishes, He does, in heaven and earth, in the seas and in all the deeps."[18]

God's omnipotence, however, is a direct corollary of the fact that He is Creator, and therefore, it need not extend beyond His creation. Thus, for example, it does not extend to His own essence. We do not ascribe to God the power to change Himself in any way. Such things as creating another similar being, annihilating Himself, or making Himself into a corporeal being, are considered categorically impossible, and are not within the scope of God's omnipotence. When we say that God is omnipotent, we are essentially saying that He can do all possible things. His omnipotence, however, does not necessitate His being able to do the categorically impossible.[19]

God is Creator of all things, and therefore, of course, is the Creator of all matter. It should therefore be obvious that God Himself does not consist of any type of matter or anything related to it. It is because God is so utterly divorced from all material concepts that He is called Pure and Holy.[20]

Furthermore, if we speak of God as Creator of all things then He is also Creator of space and time. We therefore say that God does not exist in time or space.[21]

We can also look at this on a somewhat deeper level. If God existed in the space-time continuum, we would have to assign Him a position in this continuum. We would then have to speak of two concepts with relation to God, namely, His essence and His position. This would also introduce an element of plurality, which, as we have seen, is not permissible.

The idea of God existing outside of space and time is expressed most lucidly by our sages. In any number of places, especially in Talmudic literature, we find God referred to as *Makom*, which literally means "place." The Midrash asks why He is given this name, and answers that it is because "He is the place of the universe, but the universe is not His place."[22] What this means is that the universe of space, time and matter is a creation of God, and therefore cannot contain Him.

Our minds can only think in material terms, and therefore, it is almost impossible for us to picture any existence outside of space and time. This is but another reason why God's essence is absolutely unknowable.[23]

A corollary of the concept that God exists outside of space is the fact that He has neither body, shape nor form. This should be quite obvious, since all of these are attributes of space.

The belief that God is absolutely incorporeal is a foundation of our faith. Concerning this, the Torah warns (Deuteronomy 4:15), "Take good heed of yourself, for you saw no manner of form on the day that the Lord spoke to you at Horeb (Sinai)."[24]

We therefore may not compare God to any of his creatures, even the highest angels. The Prophet thus tells us (Isaiah 40:18), "To whom will you then liken God, or to what likeness will you compare Him?" In another place we likewise find the Prophet declaring (Jeremiah 10:6), "There is none like You, O God." The Psalmist also speaks of this and says (86:8), "There are none like You among the powers, O God, and there are no works like Yours."[25]

In many places, the Torah and other writings speak of God as if He had a human body. We find such anthropomorphisms as (Deuteronomy 11:12), "the eyes of God," and (Exodus 9:25), "the hand of God." However, none of this is meant to imply that God has any sort of body, shape or form. Our sages teach us that the Torah borrows terms from God's creatures in order to describe His relationship to the world.[26]

Similarly, when the Torah says that God created man in His image, it by no means comes to imply that God looks like man. What it means is that man partakes of the very same attributes that God uses in interacting with the world.[27]

In a number of places, the Torah speaks of people hearing God's voice. Here again, this is not meant to imply that God actually speaks like a human being. When we speak of God's voice, we sometimes refer to a prophetic voice within an individual's mind. In other cases, God might actually create sound waves to convey His message.[28]

The fact that we always refer to God as "He" is also not meant to imply that the concept of sex or gender applies to God. We use the male form because there is no neuter in the Hebrew language, and the Hebrew word for God is a masculine noun. The reason for this is because, like the male, God is an active rather than a passive creative force.[29]

Just as God exists outside of space, He likewise exists outside the realm of time. As difficult as it is to imagine nonspatial existence, timelessness is even more difficult to comprehend. Nevertheless, the two concepts are very closely related.

A corollary of the concept that God exists outside of time is the fact that He is eternal. All things pertaining to time, such as beginning, end, and age, can in no way pertain to God.[30] It is therefore utterly meaningless to ask how old God is. It is equally meaningless to ask how He began.

The entire concept of change also exists only within the realm of time. Therefore, the fact that God exists outside of time implies that He is absolutely unchangeable and unchanging. This is alluded to in the words of the Prophet who said in God's name (Malachi 3:6), "I am the Lord, I do not change."[31]

As creator of time, God can make use of it without becoming involved in it. Thus, He can cause change in the world without being changed Himself.[32] Thus, some philosophers call God the "unmoved Mover."

Here again, we find statements in the Torah that appear to contradict this. Thus, for example, the Torah appears to ascribe emotions such as joy and anger to God. However, here too, we are merely speaking of God's interaction with man. We perceive God's actions, and ascribe to Him the same emotion that we ourselves would feel if we were performing the same act. Thus, for example, when God punishes we say that He is angry. None of this, however, is meant to imply any change in God Himself.[33]

Even the creation of the universe did not in anyway change God. It furthermore did not even involve any change in God's mind. We cannot say that at a particular moment He suddenly decided to create a world. A statement such as this has no meaning, since time and the very concept of change were created along with all other things.[34] God Himself, however, was exactly the same before and after creation.[35]

It is also important to realize that creation did not fill any need in God's being. God is inherently perfect, and therefore does not have any need for the universe.[36] In absolutely no way can we say that God was compelled to create the world.[37] Hence, to the extent that we can understand God's purpose, creation was nothing less than an act of absolute love and altruism on the part of God.[38]

Our understanding of God's relationship to the world is ultimately twofold. We conceive of God as being both immanent and transcendental.[39] Some of our great thinkers express this in another way, saying that God both fills and encompasses all creation.[40]

We make use of these two opposing concepts in many ways

when we speak of God. In our blessings, we speak of God as the "King of the universe," yet, at the same time, we call Him "our God." In another well-known prayer, we address God as "our Father, our King." What we are saying is that God is as close to us as a father, and yet, that He is as distant from us as an imperial monarch.

One of the clearest expressions of this is found in the *Kedushah*, the prayer we say in imitation of the song of the angels. We first repeat the verse (Isaiah 6:3), "Holy, holy, holy, is the Lord of Hosts, the whole earth is filled with His glory." Here, we are speaking of the immanence of God, saying that He fills all of creation. The second part of the *Kedushah*, however, consists of the passage (Ezekiel 3:12), "Blessed is the Lord's glory from His place." Here, we are speaking of a transcendental God, and even the highest celestial beings cannot comprehend His place.[41]

The fact that we speak of God as both transcendantal and immanent, however, does not imply any element of duality in God Himself. We perceive this dichotomy only because of our own imperfect understanding. God Himself is an absolute unity.[42]

God's immanence implies that there is no place in all creation that is devoid of His being. We therefore speak of God as being Omnipresent. The Torah thus states (Numbers 14:21), "All the earth is filled with God's glory." We likewise find (Psalms 148:13), "His glory is in heaven and earth."[43]

In a number of places, the Torah speaks of God as being in a certain place at a given time. This, however, does not mean that God is in that place and no other. What it does mean is that God wishes to bestow special honor and attention to that place, or that His action is particularly visible there. Thus, for example, God was said to dwell in the Holy Temple (Bais HaMikdash) because He bestowed special attention and honor to that particular location. Similarly, God was said to lead the Jews at the Exodus, because His activities were particularly visible in relation to them.[44]

We can understand God filling all creation on a somewhat deeper level. Nothing can exist, even for an instant, unless God wills it to exist. If God were to stop willing a particular thing to exist, it would instantaneously cease to exist. Thus, God's will must permeate all creation. However, as we discussed earlier, God's unity and simplicity require that His will be the same as His essence. Therefore, when we say that God's will permeates all creation, we are actually making the same statement regarding His essence.

An important corollary of this is the fact that the existence of all things continually depends on God's creative power. If this power were removed even for an instant, all creation would cease to exist. Scripture alludes to this when it states (Nehemiah 9:6), "You have made the heaven...the earth and all that is on it...and You give life to all." The statement here is that God continually gives existence to all things. This is likewise the meaning of what we say in our morning prayers. "In His goodness, He daily renews the act of creation."[45]

Although God's presence fills all creation, His existence is absolutely undetectable. The Prophet therefore says to God (Isaiah 45:15), "Certainly, You are a God who hides Himself."

One reason why God does not reveal Himself is because all creation would be nullified by His glory.[46] On a deeper level, we can say that He is undetectable because He fills all creation, and therefore there is no place empty of Him. We therefore have no comparison which we can use to detect His presence. Or as some have said, the reason why we cannot see God is not because He is so far, but because He is so near.

On this level, the reason why we cannot see God is very similar to the reason why we cannot see the air around us. The only time that we are aware of the atmosphere is when the wind blows and we can feel it. Similarly, the only time that we are aware of God is when He acts to reveal His presence. This may be the reason why the Hebrew language has the same word, ruach, for both wind and spirit.

Another important teaching regarding God is his omniscience.[47] We believe that God knows all our deeds and everything else that occurs in the universe. Thus, we find (Proverbs 15:3), "The Lord's eyes are in every place, beholding the evil and the good."

This, however, is also a direct consequence of God's omnipresence. God fills and sustains all creation, and therefore, is aware of everything happening in it. The Prophet spells this out, saying in God's name (Jeremiah 23:24), "Can a man hide himself in secret places, that I not see him?...Do I not fill heaven and earth?"[48]

God's knowledge extends even to the very thoughts of man. God is constantly aware of every thought in the mind of every single creature in the universe. Thus, we find (I Chronicles 28:9), "The Lord searches every heart, and perceives every urge of thought." The Psalmist puts it more succinctly when he says (44:22), "He knows the secrets of the heart."[49]

Another aspect of God's knowledge results from the fact that He exists outside of time. This is His knowledge of the future. Since God is not bound by time, He sees the future in exactly the same manner as He perceives the past and present. This concept is clearly spelled out in the words of the Prophet, who says in God's name (Isaiah 41:4), "I call the generations from the beginning, I, the Lord, I am the first, and with the last, I am the same."[50]

Since God's intellect is identical with His infinite being, it too is infinite. The Psalmist thus testifies (147:5), "His understanding is infinite." Therefore, there is no question as to how God can be constantly aware of every single human being. Beyond this, He even knows precisely what is happening to every single atom in the universe at any given instant. However great the number of events, it is nothing compared to God's infinite intellect.[51]

What we have presented here is a summary of what our great

sages have to say about God. All of this, however, is less than a drop in the ocean. Ultimately, God is so high above us that we cannot comprehend Him at all. Scripture thus says (Job 11:7), "Can you by searching find out God? Can you find out the Almighty unto perfection?" God's essence transcends our very powers of thought, as He Himself told His Prophet (Isaiah 55:8), "My thoughts are not your thoughts, neither are My ways your ways." We have neither the words nor the mental processes that would enable us to actually describe God or understand Him.[52] This is not only true of mortal man, but even of the highest celestial beings.[53]

A most important statement regarding God proclaims, "No thought can grasp you at all."[54] One great thinker explains this by saying that just as an abstract thought cannot be grasped by a physical hand, so, the essence of God cannot be grasped by the power of thought.[55]

We may be able to experience God and approach Him in prayer, but understanding Him is totally beyond our power.

NOTES

1. Cf. *Mesilas Yesharim* 1; *Zohar Chadash* 70d.
2. For classical arguments, see *Emunos VeDeyos* 1:3. See also *Bereshis Rabbah* 12:1, *Koheles Rabbah* 2:14, *Sifri, Deuteronomy* 307.
3. See *Radak* ad loc.
4. Cf. *Chovos HaLevavos* 2:5, *Shnei Luchos HaBris (Shelah)* 1:46b. See also *Bereshis Rabbah* 48:2.
5. *Moreh Nevuchim* 1:44.
6. *Chovos HaLevavos*, end of 1:6.
7. *Ramban* on Exodus 20:2, *Sefer HaChinuch* 25.
8. Cf. *Kuzari* 1:1, 2.
9. See *Avos* 4:11, 5:17.
10. See also Jeremiah 10:12, Zechariah 12:1, Psalms 33:6, 89:12, Nehemiah 9:6. Cf. *Emunos VeDeyos* 1:1, *Yad, Yesodei HaTorah* 11:111, 5.
11. *Moreh Nevuchim* 1:58, *Kuzari* 2:2, *Ikkarim* 2:22.
12. 13 Principles of Faith #2.
13. See *Yad, Yesodei HaTorah* 1:7.
14. *Moreh Nevuchim* 1:75.
15. Cf. *Targum, Metzudos David* ad loc., *Reshis Chochmah* 1:1 (9c).

16. *Ikkarim* 2:9, *Pardes Rimonim* 5:4. Cf. *Yad, Yesodei HaTorah* 1:7.
17. *Derech HaShem* 1:5. Cf. *Yad*, loc. cit. 2:10.
18. Cf. *Bereshis Rabbah* 28:2, 48:22; *Tanchuma, Sh'mos* 18, *Korach* 9, *Midrash Tehillim* 62:1, 107:3, *Nissim Gaon* on *Berachos* 32a.
19. *Moreh Nevuchim* 3·15, *Pardes Rimonim* 2:7, *Shefa Tal* 1:3. See *Yerushalmi, Taanis* 2:1 (89a), from Numbers 23:19.
20. Regarding "pure," see *Berachos* 10a, *Vayikra Rabbah* 4:8, *Devarim Rabbah* 2:26, from Habakuk 1:13. For "holy," see *Kuzari* 4:3; also Leviticus 19:2, 21:8, Isaiah 6:3; *Vayikra Rabbah* 224:9, *Tosafos, Kiddushin* 3b "*DeAsar.*"
21. *Emunos VeDeyos* 2:11, 12, *Shevil Emunah* ad loc. 2:11:12; *Moreh Nevuchim* 2:13, 30, *Ikkarim* 2:18, *Asarah Maamaros* 1:16, *Derech Mitzvosecha (Chabad)* 57b. See *Bereshis Rabbah* 3:8.
22. *Bereshis Rabbah* 68:10, *Sh'mos Rabbah* 45:6, *Midrash Tehillim* 50, *Pesikta Rabosai* 21 (104b); *Rashi* on Exodus 33:21, *Baalei Tosafos* ibid., *Radak* on Psalm 90:1, *Nefesh HaChaim* 3:1-3.

23. *Emunos VeDeyos* 1:4.

24. 13 Principles of Faith, #3; *Yad, Tshuva* 3:6, Raavad ad loc., *Iggeres Techiyas Hamesim* p. 4, *Ikkarim* 1:2, *Pardes Rimonim* 1:9.

25. See Targum ad loc. *Emunos VeDeyos* 2:1, *Yad, Yesodei HaTorah* 1:8, *Moreh Nevuchim* 1:35, 55; *Zohar* 3:225a, *Reshis Chochmah* 9a.

26. *Mechilta* (65a) Rashi, on Exodus 19:18; *Tanchuma, Yisro* 13; *Bereshis Rabbah* 27:1, *Koheles Rabbah* 2:224, *Midrash Tehillim* 1, *Pesikta DeRabbi Kahana* 4 (36b); *Yad, Yesodei HaTorah* 1:9, *Moreh Nevuchim* 1:26, 47; *Emunos VeDeyos* 2:0, *Chovos HaLevavos* 1:10, *Kuzari* 4:3 (18a). See also *Avodas HaKodesh* 3:26, *Pardes Rimonim* 22:1, *Tiferes Yisrael* (Maharal) 33, *Nefesh HaChaim* 2:2, 2:5 (note: "*Vezehu*"); Ramban on Genesis 46:1.

27. *Nefesh HaChaim* 1:1. See also *Mechilta* (33a) on Exodus 14:29, *Bereshis Rabbah* 21:5, *Shir HaShirim Rabbah* 1:46, *Yad, Tshuvah* 5:1.

28. *Moreh Nevuchim* 1:21, 65; *Kuzari* 1:89.

29. *Ikkarim* 2:11, *Akedas Yitzchak* 4 (36b); See *Berachos* 32., *Bereshis Rabbah* 13:14.

30. *Emunos VeDeyos* 2:10, *Yad, Yesodei HaTorah* 1:10, *Kuzari* 5:18 #5, Cf. *Bereshis Rabbah* 81:2, *Mechilta* (67b) to Exodus 22:3, *Vayikra Rabbah* end of 19:2, Ibn Ezra on Ecclesiastes 3:15, *Ikkarim* 2:19.

31. *Yad*, loc. cit. 1:11, *Moreh Nevuchim* 1:11, *Akedat Yitzchok* 60.

32. *Charedim* #5 (p. 42).

33. *Yad*, loc. cit., *Moreh Nevuchim* 1:54, *Emunos VeDeyos* 2:11.

34. *Shomrei Emunim* (HaKadmon) 2:17.

35. *Shnei Luchos HaBris* 1:6a note, *Charedim* #5 (p. 40). Cf. *Pirkei DeRabbi Eliezer* 3.

36. *Yad, Yesodei HaTorah* 1:2,3, *Moreh Nevuchim* 3:13, *Emunos VeDeyos* 1:4, *Shevil Emunah* ad loc.1:4:9, *Reshis Chochmah* 8d. Cf. *Pesikta* 6 (57b.

37. *Akedas Yitzchak* 4 (35B), *Likutei Moharan* (Breslov) 52.

38. *Emunos VeDeyos* 3:0, *Or HaShem* (Crescas) 2:6:2, *Sefer HaYashar* 1, *Pardes Rimonim* 2:6, *Etz Chaim*, "*Shaar HaKelalim*"#1, *Shnei Luchos HaBris* 1:21b, *Shomrei Emunim* (HaKadmon) 2:13.

39. Cf Ibn Ezra.

40. *Zohar* 3:225a, *Likutei Amarim* (Tanya) 83b, *Nefesh HaChaim* 3:4, *Reshis Chochmah* 9a.

41. *Chagigah* 13b, *Pirkei DeRabbi Eliezer* end of #4, *Moreh Nevuchim* 1:8, *Nefesh HaChaim* 3:6.

42. *Shnei Luchos HaBris* 1:44a, 64b; *Likutei Amarim* 84.

43. *Berachos* (10a), *Vayikra Rabbah* 4:8, *Devarim Rabbah* 2:26, *Midrash Tehillim* 2:45 (103a); *Bamidbar Rabbah* 12:4, *Pesikta* 1 (2b), *Zohar* 2:42b, *Tikunei Zohar* 3a, 62a, *Reshis Chochmah* 7a, 8c, 8d, Radak on Jeremiah 23:24.

44. *Mechilta* (25a), Ibn Ezra, on Exodus 3:2, *Emunos VeDeyos* 2:11, *Kuzari* 2:7, 8, *Moreh Nevuchim* 1:19, 27, Ramban on Genesis 46:1. Cf. *Succah* 53a, Rashi ad loc. "*Im.*"

45. *Kuzari* 4:26, Ibn Ezra on Exodus 3:2, Ramban on Genesis 1:4, Ralbag on Nehemiah 9:6; *Yad, Yesodei HaTorah* 2:9; *Zohar* 3:31a, 3:225a; *Tosefos Yom Tov* on *Tamid* 7:4, *Reshis Chochmah* 9b, 63d, *Likutei Amarim* 77b, *Nefesh HaChaim* 1:2. Cf. *Midrash Tehillim* 119:36; *Berachos* 10a, *VaYikra Rabbah* 2:26, *Pirkei DeRabbi Eliezer* 7, 18, end of 34, Radal ad loc. 7:6, 18:9, 34:75, 48:5. Also see *Mechilta* (59a) to Exodus 18:12, *Kiddushin* 32b, *Avodah Zarah* 3b.

46. *Chulin* top of 60a, *Yalkut* 1:396 on Exodus 33:20.

47. 13 Principles of Faith, #10.

48. *Tanchuma, Naso* 5, *Yalkut* 2:305; *Mechilta* (8a) on Exodus 12:13 *Bereshis Rabbah* 9:3, *Kuzari* #7, *Yad, Yesodei HaTorah* 2:9, 10, Cf. Psalms 33:13, 14, 139:12, Job 28:24, II Chronicles 16:9.

49. *Bereshis Rabbah* 9:3, *Sh'mos Rabbah* 21:3, *Yerushalmi, Rosh HaShanah* 1:3 (8a), *Tanna DeBei Eliahu Zuta* 23 (50b).

50. *Sanhedrin* 90b, *Avos* 3:15, Rambam ad loc., *Yerushalmi, Rosh HaShanah* 1:3 (87b), *Bereshis Rabbah* 2:5, 26:4, 27:7, *Bamidbar Rabbah* 16:22, *Tanchuma, Shelach* 5, *Pirkei DeRabbi Eliezer* 36, 38, 48, *Tanna DeBei Eliahu Rabbah* 1 (5a), Rashi on Genesis 6:6, Psalms 139:16. Cf. Isaiah 41:26, 46:10.

51. *Yad, Yesodei HaTorah* 2:10, Cf. *Bereshis Rabbah* 9:3, *Tanchuma, Yisro* 12, *Tosefos Yom Tov* on *Rosh HaShanah* 1:2 "*She-Ne'emar.*"

52. Cf. *Berachos* 33b, *Megillah* 18a, 25a, *Makkos* 10a, *Pirkei DeRabbi Eliezer* 3; *Moreh Nevuchim* 1:59, *Yad, Tefillah* 9:7, *Turei Zahav* on *Shulchan Aruch, Orach Chaim* 113:7.

53. *Yad, Yesodei HaTorah* 2:8, *Chagigah* 13b, *Sifra* (6) to Leviticus 1:1, *Sifri* 1:113, *Bamidbar Rabbah* 14:27, *Midrash Tehillim* 18, *Pirkei DeRabbi Eliezer* 4, *Tanna DeBei Eliahu Rabbah* 31 (123a), *Reshis Chochmah* 11c.

54. *Tikunei Zohar* 17a.

55. *Likutei Amarim* 86b.

Free Will and the Purpose of Creation

WHY DID GOD create the world?

The answer to this question is very simple, and yet, at the same time, involves some of the most sublime mysteries. Just as we cannot truly understand God, we cannot truly fathom His reasons. Still, we can look at God's creation and seek to comprehend its reason for existence. We can see what God Himself has taught us about the purpose of creation, both in the Torah and in our traditions.

One of the things that we can say about God is that He is good. Not only can we say that He is good, but also that He defines good. His every act involves the most pure and infinite love that can exist. His goodness and love are intertwined to bring about His purpose. The Psalmist speaks of this saying (145:9), "The Lord is good to all, His love rests on all His deeds."[1]

God Himself is intrinsically perfect, and therefore has no need for anything, even creation. We must therefore say that He had absolutely no need to create the world. Creation was therefore the most perfect possible act of altruism and love. Ultimately, God created the world in order to bestow His good upon it. The Psalmist sums this up when he says (89:3), "I have said the world is built of love."[2]

God's ability is limitless. It therefore follows that His love and altruism are likewise unlimited and must result in the greatest possible benefit for His creation.[3] Furthermore, God Himself defines all good, and therefore, the highest possible benefit is that which comes most directly from God Himself.[4]

Collegiate Hashkafa Series—1973

In order for anything to be appreciated, or for that matter, even to be detected, some degree of contrast is required.[5] Therefore, in order that the world experience the benefit of God's presence, it must first experience His absence. In order to provide the greatest possible contrast, God created the world as an environment where His essence would be absolutely undetectable.[6]

In order to fulfill His goal, God created the universe as a place for a creature to be capable of partaking of His goodness. This creature, man, would be capable of understanding joy and happiness, and of communing with God.[7] Everything in the world would then be a means through which man attains God's goodness. This is the meaning of the Talmudic statement, which teaches us that upon completing His creation, God declared, "If there are no guests, then what pleasure has the King with all the good things that He has stocked?"[8]

Man was therefore created as a creature capable of understanding and ultimately experiencing the greatest possible good, namely, God Himself.[9] We can therefore say that God's purpose in creation was to allow Himself to be experienced by a creature far removed and much lower than Himself. This is the meaning of the Midrashic teaching which states that God created the world because "He desired an abode in the lower world."[10]

In order that man fulfill God's purpose in creation and be able to accept His good, God caused man to develop a psychological makeup that gives him the greatest pleasure in doing things that he knows to be good and beneficial. This pleasure is enhanced according to the importance of the authority declaring that a particular action is good. The greatest such pleasure of accomplishment therefore comes from obeying God's express will. God is the highest possible authority, and there can be no greater spiritual pleasure than in knowingly obeying His express will.[11]

In order that man experience this pleasure of accomplishment, God revealed His will to man. This is what the Prophet teaches us in God's name (Isaiah 48:17), "I am the Lord your God, Who teaches you for your profit, Who leads you by the way that you should go."[12] When we fulfill God's will, we are ultimately also fulfilling His purpose in creation.[13] The Psalmist thus teaches us (16:11), "You make me know the path of life, in Your presence is the fullness of joy, in Your right hand, bliss forever."[14]

In order to enjoy the pleasure of accomplishment, it is imperative that man know that his accomplishment was a matter of his own free choice and not something that he was compelled to do. This is one reason why God gave man free will.[15]

Such freedom of will is certainly required by God's justice.[16] However, beyond this, it is also required by the very purpose for which He created the universe. For God arranged things so that He may give man good as a result of man's own pleasure of accomplishment, and this is only possible when man has free will.[17]

We can also understand this on a deeper level. The ultimate good is God Himself. Therefore, the greatest possible good that he can bestow is Himself. There is no greater good than achieving a degree of unity with God, the Creator of all good. Therefore, since God desires to give man the greatest good possible, He gave Him the ability to resemble Himself.

It is for this reason that God gave man free will.[18]

Just as God acts as a free being, so does man. Just as God operates without prior restraint, so does man. Just as God can do good as a matter of His own free choice, so can man. According to many commentators, this is the meaning of what the Torah says when it speaks of man as created in the "image of God."[19]

But in order for man to have true free choice, he must not only have inner freedom of will, but also an environment where a choice of obedience and disobedience exists.[20] In order that such a choice exist, God created a world where both good and evil can freely operate.[21] He thus tells His Prophet (Isaiah 45:7), "I form light and create darkness, I make peace and create evil; I am the Lord, I do all these things."[22]

The more difficult an accomplishment, the more satisfaction there is in doing it. This is again something basic built into human psychology. God therefore created this world so that it should present man with the greatest possible challenge. This world was therefore made as a place where it would be possible, but very difficult, to truly serve God. God allows evil and temptation to exist, even though they may cause people to abandon Him and completely ignore Him and His teachings.[23] Even though some may stray through their own choice, this is the price that we pay in order that the reward of those who choose good be maximized. Thus, our sages teach us that it was for the sake of the righteous that the world was created.[24]

Even the evil and temptations of the world serve the divine purpose of enhancing the satisfaction of accomplishment of those who overcome them, and in this way play a part in man's ultimate reward and God's final purpose.[25] The greater the barriers that must be overcome, the greater the satisfaction and reward in overcoming them. Thus, our sages teach us, "Reward is according to suffering."[26] God may have created evil, but He created it in order that we may overcome it. This is what Scripture means when it says (Job 28:28), "Behold, the fear of God, that is wisdom, and to depart from evil, that is understanding."[27]

Here, however, we find an important contradiction. The environment required to earn God's reward is exactly the opposite of that required to receive it. In order that man gain the maximum satisfaction of accomplishment, and therefore, maximum reward, he must serve God in an environment presenting the greatest possible challenge. This must be a world where neither God nor the divine nature of His commandments is either visible or obvious. On the other hand, the environment required for man's ultimate reward is the exact opposite. In the world of reward, both God and the divine nature of His commandments must be as obvious as possible. It is only when one truly realizes the true nature of his deeds that he obtains maximum pleasure in having done them.[28]

It is for this reason that God created two levels of existence. He created *Olam Hazeh*—This World—as an environment of challenge and accomplishment, where we earn our ultimate reward. However, He also created a second level, *Olam Haba*—The World to Come—as the world of ultimate reward. This will be a world where the true nature of our deeds will be perfectly obvious. The existence of these two worlds then resolves our dichotomy. We have This World offering the greatest possible challenge on one hand, while on the other, we have the World to Come, offering the greatest possible realization of accomplishment.[29]

The principle that man has free will, with the absolute freedom to choose between good and evil, is therefore a foundation of our faith. God therefore tells us in His Torah (Deuteronomy 30:19), "I call heaven and earth to bear witness this day, for I have set before you life and death, the blessing and the curse. Therefore, choose life, that you and your children may live."[30]

Judaism therefore teaches us that every man can choose his own path in life, whether it be good or evil. Each individual has the ability to achieve the highest human perfection, or, on the other hand, to sink to the lowest levels of evil and degradation. If man fails to heed the call of righteousness and chooses evil, then he has no cause to complain, for the decision is only his own. This is what Scripture means when it says (Lamentations 3:38-39), "Evil and good come not from the mouth of the Most High. Why then should a living man complain, a strong man because of his sins?"[31]

Of course, there are many things that may limit a person's capabilities. One's intellect or health or personality traits may place limitations on his accomplishments in the world.[32] Nevertheless, each man has the ultimate choice whether or not to serve God according to his abilities.[33] This is what our sages mean when they teach us, "All is in the hands of heaven, except the fear of heaven."[34]

It is interesting to note that according to the most modern scientific picture of the world, free will is an integral part of creation. Science teaches us that there is an element of indeterminacy or "free will" inherent in the very quantum nature of matter, and this clearly indicates that the universe was created as an arena for a free-willed creature such as man. It is this freedom of will that gives man a wider choice than merely to react to his surroundings. Although an individual's actions may be influenced by his heredity and environment, neither of these absolutely determines his actions.

There are some who might ask why God does not force man to do good and obey His commandments. However, when we understand God's ultimate purpose in creation, we can also understand why He does not force man to obey His will.[35] For, as far as we understand God's purpose, we understand that free will is one of its prime ingredients. God may desire that we do good, but only if we do so as a matter of free will. Morality as such does not apply to God. All ethics and morality only exist for the benefit of man, and this benefit is ultimately only attained when man himself acts as a free agent. Similarly, evil may act to the detriment of the one who does it, but it can never actually affect God. Thus, God tells His Prophet (Jeremiah 7:19), "Am I the one they anger?...Is it rather not they themselves, for their own shame?"[36]

Since free will is one of the prime ingredients of God's purpose, He does not do anything in this world that might destroy or diminish man's choice between good and evil. Thus, for example, He does not openly reward the good nor punish the wicked, since this would make man less free to sin. Similarly, God does not allow any obvious miracles to occur under any conditions where they would undermine one's freedom of choice.[37]

There is another paradox that is discussed by virtually every Jewish philosopher: If God is omniscient and knows what every man will do in the future, how can man have free choice to do otherwise? Ultimately, this apparent paradox stems from the fact that we cannot understand precisely how God knows the future.[38] As long as man is bound to this physical world and his mind is limited by the bonds of time, he cannot see beyond time where the resolution of this paradox exists.[39] However, to the limit of our understanding, we know that somehow God restricts His own knowledge of the future in order to give man free will.[40] The main thing is that, although we do not understand it, God's knowledge of the future in no way deprives the individual of his own free choice.[41]

We can make this plausible in one way. We know that God exists outside of time. Therefore, His knowledge of the future is *exactly* the same as His knowledge of the past and present.[42] Therefore, just as His knowledge of the past and present does not interfere with man's free will, neither does His knowledge of the future.[43] Essentially, we must say that since God created time, He can do with it as He wills. Furthermore, time was not created because God Himself needed it, but because it was needed to make this world an arena of action, for man's own ultimate benefit.

This entire concept is clearly explained by Rabbi Akiba in a Mishnah, which states, "All is foreseen, yet free will is granted. The world is judged for good, and all is according to one's works."[44]

When Rabbi Akiba says, "All is foreseen, yet free will is granted," he is presenting the paradox of free will and God's knowledge of the future. But he then concludes by giving a reason for this paradox: "The world is judged for good, and all is according to one's works." Both time and this apparent paradox were created in order for God to attain His ultimate purpose—to "judge the world for good"—and that it be an arena where "all is according to one's deeds."[45]

We find occasions where God reveals the future actions of an individual.[46] Such prophecy, however, is always contingent on the individual's free choice, and is therefore not absolutely binding.[47] What God does reveal, however, is the most probable course of future events based on the individual's nature. Still, this does not bar the individual from going against his nature, and such a change of mind is by no means precluded by any prophecy.[48] Similarly, there are cases where a prophet predicts that those not yet born will be wicked.[49] Here too, he is merely predicting their most likely future based on heredity and environment, but the ultimate choice is still up to the individual concerned.[50]

Even when God does reveal to a prophet that an individual will do evil, He does not reveal the extent of their evil. Therefore, the fact that their evil has already been predicted does not exempt them from punishment. Thus, for example, we find that God revealed to Abraham (Genesis 15:13-14), "Know that your children will be strangers in a land that is not theirs...and that nation shall afflict them...but I will also judge the nation whom they shall serve."[51] We see here, that even though the decree had been declared, individuals were still judged for their actions, and therefore, the Egyptians were punished for maximizing the suffering of the Jews. Regarding this, God told His Prophet (Zechariah 1:15), "I am sorely displeased with the nations...for I was a little displeased, but they helped add evil."[52]

Although God does not determine the conduct of individuals, He does influence the large-scale course of history. Therefore, even though each individual has free will, the collective wills of nations and societies are largely determined by God.[53] For this reason, God often guides the wills of kings and other important leaders, thereby influencing the tides of history. With regard to this, Scripture states (Proverbs 21:1), "The king's heart is in God's hand...He turns it wherever He wills."[54]

Although God does not directly influence human behavior, our sages teach us that He does often lead a person along the path that he himself has chosen to follow.[55] Thus, for example, we are taught, "One who comes to cleanse himself is helped [by God]."[56] God may plant ideas in one's mind that are conducive to helping him follow the correct path, or may otherwise bring about events to encourage him.[57] Thus, the Psalmist prayed (86:11), "Teach me Your ways, O God, that I may walk in Your truth; make my heart one to fear Your name."[58]

There are many ways in which God can bring about circumstances conducive for a righteous person to do good.[59] In a likewise manner, the wicked are given every opportunity and circumstances to continue doing evil, as our sages state, "When one comes to make himself unclean, the door is open for him."[60] However, in all these cases, the final choice ultimately rests with the individual.[61]

There are times, however, when a person is so wicked that God's ultimate purpose requires that choice be taken away from him, and that he be denied the power to repent.[62] We find an example of this when God told His Prophet (Isaiah 6:10), "Make the heart of this people fat, and make their ears heavy, and shut their eyes...return and be healed."[63] This is also the meaning of what God told Moses (Exodus 7:3), "I will harden Pharaoh's heart, and multiply My signs and wonders in the land of Egypt."[64] In all such cases, God does not decree that a person be wicked, but once his wickedness surpasses certain bounds, free choice to repent is taken away from him.[65] Accordingly, our sages teach us that God first warns a sinner many times, but if the warning is not heeded, then the gates of repentance may be closed.[66]

Ultimately, then, all of life is a test. However, there are times when God puts an individual to a special test or *nisayon*. In such a case, a person is placed in an especially difficult position, where his devotion and faith are tested.[67] However, God does not put an individual to such a difficult test unless He knows that he will pass it. Thus the Psalmist says (11:5), "God tests the righteous, but His soul hates the wicked."[68] The Midrash thus teaches us, "The potter does not test vessels that are easily broken, but only those that are strong. Similarly, God does not test the wicked, but only the righteous."[69]

There are many reasons why God puts an individual to the test. Most often this is done to bring out his latent potential.[70] This may be done to reward a person, since reward comes for action and not for potential alone,[71] as Scripture teaches us (II Chronicles 15:7), "Your *works* shall be rewarded."[72] Similarly, the test often makes a particular task more difficult, in order to increase its reward.[73]

There are other occasions when God puts an individual to the test in order to make his potential and ability known, either to himself[74] or to others.[75] It is for this reason that a person is often tested by God before he is chosen for greatness or leadership.[76]

Although God might often guide or test man, the final choice between good and evil ultimately depends on each individual. Whether a person does right or wrong, he can blame nothing and nobody but himself. Every man can control his action if only he tries hard enough. Man was created to be master of his fate, and as such, he bears the full responsibility for it.

1. Cf. *Sanhedrin* 39b, Rashi ad loc. "Oder."

2. *Emunos VeDeyos* end of 1:4, 3; *Or HaShem* (Crescas) 2:6:2, *Sefer HaYashar* 1, *Pardes Rimonim* 2:6, *Etz Chaim, Shaar haKelallim* #1, *Reshis Chochmah, Shaar Ha-Tshuvah* #1, *Shnei Luchos HaBris, Bais Yisroel* 1:21b, *Shomrei Emunim* (HaKadmon) 2:13 *Derech HaShem* 1:2:1, *Likutei Moharan* #64. See also *Zohar* 1:10b, 1:230b, 2:166b, *Sefer HaBris* 2:1:3.

3. *Tshuvos Chacham Tzvi* 18, *Likutei Amarim* (Tanya) 2:4 (79a). Cf. *Moreh Nevuchim* 3:25, 27.

4. *Derech HaShem,* ibid. See also *Shiur Kumah* (RaMaK) 1:3, *Yad, Tshuvah* 8:2.

5. *Likutei Amarim* (Tanya) 2:7 (81b).

6. See *Chulin* 60a.

7. *Mesilas Yesharim* 1.

8. *Sanhedrin* 38a, *Yerushalmi Sanhedrin* 4:9 (23b), *Bereshis Rabbah* 8:5.

9. Cf. *Bereshis Rabbah* 5:1, *Eichah Rabbah* 1:59, *Pirkei DeRabbi Eliezer* 3 (5b). Also see *Emunos VeDeyos,* end of 1:4, from Psalms 145:12.

10. *Tanchuma, Naso* 16, *Likutei Amarim* (Tanya) 1:36 (45b).

11. Cf. *Avos* 4:17; *Kiddushin* 31a, *Baba Kama* 38a, 87a, *Avodah Zarah* 3a, *Sotah* 21a.

12. *Emunos VeDeyos,* loc. cit.

13. Cf. *Shabbos* 31b, *Yalkut* 2:1069, from Ecclesiastes 3:14. Also see *Bereshis Rabbah* 1:6, 12:2, *Zohar* 2:42a, Rashi on Genesis 1:1, *Reshis Chochmah, Shaar HaTshuvah* 1 (101b).

14. See Ibn Ezra ad loc., *Emunos VeDeyos* 3.

15. *Yad, Tshuvah* 5:1, *Moreh Nevuchim* 3:17, *Emunos VeDeyos* 4:4 (64b). Cf. *Pirkei DeRabbi Eliezer* 15 (35a), *Minachos* 29b.

16. *Yad, Tshuvah* 5:4, *Moreh, Emunos VeDeyos* loc. cit.

17. *Zohar* 1:23a, *Emunos VeDeyos, Reshis Chochmah* loc. cit.

18. *Derech HaShem* 1:2:2.

19. Cf. *Mechilta* on Exodus 14:29 (33a), *Bereshis Rabbah* 21:5, *Shir HaShirim Rabbah* 1:46, *Yalkut* 1:34, *Yad, Tshuvah* 5:1.

20. *Derech HaShem* loc. cit. Cf. *Midrash Tehillim* 36:3, *Reshis Chochmah, Shaar HaYirah* 7 (22b).

21. Cf. *Moreh Nevuchim* 3:10, *Sefer HaYashar* 1, quoted in *Shnei Luchos HaBris, Bais Yisrael* (1:22a). Also see *Sanhedrin* 39b.

22. Cf. *Bereshis Rabbah* 9:12-14; Rabbi Yaakov Emden (Maharibatz) on *Baba Basra* 16a.

23. *Mesilas Yesharim* 1 (4a). Cf. *Eruvin* 13b, Tosafos, *Avodah Zarah* 5a "She'ilmalei."

24. *Emunos VeDeyos* 4:5 (66a). Cf. *Sifri* on Deuteronomy 11:9, *Yalkut* 1:872, *Reshis Chochmah* 2a.

25. *Tanna DeBei Eliahu Rabbah* 16 (77a), *Tanna DeBei Eliahu Zuta* 12 (17a), *Zohar* 2:163a, *Sefer Chasidim* 155, *Likutei Amarim* (Tanya) 1:36 (46a). See also *Bereshis Rabbah* 9:9, *Zohar* (Midrash Ne'elam) 1:138a.

26. *Avos* 5:23, *Shnei Luchos HaBris, Bais Yisrael* (1:21b).

27. Cf. *Emunos VeDeyos,* end of 4:1 (63b).

28. *Derech HaShem* 1:3:4.

29. Ibid.

30. Ramban ad loc., *Yad, Tshuvah* 5:3, *Moreh Nevuchim* 3:17, *Emunos VeDeyos* 4:4 (864b). Cf. Deuteronomy 11:26.

31. *Yad, Tshuvah* 5:2, *Sefer Chasidim* 33. Cf. Rashi ad loc., *Eichah Rabbah* 3:31, *Devarim Rabbah* 4:3, *Tanchuma Re'eh* 3.

32. *Emunos VeDeyos* 4:4 (65a), *Sh'vil Emunah* ad loc. 4:4:2, *Kuzari* 5:20:6 (54a), *Akedas Yitzchak* 28.

33. *Niddah* 16b, *Tanchuma Pikudei* 3. See also Maharsha on *Baba Basra* 17a "Al," Maharitz Chayos, *Gittin* 66a; Rambam, *Shemonah Perakim* #8.

34. *Berachos* 33b, *Megillah* 25a, *Niddah* 16b, *Yalkut* 1:455, 2,302; *Zohar* 1:59a, *Tikunei Zohar Chadash* 121b,c; *Bahir* 187, *Sefer Chasidim* 33, *Tshuvos Meil Tzedakah* 7.

35. *Yad, Tshuvah* 5:4, *Moreh Nevuchim* 3:17, *Emunos VeDeyos* 4:4 (65a), *Kuzari* 5:20 (47a), *Chovas HaLevavos,* 3:8. Cf. *Bereshis Rabbah* 22:22, *Yalkut* 1:38, *Tosefos Yom Tov* on *Avos* 3:15.

36. Radak ad loc., *Emunos VeDeyos* loc. cit.

37. *Menoras HaMaor,* end of #3 (237, quoting *Shaar HaShamayim* 1:22), *Tosefos Yom Tov* on *Avodah Zarah* 4:7. Cf. *Berachos* 20a, *Bereshis Rabbah* 9:6, *Ikkarim* 4:12 from Ecclesiastes 8:12.

38. *Yad, Tshuvah* 5:5, *Moreh Nevuchim* 3:20, *Shemonah Perakim* #8.

39. See *Likutei Moharan* 21, 64.

40. *Or HaChaim* on Genesis 6:2, *Meshech Chochmah* on Genesis 1:26. See also *Elemah Rabosai* (RaMaK), *Eyen Kol* 2:18.

41. *Emunos VeDeyos* 4:4 (65b), *Kuzari* 5:20 (47b), *Chovas Halevavos* 3:8, *Milchomos HaShem* 3:106, *Or HaShem* 2:4, *Ikkarim* 4:3, 7-10, *Akedas Yitzchak* 21, *Tshuvos Rivash* 119, *Shnei Luchos HaBris, Bais HaBechirah* (1:43a), *Tikunei Zohar Chadash* 89b; *Pardes*

Rimonim 4:9, Asarah Maamaros 16, Gevuros HaShem 2, Bachya on Exodus 15:18, Or Sameach on Yad, Tshuvah 5:5.

42. Ikkarim 2:19.

43. Rabbi Moshe Almosnino, quoted in Yesod HaEmunah (Rabbi Baruch Kasaver) #2, Sh'vil Emunah (on Emunos VeDeyos) 4:4:11; Midrash Shmuel, Tosefos Yom Tov, on Avos 3:15. See also Tanna DeBei Eliahu 1, Ramasayim Tzofim ad loc 1:8. Also see Kol Yehudah (on Kuzari) 5:20 (47b) "Ki" and Otzar Nechemad (on Kuzari) 1:1 (11b) "Kol." Cf. Tanchuma VaYeshev 4.

44. Avos 3:15, according to interpretation of Ramban, Rabenu Yonah, Bertenoro (second interpretation), Tosefos Yom Tov, Tiferes Yisrael. We find a similar expression in Pirkei DeRabbi Eliezer 26 (61b), 36 (83a), 38 (88a), and 48 (114b).

45. Cf. Otzar Nechemad loc. cit.

46. Cf. Rashi on Deuteronomy 34:1, Sefer Chasidim 1159, from II Samuel 16:21, 23, Amos 7:17.

47. Yad, Yesodei HaTorah 10:4. Cf. Jonah 3:10, II Kings 20:16; Yoma 73b, Yerushalmi Sanhedrin 11:5 (56b) Tanchuma Vayera 13, Yalkut 2:308, Rashi, Kara, Radak on Jeremiah 28:7; Radal on Pirkei DeRabbi Eliezer 10:4.

48. Tosafos, Yebamos 50a "Taida," Maharsha ibid., Shnei Luchos HaBris, Yad, Tshuvah 6:5. Bais HaBechirah (1:45a). Cf. Rashi on Genesis 21:17.

49. Cf. Berachos 10a.

50. Tosafos, Tosefos HaRosh, Niddah 16b "HaKol," Maharsha, Maharshal, Maharam ad loc. Cf. Ramban on Deuteronomy 31:21.

51. Ramban, Or HaChaim ad loc. Raavad on Yad, Tshuvah 6:5, Tosefos Yom Tov on Avos 2:6 "Metifcha."

52. Radak ad loc., Bamidbar Rabbah 10:5, Ramban, Raavad loc. cit.; Rabbi Yaakov Emden (Maharibatz) on Shemonah Perakim 8:2. See also Isaiah 47:6, Radak ad loc.

53. Yad, Tshuvah 6:5, Moreh Nevuchim 2:48.

54. Ralbag, Metzudos David ad loc. Yalkut 2:959. Cf. Berachos 55a, Rashi ad loc. "Tzerichim," Yalkut 1:860, 2:306; Emunos VeDeyos end of 4:7 (68a), Maharitz Chayos on Megillah 11a, Radak on Jeremiah 10:23.

55. Makkos 10b, Bamidbar Rabbah 20:11, Zohar 1:198b, 2:50a, 3:47a, 3:207a. Cf. Avos 4:2, Mechilta on Exodus 15:16 (46a); Maharsha, Avodah Zarah 5a "Mi".

56. Shabbos 104a, Yoma 38b, Avodah Zarah 55a, Minachos 29a, Yerushalmi Peah 1:1 (5b), Yalkut 2:936, from Proverbs 3:34; Yad, Tshuvah 6:5, Kuzari 5:20 (49b).

57. Tanchuma, Re'eh 12, Pesikta 11 (97b).

58. Yad, Tshuvah 6:4, Emunos VeDeyos 4:6 (86b), Zohar 1:59A.

59. Shabbos 32a, Sanhedrin 8a, Baba Basra 119b, Tosefta Yoma 4:11, Bamidbar Rabbah 13:17, Sefer Chasidim 45, Shnei Luchos HaBris, Bais HaBechirah (1:44a).

60. Cf. Sifra on Leviticus 18:2 (85c), Yalkut end of 1:586, Raavad.

61. Cf. Shnei Luchos HaBris, Shaar HaOsios (1:157b), Sefer Chasidim 352, Bris Olom ad loc., Yad Tshuvah 6:4.

62. Cf. Chagigah 15a.

63. Rashi ad loc., Akedas Yitzchak 36.

64. Ramban ad loc., Sh'mos Rabbah 11:2, Gevuros HaShem (Maharal) 31.

65. Yad, Tshuvah 6:3, Shemonah Perakim #8, Rambam, Tosefos Yom Tov on Avos 5:18. See Deuteronomy 2:30, Joshua 11:20.

66. Sh'mos Rabbah 13:4.

67. For a general discussion see Rabbi David Luria (Radal) on Pirkei DeRabbi Eliezer 31:2.

68. Rashi ad loc., Sh'mos Rabbah 2:2, Emunos VeDeyos 5:3 (70b).

69. Bereshis Rabbah 32:3, 34:2, 55:2, Shir HaShirim Rabbah 2:35, Midrash Tehillim 11:4, Tanchuma, VaYera 20, Yalkut 2:350. 2:654, Menoras HaMaor 5:3:1:3 (300).

70. Kuzari 5:20 (48b), Ramban on Genesis 22:1, 22:12, Exodus 16:4, Deuteronomy 13:4.

71. Ramban, Toras HaAdam, Shaar HaGamul (Jerusalem, 5715) p. 72a,b.

72. Radal, loc cit. Cf. Mechilta on Exodus 12:6 (5a), Yalkut 1:195.

73. Sh'mos Rabbah 31:2, Toras HaAdam loc cit. Cf. Mechilta on Exodus 20:17 (72a), Rashi, Ramban, ibid.

74. Pirkei DeRabbi Eliezer 31, Radal loc. cit. Cf. Sanhedrin 107a.

75. Avos 5:3, Avos DeRabbi Nathan 33:2, Berashis Rabbah 55:1, Tanchuma VaYera 23, Zohar (Midrash Ne'elam) 1:106b, Rashi on Genesis 22:12.

76. Sh'mos Rabbah 2:3, Sefer Chasidim 13. See also Sefer Chasidim 106, 161.

The Jew

T O THE BEST OF OUR UNDERSTANDING, we can say that God
created the world in order to bestow good upon it.[1]

As soon as God decided to create a world where He could bestow
good, He also created a vessel to accept this good. This vessel would
be the human race, or whatever portion of it that would be worthy to
receive God's ultimate goodness. It was given a name—Yisrael—Israel,
which according to one Midrashic interpretation means SheRah
El—"He who sees God."[2] These would be the ones who would
perceive the divine, and become the recipients of God's goodness.
This is the meaning of what our sages say when they teach us that the
concept of Israel was God's very first thought in creating the world.[3]
God thus told His Prophet (Jeremiah 2:3), "Israel is the Lord's holy portion, the first of His harvest."[4]

Besides creating Israel as a vessel to receive His good, God also
created a means through which it would receive this good. This was
the Torah, which, as such, was God's blueprint for all creation.[5] The
Torah is the way to God's goodness, as He himself said through the
wise Solomon (Proverbs 4:2), "I have given you a good thing, forsake
not My Torah." Our sages interpret this to mean that the Torah is God's
ultimate plan of good for the world, saying, "There is no good other
than Torah."[6] Thus, the Torah was also among the very first ingredients
of creation, as indeed we find it allegorically said (Proverbs 8:22),
"God made me as the beginning of His way, the first of His ways of

---

Collegiate Hashkafa Series—1973

old."[7] Nevertheless, our sages clearly teach us that even the Torah was only created for the sake of Israel.[8]

God's purpose in creation therefore required that Israel accept the Torah. Were this not to take place, all creation would lose its meaning and cease to exist.[9]

The one thing, however, that was not defined was "Israel." If Adam would have been worthy and would not have sinned, then all of his children would have been worthy of the Torah. If not for Adam's sin, all mankind would have had the status of "Israel."[10]

Because of Adam's sin, however, the Torah was restricted to the small portion of mankind who would be worthy of receiving it. The rest of the human race were given seven commandments, binding on every human being. They are:[11]

1. Not to worship idols.
2. Not to blaspheme God.
3. To establish courts of justice.
4. Not to murder.
5. Not to commit adultery or incest.
6. Not to steal.
7. Not to eat flesh from a living animal.

Of these commandments, only the first six were given to Adam himself.[12] The last commandment would have been redundant for him, since the eating of all animal flesh was forbidden until the generation of Noah.[13] Thus, the final commandment, forbidding the eating of flesh from a living animal, was given to Noah and his sons.[14]

These commandments were given in order that man receive an eternal reward for obeying them, and thus we are taught that a non-Jew who obeys these seven laws has a portion in the World to Come.[15] However, these commandments were also meant to benefit man morally in this world as well. Thus, the prohibitions against idolatry and blasphemy taught man to worship and respect God, this being the foundation of all morality and ethics. This was further strengthened by the commandments forbidding murder, incest/adultery and robbery, as well as the one requiring the administration of justice. Finally, the prohibition against eating flesh from a living animal separated man from the savage, teaching him kindness toward his fellow creatures and control of his base appetites.[16]

In the course of time, however, the world reverted to paganism and these commandments were gradually forgotten by most men.[17] There were ten generations from Adam until Noah, and throughout this period mankind was on a continual moral decline.[18] In order to give civilization a new start, God brought the flood, destroying all the descendants of Adam, with the exception of Noah and his family.[19]

Soon after the flood, however, the world again reverted to paganism, and, with very few exceptions, man again forgot the universal laws of God.[20] There were some exceptions, such as Shem, the son of Noah (father of all Semites), and his grandson Eber (father of the

Hebrews or *Ivriim*), but even they did not publicly teach God's law.[21] Again, ten generations passed with the world's morality constantly deteriorating.[22]

It was into this pagan atmosphere that a most unique individual was born. From his earliest childhood, Abraham began to realize the existence of one God over all else.[23] His keen mind saw through the sham and falsehood of the pagan idolatry of his time, and he recognized the one true God governing the world.[24]

As Abraham's faith developed, it began to overshadow everything else in his life, until he was even willing to suffer martyrdom for it.[25] Never in history had an unaided person made such a complete break with his environment, overcoming all obstacles for the sake of a yet unknown faith.[26]

As Abraham continued to seek the one true God, he finally came to the academy of Shem and Eber, and there learned the traditions that had been handed down from the times of Adam and Noah.[27] Shem also blessed Abraham and made him the bearer of these traditions.[28] Soon after this, God revealed Himself to Abraham and made a covenant with him, promising that his children would eventually grow into a great nation.[29]

By this time, Abraham's faith was not only fully developed, but he also had the courage to act on the basis of his convictions.[30] Abraham realized that one cannot live a truth while allowing others to live in ignorance of it, and thus became the first one to publicly teach about God and His laws.[31] Therefore, unlike the other righteous men, whose children quickly became re-absorbed in the paganism of their time, Abraham was able to establish his faith among his descendants, until a self-sustaining group of the faithful was firmly established.[32] The Torah thus tells us that God said of Abraham (Genesis 18:18-19), "Abraham shall surely become a great and mighty nation, and all the nations of the earth shall be blessed by him. For I have known him, and know that he will instruct his children and household after him, that they may keep God's way, and do righteousness and justice, in order that God may bring upon Abraham everything that He promised him."

Still, Abraham's environment was so corrupt that it even claimed some of his own children and grandchildren. Of his two sons, only Isaac carried on his father's tradition, while the descendants of Ishmael reverted to paganism. Similarly of Isaac's two sons, only Jacob remained true, while Esau soon abandoned God's law. Therefore, of all Abraham's children, only Jacob and his family were able to maintain the tradition intact.[33]

There was another important historical development that took place during Abraham's lifetime. God saw in Abraham a force that could possibly bring all mankind back to Him, if only humanity could be unified. He therefore brought a spirit of unity upon the world, influencing all mankind to act in one accord. However, instead of uniting to serve God, mankind united to build the tower of Babel.[34]

Man then lost the chance of all humanity coming under the category of "Israel," the vessel designated to receive God's goodness. Instead, the human race was split up into nations, each with its own language and mission. It was at this time that God decreed that the children of Abraham would also become a nation, with the special mission of serving God.[35] Regarding this, the Torah says (Deuteronomy 32:8-9):

> When the Most High gave the nations inheritance,
>   When He separated the sons of man,
> He set the borders of the peoples
>   According to the number of Israel's children;
> For the Lord's portion is His people,
>   Jacob, the lot of His inheritance.[36]

God gave Abraham and his descendants the commandment of circumcision as an everlasting covenant.[37] Both Abraham and his son Ishmael were circumcised by Shem,[38] after which Abraham himself circumcised the rest of his household.[39] According to our traditions, Abraham entered into the covenant of circumcision on Yom Kippur, and therefore, this day marks the beginning of the Jewish people.[40]

On a simple level, we can understand that circumcision was given to Abraham and his children in order that they be set apart by an indelible bodily sign, symbolic of their control over their physical passions.[41] On a deeper level, it made their reproductive organ into the "holy sign of the covenant," whereby by the act of reproduction Abraham and his children would now be able to draw down souls from the highest spiritual levels. It is for this reason that circumcision was given to take place on the eighth day after a child is born. Seven symbolizes the physical world which was created in seven days. Eight therefore indicates that which transcends the mere physical. Circumcision is therefore performed on the eighth day, showing that it gives Abraham's children the power to transcend the physical world.[42] In the beginning of creation, God made a storehouse of souls, to be given to "Israel" and to be associated with the Torah.[43] It was with the commandment of circumcision that Abraham was given access to this storehouse.

The commandment of circumcision was primarily passed on to Jacob and his children, who became the standard bearers of Abraham's teachings. It did not apply to the children of Ishmael, since it was given after his birth. Similarly, it did not apply to the children of Esau, since they rejected the distinction and responsibility that went with the covenant.[44] Therefore, of all the descendants of Abraham, only the children of Israel are bound by this commandment. Some say, however, that the later children of Abraham, born to his second wife Keturah after the commandment was given, are also bound by it.[45] Since these intermingled with all the other Arabs, the latter practice circumcision until this very day.[46]

Jacob was the first of the patriarchs who was able to lead all his children in the way of God, and it was for this reason that he was chosen to be the father of an entire people dedicated to serving Him.[47] The circumstances leading to the election and elevation of Jacob are described in a most wondrous account in the Torah (Genesis 32:25-29):

Jacob remained alone, and a man wrestled with him until daybreak. When the man saw that he could not defeat Jacob, he struck him in the hollow of his thigh, and Jacob's hip was dislocated as he wrestled. The man then said, "Let me go, for day is breaking." Jacob replied, "I will not let you go unless you bless me." The man asked him, "What is your name?" and he answered, "Jacob." The man then said, "Your name shall no longer be Jacob. From now on it shall be Israel, for you have been great with God, and you have prevailed against man."

According to most commentaries, this battle took place on a purely spiritual level, and was perceived by Jacob in a prophetic vision.[48] The man with whom he wrestled symbolized all the forces of evil in the world, and the fact that Jacob ultimately won the battle showed that he had enough spiritual fortitude to give his children the power to ultimately overcome evil.[49] Thus, Jacob was worthy that his children should be God's vehicle to ultimately overcome the evil of the world and return all things to the good.

In this episode, however, Jacob is wounded in his left thigh.[50] This symbolizes the partial victory of evil and the many persecutions that Jacob's children would have to endure as a dedicated people.[51] Jacob accepted both the responsibility and its consequences, merely asking for a blessing to give his children the strength to endure.[52]

It was at this time that God gave him the name Israel. The name indicates that his children would be "great before God" and would survive to carry the banner of God's teachings to all mankind.[53] But beyond this, Jacob was not worthy of becoming "Israel," the vessel that God had originally conceived as the recipient of His good. "Israel" was a concept that had existed even before creation, but it was only now that the descendants of Jacob became worthy of carrying both the name and the concept that goes with it.[54]

God then gave Jacob and his children the commandment not to eat of the tendon that was wounded in the "battle."[55] On the simplest level, this was given in order that Jacob's children always remember this event. It was a dietary law, given to symbolize the self-control required for their mission, especially since it would prohibit the choice hindquarters of all animals, unless the tendon was arduously removed. On a deeper level, it was forbidden because the wound symbolized the partial victory of evil, and since evil now has a grasp on this tendon, it must be avoided.[56] It is also a constant reminder that the victory of evil can never be complete, for Israel might be wounded, but never destroyed.[57]

Even the ancestry of the patriarchs, however, would not have been enough to mold Israel into a nation capable of adhering to their faith under all conditions.[58] God therefore decreed that they should spend over two hundred years in Egypt,[59] where all the spiritually weaker elements would be weeded out, while at the same time, they grew from a small desert tribe into a populous nation.[60] The Egyptian bondage thus strengthened their faith and drew them together, while at the same time exposing them to the greatest civilization of the day.[61] In many ways, the Jews proved themselves worthy of God's choice, and, even under the most degrading slavery, maintained their identity and moral values.[62] Out of the crucible of Egypt, Israel then emerged, refined and ready to be made into the torchbearers of God and His Torah.[63]

Nevertheless, in many ways, the Jews did fall into the pagan ways of the Egyptians.[64] Thus, in describing the Exodus to His Prophet, God says (Ezekiel 20:8-9), "They rebelled against Me and would not listen to Me. Not one of them rejected the detestable things that attracted them, nor did they give up the idols of Egypt. I would have decided to pour out My anger against them...but I acted for the sake of My name...For I had given My word that in the sight of the nations I would lead My people out of the land of Egypt."

Ultimately, the Jewish people were chosen by God primarily because of the merit of the patriarchs. The Torah thus states (Deuteronomy 10:15), "Only in your fathers did God delight, and He loved them and chose their children after them, namely you, above all peoples, as it is this day."[65] It was because of this that they were led into Egypt, only to be redeemed amid the greatest miracles ever witnessed by mankind. We thus find (ibid. 7:7-8), "God did not set His love over you, nor choose you, because you were greater in number than any other people, for indeed, you were fewest of all people. But because God loved you, and because He kept the oath that He swore to your fathers, God brought you out of the house of bondage."[66]

Although the Exodus took place more than three thousand years ago, it still plays a most important role in Judaism. It was at this time that God revealed Himself to an entire people and literally changed the course of both nature and history. This was an event unique in the annals of history, as the Torah states (ibid. 4:34-35), "Did God ever venture to take a nation for Himself from another nation, with a challenge, with signs and wonders, as the Lord your God did in Egypt before your very eyes? You have had sure proof that the Lord is God, there is no other."[67] Thus, the Exodus not only made us uniquely aware of God, but it also showed Him profoundly involved in the affairs of man.

It was also the Exodus and the events surrounding it that makes Judaism unique among all other religions. Other faiths begin with a single individual who claims to have a special message and gradually gathers a following. His followers then spread the word and gather converts, until a new religion is born. Virtually every major world religion follows this pattern.

The only exception to this is Judaism. Here God gathered an entire people, some three million strong,[68] to the foot of Mount Sinai and proclaimed His message. Every man, woman and child heard God's voice, proclaiming the Ten Commandments, and thus a bond was forged between God and Israel.[69]

This was an event unique in the history of mankind. It remained deeply imprinted in the Jewish soul throughout all of our history, and was something that was not to be forgotten. The Torah thus tells us (Deuteronomy 4:9-10), "Be most careful and watch yourselves, that you not forget the things that you saw with your own eyes. Do not let them pass from your minds as long as you live. Teach them to your children and your children's children: The day when you stood before the Lord."

The Torah likewise warns us never to forget the Exodus. We thus find (ibid. 6:12), "Beware, that you do not forget the Lord, Who brought you out of the land of Egypt, from the house of bondage." There are some authorities who count both of these statements among the commandments of the Torah.[70]

God ultimately knew that of all the nations of the earth, only Israel would have the great faith and intrinsic tenacity[71] to adhere to His teachings through all the vicissitudes of history.[72] The Talmud expresses this most clearly by stating that God asked all the nations to accept the Torah, and found them to refuse.[73] Of all peoples, only Israel responded with the unequivocal statement (Exodus 24:7), "All that God has spoken, we will do and we will obey."[74]

It was primarily because of this ready acceptance of the Torah that Israel was chosen for a position of moral leadership in the world.[75] God thus told us before the giving of the Ten Commandments (ibid. 19:5-6), "Now therefore, if you will hearken to My voice and keep My covenant, then you shall be My own treasure among all peoples, for all the earth is Mine. You shall be My kingdom of priests and holy nation."[76]

Because of the unique dedication to God, the Jewish people thus became utterly separated from the rest of the world, almost like a distinct species of humanity.[77] God thus told us in His Torah (Leviticus 20:26), "You shall be holy unto Me, for I, God, am Holy, and I have set you apart from all other peoples, that you should be Mine."[78]

But being chosen is more of a responsibility than a mere privilege, and Israel has the incessant mission of proclaiming God's teachings to the world.[79] God thus speaks to us through His Prophet (Isaiah 42:6), "I, the Lord, have called you in righteousness... and have set you as a covenant of the people, for a light to the nations."[80] Israel's mission is to bear witness to God, as again we find (ibid. 43:10), "You are My witnesses, says the Lord, and My servant whom I have chosen."[81] We are thus taught that Israel is like the heart of humanity, constantly beating and infusing all mankind with faith in God and His teachings.[82]

This universal message was often to be proclaimed even at the price of suffering and persecution. The Midrash tells us that Israel is likened to an olive tree, for just as an olive must be crushed to bring forth its oil, so Israel is often persecuted before its light shines forth.[83] The Talmud teaches us that even the dispersion of Israel among the nations was primarily to teach the world how to serve God.[84]

Furthermore, because of Israel's unique place in God's plan, they must constantly be corrected when they stray from the true path. God thus tells us through His Prophet (Amos 3:2), "Only you have I known of all the families of the earth, therefore I will punish you for all your sins."[85] God might punish the Jews, but He does so to correct them, just as a father might chastise his children. The Torah therefore tells us (Deuteronomy 8:5), "Consider this in your heart: Just as a man chastises his son, so the Lord your God shall chastise you."

Nevertheless, God promised that despite all these sufferings, Israel would always continue to exist to fulfill His purpose. He thus told His Prophet (Isaiah 54:10), "The mountains may depart, and the hills be removed, but My kindness shall not depart from you, neither will My covenant of peace be removed." He continues (ibid. v. 17), "No weapon that is raised against you shall prosper, and every tongue that shall rise against you in judgment shall be condemned by you. This is the heritage of God's servants, and their reward from Me."

God thus made a covenant with Israel that they would continue to be the bearers of His word for all times. We find this in His words to His Prophet (ibid. 59:21), "As for Me, this is My covenant with them...My spirit that is with you, and My word that I have placed in your mouth, shall not depart from your mouth, nor from the mouth of your children, nor from the mouth of your children's children...now and forever."

Although the Jews have been persecuted and degraded throughout history, they will ultimately be vindicated, as the Prophet continues (ibid. 60:15), "Where you have been hated and forsaken, so that no man passed through you, I will make you an eternal pride, and a never-ending joy." It is God's promise that Israel will ultimately restore the world to good and therefore cannot be destroyed. This is His message (ibid. 42:4), "He shall not fail nor be crushed, until he has set the right in the earth, for the islands await his teachings."[86]

Israel's unique position makes it a prime ingredient in God's purpose of creation.[87] Here again, God told His Prophet (ibid. 51:16), "I have put My words in your mouth, and kept you safe under the shelter of My hand, that I may plant the heavens and lay the foundations of the earth, and say to Zion: You are My people."[88] Our sages thus teach us that God, Israel and the Torah are uniquely linked together.[89] In one place, they say that the Torah is like the oil in a lamp, with Israel as its wick, causing the light of God to shine forth upon all creation.[90]

1. *Emunos VeDeyos* 3, end of 1:4, *Or HaShem* (Crescas) 2:6:4, *Sefer HaYashar* 1, *Pardes Rimonim* 2:6, *Etz Chaim*, *Shaar HaKelallim* #1, *Reshis Chochmah*, *Shaar HaTshuvah* #1, *Shnei Luchos HaBris*, *Bais Yisroel* (1:21b), *Shomrei Emunim* (HaKadmon) 1:1:41, 2:13, *Derech HaShem* 1-2-1, *Likutei Moharan* #64.
2. *Tanna DeBei Eliahu Rabbah* 27.
3. *Bereshis Rabbah* 2:1. Cf. *Sh'mos Rabbah* 38:5, *Bamidbar Rabbah* 20:2.
4. *Rashi on Genesis* 1:1.
5. *Bereshis Rabbah* 1:2.
6. *Avos* 6:3, *Berachos* 5a, *Kallah* 8, *Yerushalmi Rosh HaShanah* 3:8, *Tanchuma Re'eh* 11, *Tanna DeBei Eliahu Zuta* 17, *Pesicha Eichah Rabbah* 2.
7. *Rashi on Genesis* 1:1.
8. *Koheles Rabbah* 1:9, *Sifri Ekev* 47, *Tanna DeBei Eliahu Rabbah* 14.
9. *Shabbos* 88a, *Avodah Zarah* 3a, *Rashi on Genesis* 1:31.
10. *Derech HaShem* 2:4:2. Cf. *Tiferes Yisroel* (Maharal) 17, *Tosefos Yom Tov on Avos* 5:2.
11. *Sanhedrin* 56b, *Tosefta Avodah Zarah* 9:4, *Berashis Rabbah* 16:9, *Devarim Rabbah* 2:17, *Shir HaShirim Rabbah* 1:16, *Pesikta* 12 (100b), *Zohar* 1:35b, *Yad*, *Melachim* 9:1, *Moreh Nevuchim* 1:2, *Kuzari* 3:73 (75b).
12. Ibid. *Bereshis Rabbah* 24:5, *Sh'mos Rabbah* 30:6, *BaMidbar Rabbah* 14:24, *Midrash Tehillim* 1:10, *Yalkut* 1:272, 2:964; *Kesef Mishneh*, *Lechem Mishneh on Yad*, *Melachim* 9:1.
13. *Sanhedrin* 59b, *Bereshis Rabbah* 34:18, from Genesis 1:29, *Etz Yosef* (on *Eyin Yaakov*) *Sanhedrin* 100. However, others hold that Adam was also given this commandment, cf. *Sanhedrin* 56b, *Zohar* 1:35b. According to this opinion, Adam was allowed to eat flesh, but not kill for food. The prohibition against flesh from a living animal then applied even if it was not cut from the animal by man. See Rashi, *Sanhedrin* 57a *"Le Mishri,"* *Tosafos*, *Sanhedrin* 56b *"Achal,"* Rashi on Genesis 1:19 and *Sifsei Chachamim* ad loc. However, in *Bereshis Rabbah* 16:9, we find that this prohibition was hinted to Adam, even though it did not actually apply to him.
14. Genesis 9:3, 4, Rashi ad loc. Cf. *Shir HaShirim Rabbah* 1:16, *Pesikta* 12 (100b), *Yad*, *Melachim* 9:1.
15. *Sanhedrin* 105a, *Tosefta Sanhedrin* 13:1, *Midrash Tehillim* 9:15; *Yad*, *Tshuvah*, end of 3:5, *Edus* 11:10, *Melachim* 8:11; Rambam on *Sanhedrin* 10:2.
16. Cf. *Moreh Nevuchim* 3:48.
17. Cf. *Sanhedrin* top of 57a, *Bereshis Rabbah* 31-6, Rashi on Genesis 6:11, *Yad*, *Avodas Kochavim* 1:1.
18. *Avos* 5:2.
19. Genesis 6:9 ff.
20. *Yad*, *Avodas Kochavim* 1:2.
21. Ibid. Cf. *Bereshis Rabbah* 63:8, *Tanna DeBei Eliahu Rabbah* 20 (93b), 28 (109a), Rashi on Genesis 10:25, 25:22, *Kuzari* 1:49 (35a), *Moreh Nevuchim* 2:39.
22. *Avos* 5:2.
23. Some say from the age of three, cf. *Nedarim* 32a, *Bereshis Rabbah* 30:8, 64:4, 95:2, *Bamidbar Rabbah* 18:17, *Shir HaShirim Rabbah* 6:1, *Esther Rabbah* 6:5, *Tanchuma Lech Lecha* 3, *Zohar* 3:302a, *Raavad on Yad*, *Avodas Kochavim* 1:3, *Kesef Mishneh*, *Migdal Oz*, *Hagahos Maimoni* #1, ibid.; *Seder HaDoros* 1958.
24. *Bereshis Rabbah* 39:1, *Bamidbar Rabbah* 14:7. We also have the account how he ridiculed and destroyed his father's idols, *Bereshis Rabbah* 38:19, *Tanna DeBei Eliahu Zuta* 25 (57a), *Seder HaDoros* 1998.
25. Like, for example, when he was thrown into the furnace by Nimrod for the sake of his faith, cf. *Eruvin* 53a, *Pesachim* 118a, *Bereshis Rabbah* 38:19, *Midrash Tehillim* 118:11, *Pirkei DeRabbi Eliezer* 26 (61a), *Tanna DeBei Eliahu Zuta* 25 (58a); Rashi on Genesis 11:28, 14:1, *Seder HaDoros* loc. cit.
26. Cf. *Avos* 5:3, Rambam, Bertenoro ad loc.
27. *Seder HaDoros* 1958. Cf. *Pirkei DeRabbi Eliezer* 8.
28. See Genesis 14:19, *Nedarim* 32b, Ran ad loc. *"U'Malki Tzedek."*
29. According to most sources, this occurred when Abraham was seventy years old, before God told him to leave Ur at the age of seventy-five. See *Seder Olom Rabbah* #1, *Mechilta on Exodus* 12:40 (15b), Rambam, *Sifsei Chachamim*, ibid., Rashi, *Sanhedrin* 92b *"U'Ta'u,"* *Tosafos*, *Shabbos* 10b *"VeShel,"* *Avodah Zarah* 9a *"U'Gemiri,"* *Rosh Yebamos* 6:12. For further discussion, see HaGra on *Seder Olam*, Abarbanel on Genesis 12:2, *Baalei Tosafos on Genesis* 12:4.
30. According to those who hold that Abraham was 40 or 48 years old when he discovered God. See *Yad*, *Avodas Kochavim* 1:3; above, note 23.
31. *Berachos* 7b, *Sotah* 10b, *Bereshis Rabbah* 39:21, Rashi on Genesis 12:5, *Maharitz Chayos on Chagigah* 3a. Cf. *Yalkut* 1:766.
32. *Yad*, loc. cit. Cf. *Yoma* 28b.
33. Cf. *Nedarim* 31a, *Yad*, *Nedarim* 9:21,

Yoreh Deah 217:40, Tshuvos Rivash 31, Magen Avraham 591:8, Turei Zahav 591:3.

34. Alshich on Genesis 11:1.

35. Derech HaShem 2:4:3.

36. See Sifri (311), Alshich, Bachya, Or HaChaim and Klei Yakar ad loc.

37. Genesis 17:9. See Pesikta 12 (100b), Shir HaShirim Rabbah 1:16; Yad, Melachim 9:1.

38. Cf. Moreh Nevuchim 3:49.

39. Pirkei DeRabbi Eliezer 29 (64a), Radal ad loc. 29:1.

40. Ibid. Cf. Tosafos, Rosh HaShanah 11a "Elah" Baalei Tosafos on Genesis 17:26.

41. Radal loc. cit. 29:2.

42. Tiferes Yisrael (Maharal) #2. Cf. Vayikra Rabbah 27:10, Derech Mitzvosecha (Chabad) p. 9b.

43. See Zohar Chadash 74d, Likutei Moharan 52. See also Niddah 13b, Chagigah 12b, Akedas Yitzchak 6, Nishmas Chaim 2:16.

44. Sanhedrin 59b, Yerushalmi Nedarim 3:8 (12a), Yad, Melachim 10:7.

45. Yad, Melachim 10:8. However, Rashi, Sanhedrin 59b "B'nai" holds that this only applied to Abraham's actual children, and not to their descendants. See also Mishneh LaMelech ad loc., Tshuvos Shaagas Aryeh 49, Maharitz Chayos on Nedarim 31a, 32a.

46. Yad, loc. cit., Tshuvos Nodeh BeYehudah, Even HaEzer 42.

47. Cf. Tanna DeBei Eliahu Rabbah 27 (107b), from Hosea 9:10; Kuzari 1:47 (33b), 1:95 (47b).

48. Moreh Nevuchim 2:42, Bachya, Abarbanel ad loc. Cf. Chulin 90b, Zohar 1:14a.

49. Tanchuma VaYishlach 8, Zohar 1:170a. Also see Chulin 91b, Bereshis Rabbah 77:2, 78:6. However, others write that it was the angel Michael, cf. Targum J. on Genesis 32:25, Yalkut 1:142. See Hosea 12:5.

50. Zohar, 3:243a, Pardes Rimonim 17, Etz Chaim Shaar HaYereach 50. However, in Chulin 90b, 91a, we find an opinion that it was the right leg. See also Likutei Torah HaAri ad loc.

51. Bereshis Rabbah 77:4, Zohar 1:170b, Ramban on Genesis 32:26, Sefer HaChinuch #3.

52. Cf. Rashi ad loc.

53. See Bereshis Rabbah 78:6.

54. See Bachya ad loc.

55. That is, the sciatic tendon. This commandment was actually given to Jacob, see Pesikta 12 (100b), Shir HaShirim Rabbah 16, Yad, Melachim 9:1, Lechem Mishneh ad loc. In Chulin 7:6 (100b) this appears to be the opinion of Rabbi Yehudah which is disputed by the majority. However, Ramban, ad loc., writes that they do not dispute its origin with Jacob, but whether our obligation originates

from Jacob or from Sinai. According to Rashi, however, the accepted opinion would be that this commandment was not given until Sinai.

56. Zohar 1:170b, Or HaChaim on Genesis 32:33.

57. Sefer HaChinuch 3.

58. Hence we find that the Egyptian exile was due to a lack of faith on the part of Abraham, cf. Genesis 15:16, Targum J., Daas Ziknei Baalei Tosafos ad loc.; Pirkei DeRabbi Eliezer 48 (23b), Yalkut 1:77, Ramban on Genesis 12:10.

59. Actually 210 years, Pirkei DeRabbi Eliezer 48 (114a), Seder Olom Rabbah #3, Yalkut 77; Rashi on Genesis 15:13, Exodus 12:40; Megillah 9a, Rashi ad loc. "U'VeShaar," Rashbam, Baba Basra 120a "Asher."

60. Such as those who died during the three days of darkness, Targum J., Rashi on Exodus 10:23, Sh'mos Rabbah 14:3, Tanna DeBei Eliahu Rabbah 7 (60a). According to our traditions, less than one out of five of the Jews in Egypt were worthy of leaving, see Mechilta (24a), Rashi on Exodus 13:18, Yalkut 1:227, Zohar 3:108b, Rashi on Ezekiel 20:8, Radak ibid. 20:9.

61. Cf. Sh'mos Rabbah 1:1, Tanchuma Sh'mos 1, Yalkut 2:950.

62. That is, they did not change their names or language, and avoided the sexual immorality and malicious talebearing of the Egyptians. See Mechilta (5a) on Exodus 12:6, Sh'mos Rabbah 1:33, Vayikra Rabbah 32:5, Bamidbar Rabbah 20:21, Shir HaShirim Rabbah 4:24, Tanchuma Balak 16, Midrash Tehillim 114:4, Pesikta 10 (63b), Pirkei DeRabbi Eliezer 48 (108b), Tanna DeBei Eliahu Rabbah 10, 23, 24, Yalkut 1:657. The common expression that they changed neither their names, language, nor clothing is not found in any Midrashic source, cf. Buber on Pesikta loc cit. 10:66.

63. See note 61. Cf. Berachos 5a, Mechilta (73a) on Exodus 20:20, Sifri VaEsChanan 32, Midrash Tehillim 94:2, Yalkut 2:850.

64. See Yalkut 1:243, Zohar 2:170b. See Ramban on Exodus 12:2, Radak on Ezekiel 16:7.

65. Rambam, Igeres Taiman (Jerusalem, 5721) p. 6. See also Genesis 12:2, 17:6, 18:18.

66. Igeres Taiman loc. cit. Cf. Genesis 15:13, Exodus 6:5, Deuteronomy 4:37.

67. Moreh Nevuchim 2:35.

68. See Targum J., Mechilta (15a) on Exodus 12:37.

69. Yad, Yesodei HaTorah 8:1, Kuzari 1:87.

70. Rambam, additions to Sefer HaMitzvos, negative commandments #1 and #2, Sefer Mitzvos Gadol (Smag), negative commandments #13 and #64. See also Ramban on Deuteronomy 4:9.

71. *Betzah* 25b, Ramban on Deuteronomy 7:6.

72. Nevertheless, other nations can also occasionally serve God in truth. Cf. *Kuzari* 4:3 (8a), *Kol Yehudah* ad loc. 3:23 (32a) "VeKavar," from Malachi 1:11. Also see *Tanchuma Ekev* 2.

73. *Avodah Zarah* 2b, *Mechilta* (65a) on Exodus 20:2, *Sifri* (2:343) *Targum J.*, Rashi, Ramban, on Deuteronomy 33:2; *Sh'mos Rabbah* 27:8, *Bamidbar Rabbah* 14:22, *Eichah Rabbah* 3:3; *Tanchuma Yisro* 14, *Shoftim* 9, *Zos HaBerachah* 4; *Pirkei DeRabbi Eliezer* 41 (95b), *Pesikta* 29 (186a), *Yalkut* 1:551, *Zohar* 2:3a, 3:192b.

74. *Eichah Rabbah* 3:3. Cf. *Shabbos* 88a, *Vayikra Rabbah* 2:4.

75. Cf. *Sh'mos Rabbah* 47:4, *Ruth Rabbah* 1:1, *Yalkut* 1:760; *Emunos VeDeyos* 3:7 (48a).

76. Cf. *Mechilta* (62b) ad loc. Also see Deuteronomy 7:6.

77. *Kuzari* 1:103 (70a), 5:20 (53b), *Tiferes Yisroel* (Maharal) #1. Also see *Tiferes Yisroel* on *Avos* 3:14. Cf. *Baba Metzia* 114b, *Yebamos* 61a, from Ezekiel 34:31, Radak ad loc.; *Tosefos Yom Tov* on *Negaim* 12:1; *Berachos* 26a, *Shabbos* 15a, *Yebamos* 98a, from Ezekiel 23:20 Maharitz Chayos on *Yebamos* 61a.

78. Rashi ad loc. Cf. Leviticus 19:2.

79. Cf. *Vayikra Rabbah* 6:5.

80. This is from the famous "suffering servant" passage. According to Rashi and Kara in some places, this refers to Israel, cf. *Midrash Tehillim* 2:9. Others, however, allude this to the Messiah, cf. *Targum*, Radak, *Metzudos*, ad loc., *Midrash Tehillim* 433:1. Others write that it refers to Cyrus (Kara) or to the Prophet himself (Ibn Ezra). Cf. Isaiah 49:5.

81. Kara ad loc., *Ikkarim* 1:2. Cf. Isaiah 43:21, 44:8.

82. *Zohar* 2:221b, *Kuzari* 3:36 (51b), 2:12 (13a).

83. *Sh'mos Rabbah* 36:1, *Yalkut* 2:289.

84. *Pesachim* 87b, Maharsha ad loc. "Lo."

85. *Avodah Zarah* 4a, *Tanna DeBei Eliahu Rabbah* 15 (75b), *Zohar* 2:17b, *Chovos HaLevavos*, *Avodas Elokim* 6, *Yichud HaMaaseh* 5; *Kuzari* 2:44 (53b).

86. Kara ad loc. Cf. *Minachos* 53b.

87. Cf. *Shabbos* 88a, *Avodah Zarah* 3a, 5a; *Tanchuma Bereshis* 1, from Jeremiah 33:25; Rashi on Genesis 1:1, 1:31.

88. *Zohar* 1:5a, *Tikunei Zohar* 69 (104a, 118a), *Nefesh HaChaim* 1:12. Cf. *Sanhedrin* 99b, *Yerushalmi Taanis* 4:2 (21a), *Megillah* 3:6 (26a), *Pesikta* 19 (140b); *Tanchuma Yisro* 14, *Re'eh* 1; *Avos* 1:2, *Shabbos* 10a.

89. *Zohar* 3:73a, 3:93a, *Nefesh HaChaim* 1:16 (note: "Af Al Pi").

90. *Tikunei Zohar* 21 (60a).

On Extraterrestrial Life

ONE OF THE UNIQUE ASPECTS of Judaism is its far-reaching univer-
sality. Not only does Judaism provide a lesson for every human
being, its teachings extend to the very boundaries of the universe.

It is an axiom of Judaism that the entire universe was created for
the sake of man.[1] In one place, the Talmud reckons that there are some
10^{18} stars in the observable universe,[2] and explicitly states that they
were all created for the sake of man. It goes further to state that all the
angels and spiritual worlds also only exist for this purpose.[3]

Of course, this immediately raises a question that many find quite
difficult. How is it possible that man, living on a dust mote called the
planet Earth, should be the center of the universe? Our Sages realized
the vast number of stars in the universe, and also realized that many of
them were many orders of magnitude larger than the Earth.[4]

Actually, this question was first raised in the eighth Psalm:[5]

> When I behold Your heavens,
>   the work of Your fingers,
> The moon and the stars
>   that You have established;
> What is man that You consider him?
>   Or the son of man that You think of him?
> Yet You have made him a little lower than the angels,[6]
>   You have crowned him with glory and honor,
> You made him master of Your creation,
>   You placed all under his feet.

Intercom—December 1972

It should be quite simple to understand that size and quantity alone are meaningless to an infinite God. There is absolutely no question that the human brain is vastly more complex than the greatest galaxy, and furthermore, that it contains more information then the entire observable inanimate universe. Beyond that, man is endowed with a Divine soul that towers over even the highest angels.[7]

Although the creation of such a vast universe for the sake of man does not defy logic, we still need to seek out a reason for its necessity. Some sources[8] state that by contemplating the greatness of the universe, one can begin to comprehend that of God, and thereby fear Him all the more. However, if we speak of the possibility of extraterrestrial life, we must explore the question somewhat further.

One of the first to discuss the question of extraterrestrial life in general was Rabbi Chasdai Crescas.[9] After a lengthy discussion, he comes to the conclusion that there is nothing in Jewish theology to preclude the existence of life on other worlds.

As possible evidence for extraterrestrial life, he then quotes the Talmudic teaching that God flies through 18,000 worlds.[10] Since they require His providence, we may assume that they are inhabited.

Of course, this Talmudic quotation is by no means absolute proof, for it may be speaking of spiritual worlds, of which an infinite number were created.[11]

One could also attempt to support this opinion from the verse (Psalms 145:13), "Your kingdom is a kingdom of all worlds."[12] However, here, too, this may be speaking of spiritual universes.

The exact opposite opinion is that of Rabbi Yosef Albo, author of the *Ikkarim*.[13] He states that since the universe was created for the sake of man, no other creature can exist possessing free will. Since any extraterrestrial life would neither have free will nor be able to serve a creature having free will (as terrestrial animals and plants serve a terrestrial man), they would have no reason for existing and therefore be totally superfluous.[14]

One could bring some support to this second opinion from the Talmudic teaching that every land where it was not decreed for man to live was never subsequently inhabited.[15] However, here again, it is not absolute proof, since this may only refer to our planet.[16]

Between these two extremes, we find the opinion of the *Sefer Habris*[17] who states that extraterrestrial life does exist, but that it does not possess free will. The latter is the exclusive possession of man, for whom the universe was created. The 18,000 worlds mentioned earlier, in his opinion, are inhabited physical worlds.

The proof that he brings for his thesis is most ingenious. In the song of Deborah, we find the verse (Judges 5:23), "Cursed is Meroz...cursed are its inhabitants." In the Talmud,[18] we find an opinion, that Meroz is the name of a star. According to this opinion, the fact that Scripture states, "Cursed is Meroz...cursed are its *inhabitants*" is clear proof from the words of our Sages for extraterrestrial life.

Of course, even this proof is subject to refutation. For the Zohar[19] also follows the opinion that Meroz is a star, yet states that "its inhabitants" refers to its "camp," that is, most probably, to the planets surrounding it. Nevertheless, the simple meaning of the verse seems to support the opinion of the Sefer Habris.

The Sefer Habris goes on to say that we should not expect the creatures of another world to resemble earthly life, any more than sea creatures resemble those of land.

He further states that although extraterrestrial forms of life may possess intelligence, they certainly cannot have freedom of will. The latter is an exclusive attribute of man, to whom was given the Torah and its commandments. He proves the latter thesis on the basis of the above-mentioned Talmudic teaching that all the stars in the observable universe were created for the sake of man.

One may ask: if the inhabitants of extraterrestrial worlds, such as Meroz, have no free will, why were they cursed? However, we do find that beings, such as angels, can be punished for wrongdoings even though they do not have free will.[20]

However, the basic premise that of all possible species only man has free will, is well supported by the great Kabbalist, Rabbi Moshe Kordevero in his Pardes Rimonim.[21] Using tight logical arguments, he demonstrates that there can be only one set of spiritual worlds. Although God would want to maximize the number of recipients of His good, His very unity precludes the existence of more than one such set. Since this set of worlds deals specifically with God's providence toward man because of his free will, this also precludes the existence of another species sharing this quality.

The basic premise of the existence of extraterrestrial life is strongly supported by the Zohar. The Midrash teaches us that there are seven earths.[22] Although the Ibn Ezra tries to argue that these refer to the seven continents,[23] the Zohar clearly states that the seven are separated by a firmament and are inhabited.[24] Although they are not inhabited by man, they are the domain of intelligent creatures.[25]

We therefore find the basic thesis of the Sefer Habris supported by a number of clear-cut statements by our Sages. There may even be other forms of intelligent life in the universe, but such life forms do not have free will, and therefore, do not have moral responsibility.

Freedom of will, however, is not at all an observable quantity. Even its existence in man has been hotly debated by the secular philosophers. Indeed, the main proof that man does indeed have free will comes from the fact that God has given him moral responsibility, namely the Torah.[26] It is in this sublime, yet unobservable quality, that man is unique.

However, if we assume this to be true, we would return to the basic question of Rabbi Yosef Albo, mentioned earlier: If such creatures never have any utility for man, what is their reason for existence?

We find a most fascinating answer to this question in the Tikunei

Zohar.[27] Speaking of the verse (Song of Songs 6:8), "Worlds [28] without number" the *Tikunei Zohar* states, "The stars certainly are without number. But each star is called a separate world. These are the worlds without number."

The *Tikunei Zohar* further states that every *Tzaddik* (righteous man) will rule over a star, and therefore have a world to himself.[29] The 18,000 worlds mentioned above would therefore be that number of stars, presided over by the 18,000 *Tzaddikim* that are alluded to in the verse (Ezekiel 48:35), "Around Him are eighteen thousand."[30] However, these may only refer to those worlds visited daily by the Divine Presence, but there may be innumerable worlds for the lesser *Tzaddikim*.

We therefore have a most fascinating reason why the stars were created, and why they contain intelligent life. Since an overcrowded Earth will not give the *Tzaddikim* the breadth they require, each one will be given his own planet, with its entire population to enhance his spiritual growth.

Once we know that the stars and their planets were created as an abode for the *Tzaddikim*, we might naturally wonder how they will be transported to them. However, the Talmud even provides an answer to this question. Discussing the passage (Isaiah 40:31), "They shall mount up with wings as eagles," the Talmud states that in the Future World, God will grant the *Tzaddikim* wings to escape the Earth.[31] The *Zohar* goes a step further and states that "God will give them wings to fly through the entire universe."[32]

In a way, this teaching predicts the event of space travel. But more than that, it provides us with at least one of the reasons why space flight would be inevitable as part of the prelude to the Messianic age. This, of course, could bring us to a general discussion of the role of modern technology in Torah *hashkafah* (perspective), a lengthy subject in its own right.

NOTES

1. *Bereshis Rabbah* 1:6, *Koheles Rabbah* 1:9, *Tanna DeBei Eliahu Rabbah* 14; *Emunos VeDeyos* 4. Cf. *Sanhedrin* 4:5 (37a).

2. *Berachos* 32b. The exact number given there is 1.0643 x 10^{18}, very close to the number of stars in the observable universe.

3. Cf. *Chagigah* 12b, *Chulin* 91b, *Esther Rabbah* 7:18.

4. *Pesachim* 94a, *Yad,, Yesodei HaTorah* 3:8.

5. Cf. *Malbim* ad loc., *Akedas Yitzchak* 5 (43a).

6. Cf. *Zohar* 1:57b top.

7. Cf. *Emunos VeDeyos* 4:2, *Shaarei Kedushah* 3:2. *Nefesh HaChaim* 1:10.

8. *Zohar* 1:11b, *Reshis Chochmah* 1:2; *Yad, Yesodei HaTorah* 2:2, 4:12. Cf. *Shabbos* 32b, *Berachos* 57a.

9. *Or HaShem* 4:2, Rabbi Chasdai Crescas was the mentor of Rabbi Yosef Albo, author of the *Ikkarim*.

10. *Avodah Zarah* 3b.

11. Cf. *Etz Chaim* 3:1.

12. Cf. *Targum* ad loc.

13. Quoted in *Sefer HaBris* 1:3:4.

14. Cf. *Emunos VeDeyos* 1:1, *Kuzari* 1:67, *Moreh Nevuchim* 2:13.

15. *Berachos* 31a.

16. Cf. *Kol Yehudah* on *Kuzari* 2:20 (34a).

17. 1:3:3.

18. *Moed Katan* 16a.

19. *Zohar* 3:269b end.

20. Cf. *Bechaya* on Genesis 3:6, Exodus 23:21; *Sefer Chasidim* 530.

21. *Pardes Rimonim* 2:7. Cf. *Shefa Tal* 1:3.

22. *Vayikra Rabbah* 29:9, *Shir HaShirim Rabbah* 6:19 *Avos DeRabbi Nassan* 37. Cf. *Pirkei DeRabbi Eliezer* 18, but see HaGra on *Sefer HaYetzirah* 4:15 that these refer to spiritual worlds.

23. Ibn Ezra on Gen. 1:2.

24. *Zohar* 3:10a.

25. Ibid. 1:9b, 1:157a, *Pardes Rimonim* 6:3. See also *Tosafos, Minachos* 37a "O Kum." The Chida in his *Pesach Eynayim*, ad loc., states that since he did not live on this earth, he was exempt from all *Mitzvos*.

26. Cf. *Yad, Tshuvah* 3:4.

27. *Tikunei Zohar* 14b.

28. The Hebrew word here is *Almos*, young maidens. However, it can also be vocalized as *Olamos* or worlds.

29. *Sh'mos Rabbah* 52:3. Cf. *Uktzin*, end.

30. *Succah* 45b. Cf. *Iyun Yaakov* (on *Eyen Yaakov) Avodah Zarah* #5.

31. *Sanhedrin* 92b.

32. *Zohar* 1:12b.

On Immortality
and the Soul

❧ Meet the Real You

L OOK AT YOUR HAND. What do you see? A part of your body, an appendage made of bone and sinew covered with flesh and skin. It is filled with nerves, blood vessels and lymph ducts which run through it and connect it to your body, making it part of you.

You can open and close your hand. It obeys every command that your mind sends to it. It is yours—a part of you. But what are you? Who is the real you? What happens when you tell your hand to open and close? How does your mind will it to obey its commands?

Now point a finger at yourself. If you are an average person, you will point a finger at your chest. You think of yourself as your body. But is your body the real you?

Not too long ago, a person could consider his own body an integral part of himself. You were your body and your body was you. But this is no longer the case. Scientific progress has changed the entire concept of human personality and identity.

Heart transplants are now an almost commonplace occurrence. They do not even make the news any more. A man can live with another person's heart beating in his breast. If we would ask such a man to point to himself, would he point at his heart? Is this transplanted heart really part of him? Is the heart that beats within your breast the real you? Or is it something else entirely?

Intercom—May 1972

Researchers are predicting that within the next decade or two, brain transplants may be possible. This would force us to completely re-evaluate the concept of human personality.

Imagine what it would be like to undergo a brain transplant. A man might be suffering from an incurable disease in his body, but still have a healthy brain. The donor, on the other hand, would have suffered irreparable brain damage, but otherwise have a perfectly sound body. The brain is removed from the sick body and placed in the healthy one.

Who is the new man? We have an old brain with all its memories, personality traits and behavior patterns. But it has a brand new body. The old body might have been old and sick, while the new one may be young and full of energy.

Let us ask this man to point to himself. Will he point to his body? Is the real you your body or your brain?

(Actually, an analogous question is raised in the Talmud. As is well known, in the case of an unsolved murder, a special sacrifice, the *Eglah Arufah*, was brought by the city nearest the corpse.[1] The Mishnah raises two questions. What if the head is found in one place and the body in another?[2] And, if the body is equidistant from the two cities, from what portion of the body do we measure?[3] In both cases, Rabbi Eliezer states that we measure from the body, while Rabbi Akiba states that we measure from the head. The *Halachah* follows Rabbi Akiba.[4])

A brain transplant raises enough questions. How about a memory transfer? The science of cybernetics has discovered many similarities between computers and the human brain. Computer technology allows one to program a memory transfer, taking all the information contained in one computer and transferring it to another. All that passes from one computer to the other is information.

What if this were done with the human brain? This may lie in the realm of science fiction, but even if it will never be possible in practice, it is certainly possible in theory.

Let us try to envision such a memory transfer. Assume we have a person with an incurable disease where neither his body nor his brain can be salvaged. We clone a new body for this individual, brain and all. The possibilities of doing this have already been discussed at length in scientific literature. This new body has a blank new brain, capable of functioning, but without any memories or thought patterns. As a final step, we accomplish a memory transfer, bringing all the information from the sick person into the brain of the new body.

We now have a fascinating situation. If all of a man's memories, thought patterns and personality traits are transferred to a new body and brain, this person literally exists in his new body. But nothing physical has been transferred. No physical part of him has been placed in the new body. All that has been placed in this new body is information that previously existed in the old brain. Yet this information contains the sum total of this person's personality.

But if this is true, then it offers us tremendous new insight into our original question: Who is the real you?

The real you is not your body or brain, but the information contained in your brain—your memories, personality traits and thought patterns.

[The philosophical Kabbalists write that the spiritual world is a realm whose substance is information. It is an arena where information can interact without being attached to or dependent on matter. Thus, an angel, for example, can interact with another angel, even though they have no connection with anything material. Angels can also interact with material objects. Such a spiritual world would also be able to interact with the information comprising the human persona.]

What happens then when a person dies? We know that the body ceases to function. The brain becomes inert and the physical man is dead. But what happens to the real you—the human personality? What happens to all this information—the memories, thought patterns and personality traits? When a book is burned its contents are no longer available. When a computer is smashed, the information within it is also destroyed. Does the same thing happen when a man dies? Are the mind and personality irretrievably lost?

We know that God is omniscient. He knows all and does not forget. God knows every thought and memory that exists within our brains. There is no bit of information that escapes His knowledge.

What, then, happens when a man dies? God does not forget, and therefore all of this information continues to exist, at least in God's memory.

[An allusion to this is also found in the Kabbalah. *Gan Eden* (Paradise) is said to exist in the *sephirah* of *Binah* (Divine understanding).[5] This may well be related to the concept of memory. Souls, on the other hand, are conceived in the *sephirah* of *Daas* (knowledge).[6] One may say that while we live, we exist in God's knowledge *(Daas)*, while after death we exist in His memory *(Binah)*.]

We may think of something existing only in memory as being static and effectively dead. But God's memory is not a static thing. The sum total of a human personality may indeed exist in God's memory, but it can still maintain its self-identity and volition, and remain in an active state. This sum total of the human personality existing in God's memory is what lives on even after a man dies.

[This may well be why the Kabbalists speak of this as *Binah* (understanding), rather than memory. For understanding is a dynamic process, where information contained in one's memory interacts in an active manner. The soul is not in a passive state of memory, but in a dynamic state of *Binah*.]

The concept of immortality and of the soul may well be outside the realm of human comprehension. "No eye has seen it other than God." However, our limited understanding of both God and man can provide us with some degree of perception into our ultimate future.

[In a Kabbalistic sense, we are here speaking about the lowest level of the soul, the *Nefesh HaBehamis* or "animal soul."[7] This most probably can be identified with the information contained in the human brain. However, this interacts with the higher parts of the soul, *Nefesh, Ruach* and *Neshamah*.]

To speak of a concept such as God's memory is indeed very difficult. It involves a deep discussion of the entire transcendental sphere. We therefore give it names that have meaning to us, such as *Gan Eden*, Paradise, the World to Come, the World of Souls,[8] or the bond of eternal life. However, the Bible speaks of immortality as a return to God Himself (Ecclesiastes 12:7): "The dust returns to the dust as it was, but the spirit returns *to God* Who gave it."

⇜ Naked before God

We have seen that our knowledge of the mind and our traditions regarding God can give us some handle on the question of immortality. But what is immortality like? What is it like to be a disembodied soul? How does it feel to be in the World of Souls?

We know that the human brain, marvelous organ that it is, is still very inefficient as a thinking device. Henri Bergson has suggested that one of the main functions of the brain and nervous system is to eliminate activity and awareness, rather than produce it.

Aldous Huxley[9] quotes Prof. C. D. Broad's comments on this. He says that every person is capable of remembering everything that has ever happened to him. He is able to perceive everything that surrounds him. However, if all this information poured into his mind at once, it would overwhelm him. So the function of the brain and nervous system is to protect us and prevent us from being overwhelmed and confused by the vast amount of information that impinges upon our sense organs. They shut out most of what we perceive and remember. All that would confound us is eliminated and only the small, special selection that is useful is allowed to remain.

Huxley explains that our mind has powers of perception and concentration that we cannot even begin to imagine. But our main business is to survive at all costs. To make survival possible, all of our mind's capabilities must be funneled through the reducing valve of the brain.

Some researchers are studying this effect. They believe that this reducing-valve effect may be very similar to the jamming equipment used to block out offensive radio broadcasts. The brain constantly produces a kind of static, cutting down our perception and reducing our mental activity.

This static can actually be seen. When you close your eyes, you see all sorts of random pictures flashing through your mind. It is impossible to concentrate on any one of them for more than an instant, and each image is obscured by a host of others superimposed over it.

This static can even be seen when your eyes are opened.

However, one usually ignores these images, since they are so faint compared to our visual perception. However, they still reduce one's perception, both of the world around him and of himself.

Much of what we know about this static is a result of research done with drugs that eliminate it. According to a number of authorities, this is precisely how the psychedelic drugs work.

Now imagine the mental activity of a disembodied soul, standing naked before God. The reducing valve is gone entirely. The mind is open and transparent. Things can be perceived in a way that is impossible to a mind held back by a body and a nervous system. The visions and understanding are the most delightful bliss imaginable (as per: "the righteous, sitting with their crowns on their heads, delighting in the shine of the *Shechinah*").[10] This is what Job meant when he said (19:26), "And when after my skin is destroyed, then without my flesh shall I see God."

But then, an individual will also see himself in a new light. Every thought and memory will be lucid, and he will see himself for the first time without the static and jamming that shuts out most thoughts.

Even in our mortal physical state, looking at oneself can sometimes be pleasing and at other times very painful. Certain acts leave us proud and pleased with ourselves. Others cause excruciating pains, especially when we are caught.

Imagine standing naked before God, with your memory wide open, completely transparent without any jamming mechanism or reducing valve to diminish its force. You will remember everything you ever did and see it in a new light. You will see it in the light of the unshaded spirit, or, if you will, in God's own light that shines from one end of creation to the other. The memory of every good deed and *mitzvah* will be the sublimest of pleasures, as our tradition speaks of *Olam Haba*.

But your memory will also be open to all the things of which you are ashamed. They cannot be rationalized away or dismissed. You will be facing yourself, fully aware of the consequences of all your deeds. We all know the terrible shame and humiliation experienced when one is caught in the act of doing something wrong. Imagine being caught by one's own memory with no place to escape. This, indeed, may be what Daniel is alluding to when he says (Daniel 12:2), "And many of them that sleep in the dust shall awake, some to everlasting life, and some to reproach and everlasting shame."

A number of our great teachers[11] write that the fire of *Gehinnom* is actually the burning shame one experiences because of his sins. Again, this may be alluded to in the words of the Prophet (Isaiah 66:24), "And they shall go forth and look upon the carcasses of the men that have rebelled against Me; for their worm shall not die, nor shall their fire be quenched, and they shall be ashamed before all flesh." We find that evil leads to shame, as it is written (Jeremiah 7:19-20), " 'Are they angering Me?' says God. 'Are they not provoking themselves, to their own

shame?..Behold My anger...shall burn, and shall not be quenched.' "
The main concept of reward is that it be without shame, as we find (Joel 2:26), "And you shall eat and be satisfied...and My people shall never be ashamed."

The Talmud provides us with even stronger evidence that shame burns like fire. It states, "Rabbi Chanina says; this teaches us that each one (in the World of Souls) is burned by the canopy of his companion. Woe, for that shame! Woe, for that humiliation."[12] We find (that shame is a major form of punishment) in the Midrash on the verse (Psalms 6:11), "All your enemies shall be ashamed and very confounded:" Rabbi Joshua ben Levi says, "God only curses the wicked with shame."[13] This is also alluded to in the Talmudic statement, "It is better for Amram to suffer shame in this world, and not in the World to Come."[14] Similarly, "Blessed is God who gave him shame in this world and not the next."[15] When the Zohar speaks of the future reward, it says, "Happy is he who comes here without shame."[16]

Of course, these concepts of fire and shame, as used by our Sages, may also contain deeper mysteries and meanings. But taken literally, one says that a major ingredient of fire may be shame.[17] How else could one characterize the agony of unconcealed shame upon a soul?

We are taught that the judgment of the wicked lasts twelve months[18.] Even the naked soul can gradually learn to live with this shame and forget it, and the pain eventually subsides. It may be more than coincidence that twelve months is also the length of time required for something to be forgotten in Talmudic law. Thus, one mourns a parent for twelve months,[19] and says a special blessing upon seeing a close friend after this period of time.[20] (Of course, there is an exception to this rule. There are some people whose entire life is shameful and meaningless. They are the nonbelievers and worst of sinners reckoned in the Talmud.[21] These individuals have nothing else but their shame and have no escape from everlasting torment.)

But even temporary torment is beyond our imagination. The Ramban (Nachmanides) writes that all the suffering of Job would not compare to an instant in *Gehinnom*.[22] Rabbi Nachman of Breslov says the same of a man who suffered for years from the most indescribable torments: it is still better than a single burn in *Gehinnom*.[23] Mental torture cannot be compared to the mere physical.

Here again, when we speak of *Gan Eden* and *Gehinnom*, we find that we are not discussing mystical concepts, but ideas that are well within the realm of scientific psychology, such as shame. We can now proceed a step further.

⇜ What the Dead Think of Us

There is another dimension of immortality discussed in the Talmud. It asks: Do the dead know what is happening in the world of the living?[24]

After an involved discussion, the Talmud concludes that they do have this awareness.[25] The Kabbalistic philosophers explain that the soul achieves a degree of unity with God, the source of all knowledge, and therefore also partakes of His omniscience.

When a man dies, he enters a new world of awareness. He exists as a disembodied soul and yet is aware of what is happening in the physical world. Gradually, he learns to focus on any physical event he wishes. At first this is a frightening experience. You know that you are dead. You can see your body lying there, with your friends and relatives standing around crying over you.

We are taught that immediately after death, the soul is in a great state of confusion.[26] What is the main source of its attention? What draws its focus more than anything else?

We are taught that it is the body. Most people identify themselves with bodies, as we have discussed earlier. It is difficult for a soul to break this thought habit, and therefore, for the first few days, the soul is literally obsessed with its previous body. This is alluded to in the verse (Job 14:22), "And his soul mourns for him."[27]

This is especially true before the body is buried.[28] The soul wonders what will happen to the body. It finds it to be both fascinating and frightening to watch its own body's funeral arrangements and preparation for burial.

Of course, this is one of the reasons why Judaism teaches us that we must have the utmost respect for human remains. We can imagine how painful it is for a soul to see its recent body cast around like an animal carcass. The Torah therefore forbids this.

This is also related to the question of autopsies. We can imagine how a soul would feel when seeing its body lying on the autopsy table, being dissected and examined. The disembodied soul spends much of its time learning how to focus. It is now seeing without physical eyes, using some process which we do not even have the vocabulary to describe. The Kabbalists call this frightening process Kaf HaKela—it is like being thrown with a sling from one end of the world to another.[29] It is alluded to in the verse (I Samuel 25:29), "The soul of my master shall be bound up in the bundle of life with the Lord, your God, and souls of your enemies shall He sling out, as from the hollow of a sling." The soul perceives things flashing into focus from all over, and is in a state of total confusion and disorientation.

One of the few things that the soul has little difficulty focusing on is its own body. It is a familiar pattern and some tie seems to remain. To some extent, it is a refuge from its disorientation.

Of course the body begins to decompose soon after it is buried. The effect of watching this must be both frightening and painful. The Talmud teaches us, "Worms are as painful to the dead as needles in the flesh of the living, as it is written (Job 14:22), 'His flesh grieves for him.' "[30] Most commentaries write that this refers to the psychological anguish of the soul in seeing its earthly habitation in a state of decay.[31] The Kabbalists call this Chibut HaKever,[32] the punishment of the grave.

We are taught that what happens to the body in the grave can be an even worse experience than *Gehinnom*.[33]

This varies among individuals. The more one is obsessed with one's body and the material world in general during one's lifetime, the more one will be obsessed with it after death. For the man to whom the material was everything, this deterioration of the body is most painful. On the other extreme, the person who was immersed in the spiritual may not care very much about the fate of his body at all. He finds himself very much at home in the spiritual realm and might quickly forget about his body entirely. This is what we are taught. *Tzaddikim* are not bothered by *Chibut HaKever* at all, since they never consider their worldly body overly important.[34]

In general, adjustment to the spiritual world depends greatly on one's preparation in this world. Our traditions teach us that the main preparation is through Torah.

Many of us think of death as a most frightening experience. *Tzaddikim*, on the other hand, have looked forward to it. Shortly before his death, Rabbi Nachman of Breslov said, "I very much want to divest myself of this garment that is my body."[35] If we truly believe and trust in a merciful God, then death has no terror for us.

*   *   *   *

This is a description of what our tradition teaches us about the soul's existence. Most of these facts are from the teachings of the Sages in the Talmud and Midrash as interpreted by the Kabbalists. Here we have synthesized their interpretations with the terminology of modern scientific concepts. The result is a consistent view of soul and human personality as realities which do not possess the body's temporal discontinuity called "death."

NOTES

1. Deuteronomy 21:1-9.
2. Sotah 9:3 (45b).
3. Ibid. 9:4.
4. Yad Chazakah, Rotzeach 9:9.
5. Shaarei Orah 8; Pardes Rimonim 8:9, 23:3.
6. Etz Chaim, Shaar MaN U'MaD 4, Shaar HaKlipos 2.
7. Cf. Zohar 2:94b.
8. See Derech HaShem 1:3:11.
9. Aldous Huxley, The Doors of Perception (Harper, Row, N.Y. 1970) p. 22f.
10. Berachos 17a.
11. Ikkarim 4:33, Nishmas Chaim 1:13.
12. Baba Basra 75a.
13. Midrash Tehillim a.l.
14. Kidushin 81a.
15. Yevamos 105b.
16. Zohar 1:4a.
17. Toras HaAdam, Shaar HaGamul (Jerusalem, 5715) p. 78a.
18. Eduyos 2:10
19. Moed Katan 22b.
20. Berachos 58b.
21. Rosh HaShanah 17a.
22. Ramban, introduction to Job.
23. Sichos HaRan 235.
24. Berachos 18b.
25. See Tosafos, Shabbos 153a "VeNishmaso," Sotah 34b "Avoi," Maaver Yabok 2:25, Nishmas Chaim 2:22.
26. Taz, Yoreh Deah 339:3. Cf. Avodah Zarah 20b, Pirkei DeRabbi Eliezer.
27. Shabbos 152a, Midrash Ne'elam, Zohar 1:222b.
28. Shabbos 152b, Sefer Mitzvos Gadol, Esin DeRabanan 2 (Vinitzia, 5307) p. 246a.
29. Shabbos, ibid., Maharsha ad loc., Zohar 1:217b, 3:3185b, 222b.
30. Berachos 18b, Shabbos 152a.
31. Emunos VeDeyos 6:7, Tshuvos Rashba 369, Sefer Chasidim 1163, Tosefos Yom Tov 2:7, Tshuvos Sh'vus Yaakov 2:97, Zvi Hirsh Chayos on Shabbos 13b. Cf. Tanchuma, Vayikra 8.
32. Emunos VeDeyos, ibid, Nishmas Chaim 2:24, Maaver Yabok 2:7.
33. Midrash Chibut HaKever in Reshis Chochmah, Shaar HaYirah 12, #3.
34. Emunos VeDeyos, ibid. Cf. Midrash Ne'elam, Zohar 1:123a.
35. Sichos HaRan 179.

On the Resurrection

IN ORDER TO UNDERSTAND the significance of the Resurrection (*Techiyas Hameisim*) it would be instructive to look at the first two blessings of the Amidah (*Shemoneh Esrei*), a prayer that is recited three times daily by every Jew.

The first blessing of the Amidah deals with our relationship to God; indeed, one can say that it establishes our relationship with God for the rest of this fundamental prayer. Thus the first blessing speaks of God as, "the Great Mighty, Awesome, Highest God, Who bestows bountiful kindness, Who is Master of all, Who recalls the love of the Patriarchs and will bring a redeemer to their children's children..."

The second blessing begins with the words, "You are eternally Mighty, O God, You bring the dead back to life..." The second blessing of this most important prayer thus deals with the Resurrection. From this alone, one would see that it is a key teaching of Judaism.

✑ The Meaning of Life

The first two blessings of the Amidah actually deal with the two most important concerns of man regarding his own existence. The two primary questions that a person can ask are:

(1) What is the meaning of life?
(2) What happens after life in this world ends?

This article was originally transcribed from Rabbi Kaplan's lecture notes, for publication in the Crown Heights Chronicle—December 1982.

The first blessing of the Amidah brings us into contact with the answer to the first question. The meaning of life is defined by God's existence and our relationship to Him. If a person can establish a relationship to the One Author of all existence, then his own existence will have meaning.

However, no matter how meaningful life would be, if it would all end with death, its meaning would only be temporary. Therefore, the second blessing of the Amidah gives us the answer to the second question, "What happens after life in this world ends?" It also teaches that when one finds meaning in life, it is permanent, not temporary. Although life in this world may be temporary, there is another life, beyond the Resurrection, which will be permanent.

⋇§ Influence of the Patriarchs

A key teaching of Judaism is that the actions of the Patriarchs, Abraham, Isaac, and Jacob, continue to serve as a spiritual inheritance to their descendants today. Every Jew is to some degree markedly influenced by the past acts of the Patriarchs.

Again, this is evident in the first blessing of the Amidah, which begins with the words, "Blessed are You, O Lord our God, God of our fathers, God of Abraham, God of Isaac, and God of Jacob..." Here, we attempt to elevate our own conception of God to that of the Patriarchs.

In order to understand this, it would be useful to repeat a teaching of the Baal Shem Tov (founder of Chassidism). He asks, why does the Amidah begin by saying, "Our God, God of our fathers"? The first term implies that we have discovered His existence by our own efforts—He is "our God." The expression, "God of our fathers," however, implies that we were taught about His existence. Thus, the two phrases seem to contradict each other. The Baal Shem Tov explains that every person must develop his own perception of God, since it is something that cannot be communicated totally to another. Hence, we speak of Him as "our God." But still, one must be able to determine whether one's perception of God is authentic, and one must therefore relate it to the perceptions of past generations. We thus add, "God of our fathers." Both are needed: the person's individual perception, and the historical perception of past generations. And since the paradigm of perception of the Divine was that of the Patriarchs, Abraham, Isaac and Jacob, when we say, "God of Abraham, God of Isaac, and God of Jacob," we acknowledge that our ultimate goal would be to reach their level of spiritual perception.

⋇§ Four Degrees of Closeness to God

Moreover, in the last four words of the blessing of the Patriarchs, we establish an increasingly closer relationship with the Divine. In these words we address God as: "King, Helper, Rescuer, and Shield." Each of these words relates to a degree of closeness to God.

First, we speak to God as our "King." A king rules over his subjects, and in a general sense, is concerned with their welfare. However, the king is not available to help each subject on an individual basis, except in the most general terms. Therefore, a person who relates to God as "King" is quite distant from Him.

The next level is that of a helper (*ozer*). Imagine a situation where you are in financial straits and need a loan. You could not go to the king for it, but you could go to someone to whom you feel close. Such a person is your "helper." The relationship between a person and a "helper," then, is much closer than his relationship to a king.

The third level is that of rescuer (*moshia*). A helper can send assistance from a distance, but a rescuer must be right there on the spot. If a person is drowning, then his rescuer must be close enough to jump in and save him. So the level of rescuer is closer than that of the helper.

Finally, the fourth level is that of shield (*magen*). A rescuer can be a few hundred feet away when the person needs him. However, when an arrow is shot at a person, his shield must be directly in front of him, to intercept the arrow. Therefore, when a person has a conception of God as his "Shield," his perception is that of God right in front of him and surrounding him from all sides, protecting him from all danger.

The first person to attain this fourth level was Abraham. God explicitly told him, "Do not fear, Abram, I am your Shield" (Genesis 15:1). We recognize that Abraham reached the ultimate of this level of closeness to God when we conclude the first blessing, "Blessed are You, O Lord, Shield of Abraham." We strive to attain this degree of closeness with God, using Abraham as the paradigm.

This was also the level attained by King David, and hence, the *Haftorah* blessings contain a section which concludes, "Blessed are You, O Lord, Shield of David." David was on this level when he said, "I have placed the Lord before me at all times" (Psalms 16:8).

In any case, after completing the first blessing of the Amidah, one may wonder why the relationships that the Patriarchs had with God should be significant, since they belong to a generation that is dead and buried. If the Patriarchs are dead and we are alive, how can we relate to their spiritual experiences?

The second blessing of the Amidah therefore speaks of the Resurrection. It teaches that death is not a permanent situation, and that the experiences of the Patriarchs are as alive today as they were during their actual lifetimes.

⊷ Two Conceptions of the Resurrection

There are two basic opinions regarding the Resurrection, those of the Rambam (Maimonides), and the Ramban (Nachmanides).

The Rambam's opinion is that when a person dies, he immediately goes to *Olam Haba* (the "World to Come" or the "Future World"), so-called because it comes after life in this world. Thus, according to the Rambam, the "World to Come" promised in Torah literature involves only the soul, and is completely spiritual.

According to the Rambam then, the Resurrection, of necessity, involves a *temporary* return to the physical plane. Some advance a possible reason for the Resurrection, that the righteous will be able to see the Messianic world with physical eyes. In any case, according to the Rambam, the resurrected dead will die once again and will return to the "World to Come."

The Ramban, on the other hand, maintains that the World to Come is the world that will exist after the Resurrection, and that it will be a world that includes both body and soul. This is also the opinion of the *Zohar* and of most of the major Kabbalists. According to this opinion, a whole person consists of body and soul, and therefore, a person cannot attain maximum perception of the Divine without his body as well as his soul. Thus, the Resurrection is a key element in God's ultimate reward for mankind. It is seen as the inception of the World to Come.

This opinion states that when a person dies, his soul goes to the "World of Souls" (*Olam Haneshamos*). There it has a certain degree of perception of the Divine, and it waits there until the Resurrection. It is only after the Resurrection, however, in the World to Come, that this perception reaches its ultimate.

◆§ The Meaning of Death

The first mention of death in the Torah is in relation to the Tree of Knowledge, where God tells Adam, "And from the Tree of Knowledge of Good and Evil, do not eat from it, for on the day you eat from it, you will be bound to die" (Genesis 2:17). Hence, on the simplest level, death is seen as punishment for Adam's original sin.

It is significant that in the very next verse, God says, "It is not good for man to be alone, I will make him a helpmate as his counterpart" (ibid. 2:18). On a simple level, this means that once the possibility of death exists, God must make arrangements for the continuation of the species. When the possibility of death came into existence, then Adam would have to have a wife if mankind was not to become extinct with his death.

However, this can also be understood on a much deeper level. From a number of Midrashic sources, we see that the spiritual realm is looked upon as masculine, while the physical world is feminine. Thus, in the overall scheme of creation, the spiritual realm fertilizes the physical while the physical realm acts as the womb, through which God's purpose is brought to fruition.

Life, of course, is the connection of the body and the soul. Since the body, as part of the physical realm, is feminine and the soul masculine, death is a separation of the masculine from the feminine.

Hence, after the possibility of death came into existence in the world, God said, "It is not good for man to be alone" — it is not good for the soul, the masculine component of the body-soul unit, to be isolated from bodily existence through death.

Thus, there are two male-female relationships that a person can have. One is immortality, while the other is marriage. Either one can guarantee the existence of the species. If man was to lose immortality, then he would have to marry and beget children.

The Tree of Knowledge was closely related to the male-female relationship; indeed, "knowledge" to some degree defines the male-female relationship. In Hebrew, "knowledge" is daas, a word which connotes "togetherness" and "unity." Thus, the Torah says "Adam knew his wife, Eve..." (ibid. 4:1).

Therefore, before eating of the Tree of Knowledge, "the man and the woman were naked, but they were not ashamed of themselves" (ibid. 2:25). Since the male-female relationship was perfect there was no cause for shame (see Ramban, etc.). And indeed, in the Torah we see that the relationship between man and woman was damaged by eating from the Tree of Knowledge, as God told Eve, "To your husband will be your desire, and he will dominate you" (ibid. 3:16).

If life itself is a male-female relationship, then after man ate from the Tree of Knowledge and damaged this relationship, death was inevitable. It was for this reason that death was punishment for the first sin.

The World to Come, however, is seen as a time when all the effects of Adam's sin will be eradicated. Thus, the relationship between body and soul will also be perfected. Therefore, it will (according to the Ramban and the Kabbalists) be a time when man will live immortally with body and soul together.

∾§ The Mystery of Life

One can look at the entire Amidah as being the vehicle through which a person perfects his life. In the Amidah one develops a relationship with God and with life, and then asks God to provide everything needed for the good life.

Indeed, that is one reason that the Amidah has eighteen blessings. (The Amidah is called the Shemoneh Esrei, which literally means "eighteen.") The Hebrew word for "life" is chai, which has a numerical value of eighteen (see Avodas Hakodesh).

This may be yet another reason why the Resurrection is the second blessing of the Amidah. Living in the physical world, we may see ourselves as spiritually dead. Therefore, as soon as we develop a close relationship with God in the first blessing, we ask that He resurrect us spiritually. This is then accomplished through the eighteen (which equals chai, life) blessings of the Amidah. By drawing ourselves close to God, we can experience a taste of the World to Come.

Davening with Kavana

ᴥᶘ Prologue

SEVERAL YEARS AGO, I received a telephone call from Moishe, a senior yeshivah student whom I knew for some time. A problem that had been bothering him for a number of years was becoming especially troublesome. He complained that since *davening* involved saying the same words day after day, praying had become meaningless to him. How can one say the same words three times a day, day after day, and still find them meaningful?

A week or two after that, a rabbi from a town in Long Island asked me to speak to Lisa, who had become involved with TM (Transcendental Meditation). When she came to my house I asked her to explain TM to me. She replied that it consisted of repeating a mantra over and over. The mantra was a special phrase given to her by her master.

"That's all there is to it?" I asked her, incredulously.

"That's it," Lisa replied. "If you repeat the same phrase over and over, and do it in the right manner, it can bring you to higher states of consciousness."

To be sure, TM, which is a type of *avodah zarah* (idolatry), bears absolutely no relationship to *davening*. Nonetheless the range of psychological responses TM provokes may help us understand human reactions. If repeating a meaningless phrase can have a certain psychological effect, then repeating a very highly meaningful prayer may well have an even stronger effect. Didn't Reb Shraga Feivel Mendlowitz, of blessed memory, teach a generation of yeshivah

The Jewish Observer—February 1983.

bachurim that for a nigun (song, especially one of religious devotion) to be savored, it should not be sung for three minutes and then be discarded for a fresh one, but that it should be repeated for as long as forty-five minutes at a time? Then the meaning of the words begins to sink in and penetrate the emotions. The repetition of key phrases over a period of time can also be effective.

ᵉ§ Davening and Prophecy: Shedding the Physical

The two incidents brought to mind a phrase that I had seen in the Shulchan Aruch (Code of Jewish Law, 98:1) in reference to the Chassidim Harishonim (pious men of old) who made a practice of being misboded (see below) before they recited the Amidah (Shemoneh Esrei). This was similar to the Rambam's comment that the prophets would be misboded when they would want to attain prophecy, suggesting a link between davening and the prophetic state.

Understanding the word misboded, which is fascinating in itself, is a key to preparing for prayer. Literally, misboded means to isolate oneself, from the root boded, meaning "to be alone." But as the Rambam's son Rabbi Avraham points out (in his Sefer Hamaspik), self-isolation can be external or internal. External isolation is simply leaving society and being by oneself. By contrast, "internal isolation" consists of "a cessation of activity on the part of the perceptive faculty...isolating it from the soul." The Ralbag (Rabbi Levi Ben Gershon) echoes this and writes that being misboded required the isolation of the consciousness from the imagination, or of both (the consciousness and the imagination) from the other perceptive mental faculties.

This fits well with the Shulchan Aruch's comment about attaining "divestment from the physical" (hispashtus hagashmius) through the Amidah. Totally divorced from the physical, one would be more ready to be in tune with the spiritual. This seems to offer an approach to attaining in a genuine manner the very experience that people sought from Eastern types of meditation, but could only achieve in a shallow way.

It has been said that many people never develop in their davening past the ten-year-old level. While this might be true generally, there are surely others who do attain the levels of concentration suggested by the Shulchan Aruch. I have consulted with many great rabbis and tzaddikim for hints on how to daven effectively. In addition, I searched through every available sefer that dealt with the subject, especially the commentaries on the Shulchan Aruch. Gradually a pattern began to emerge.

ᵉ§ Setting the Atmosphere

The first requisite is setting the atmosphere. The many laws regarding the respect that one must have for the synagogue are designed to make the synagogue a place with a worshipful, meditative atmosphere. Just walking into the synagogue should be an experience that prepares a person to commune with his Maker. Merely being there should be enough to remove all extraneous thoughts from one's mind.

This entails developing proper synagogue habits, which begin with accepting that the synagogue is not a place for socializing. One would do well to emulate the many Sephardim who do not utter a single irrelevant word from the time they enter the synagogue until they leave. This would be an excellent habit to develop for its own sake, but at least attempting to keep synagogue conversation to a minimum is absolutely essential if one expects to learn how to develop *kavanah*.

Incidentally, it may be useful to understand the word *kavanah* before going any further. The word has variously been translated as "feeling," "emotion," "concentration," or "devotion." Its root, however, is *kiven*, which means "to aim," suggesting "directed consciousness" as perhaps the most literal translation of *kavanah*. Indeed, it does consist of directing all of one's thoughts toward a single goal.

Most people may find it very difficult to manage this for the entire Amidah, but they should find it feasible in regard to the first blessing of the Amidah. In any case, it is the most important of the blessings, and according to the strict letter of the law, if one says it without proper *kavanah*, the entire Amidah is not valid, and should be repeated.

As an additional consideration, concentrating on the first blessing gives one a realistic goal in prayer. The first blessing is referred to as *Avos*, which literally means "fathers," because it speaks of the perception of God as attained by the Patriarchs. Actually the blessing is an introduction to achieving one's own individual relationship with God. When people ask me what the Jewish concept of God is on an I-Thou level, I refer them to this first blessing of the Amidah. On a practical level, this first blessing serves to bring a person near to God and leads him into the door of the spiritual.

✍️ Slowly, Into A Higher Consciousness

To make the Amidah a genuine spiritual experience, one must say it slowly. The Talmud relates that the *Chassidim Harishonim* would spend a full hour (3600 seconds) reciting the Amidah. Since there are approximately five hundred words in the Amidah, this would allot an average of seven seconds for each word. This is an extremely slow pace, but it gives a frame of reference for understanding that one must daven slowing to attain true *kavanah*. If one begins by taking three or four seconds per word for at least the first blessing, this in itself can be an extremely intense spiritual experience.

Reciting the words slowly always introduces the possibility that one's mind will wander from the Amidah. As soon as one is aware that this is happening, advises the *Shulchan Aruch*, he should gently push the thoughts out of his mind. At the same time, he might consider the Mezricher Maggid's teaching that extraneous thoughts enter a person's mind to teach him what he must rectify through his worship...

It is also helpful to close one's eyes, at least during this first bless-ing. The Baal Shem Tov taught that when a person is in a state of "ex-panded consciousness" (mochin degadlus), he should worship with his eyes closed, but while in a state of "constricted consciousness" (mochin dekatnus), one should daven from a Siddur. Since one is trying to attain a state of expanded consciousness during this first blessing, it follows that he should recite it with his eyes closed.

Another means for helping a person achieve a deep state of kavanah is standing absolutely still during the Amidah. Many people have the habit of swaying and bowing, but, as Rabbi Yishaya Horowitz (the Shelah Hakadosh) writes, such movement may actually interfere with kavanah. On a superficial level, swaying and shaking may make a person feel more emotional about the words he is saying, but drawing upon the deepest emotions often requires remaining perfectly still. Observing many great roshei yeshivah davening would seem to bear this out: they remain perfectly still during the Amidah.

◆§ The Four Occasions For Bowing

There is, however, one important exception to this—the four times dur-ing the Amidah when one is required to bow. It may take a while to ap-preciate this, but practical experience will demonstrate how they help one achieve the proper frame of mind for the Amidah. The Talmud states that when bowing, one should bend like a rod, and rise up like a snake (Berachos 12b). As the Shulchan Aruch explains, this means that one should bow down quickly, but rise up, head first, very slowly (Orach Chaim 113:6). Observing our senior roshei yeshivah one can see them follow this procedure very closely.

Obviously, there are many very deep reasons for bowing in this fashion. There are meanings, however, on a simpler level. When one raises himself very slowly, he is not only slows down the tempo of his body, he also puts his mind into a more contemplative framework. The bowing thus has the effect of hushing the mind, and putting it into a more receptive mood for kavanah.

Reciting the Amidah in this manner is a highly effective means of entering a deep spiritual state. One says the words, especially those of the first blessing, very slowly, either drawing out each word, or pausing silently after it to permit its meaning to sink in. One should not be think-ing of anything other than the simple meaning of the word itself. The word penetrates one's inner being, and draws him into the spiritual. During the silent pause between words, the mind is hushed in anticipa-tion of the next word.

Once a person has recited the first blessing (which includes the first two occasions for bowing) in this manner, the rest of the Amidah flows relatively easily. It is then much more possible to recite the entire

Amidah with a feeling of closeness to God, without extraneous thoughts.

One may be under the impression that such achievements are only within the reach of very great *tzaddikim*. There are, however, many relatively simple people who have learned to *daven* with such *kavanah*. The very fact that the Amidah is said three times every day makes the experience all the deeper through reinforcement. Indeed, experience has borne out that it is something that everyone can do.

◄§ Epilogue

It is interesting to note that my friend, Moishe, began to *daven* in the manner mentioned above, and gradually learned to make prayer an extremely profound experience. As his *davening* improved, so did his sense of closeness to God, which in turn helped his learning. Indeed, the Talmud says that the learning of the *Chassidim Harishonim* was blessed because of the great amount of time they spent in worship.

Even more interesting is what happened to Lisa, the girl from Long Island. Before she was ready to make a commitment to *Yiddishkeit*, she was willing to *daven*. She knew how to read Hebrew, and even went as far as to memorize the first blessing of the Amidah so as to be able to say it in the most effective manner. She soon admitted that she was finding *davening* a deeply spiritual experience...She eventually enrolled in a girls' seminary, and married a *kolel* man. She still finds her *davening* profoundly spiritual and a means of actually experiencing a closeness to HaShem.

Love and the

Commandments

I T IS A BASIC TEACHING of Judaism that God created the world as an act of love. Since He had no need for creation, it was the most perfect possible act of love and altruism. The Psalmist thus said (89:3), "I have said: The world is built of love."[1] The Prophet echoes these words when he says (Jeremiah 31:2), "I have loved you with an infinite world of love, therefore I have drawn you to Me with affection."

Love is therefore the ultimate bond between God and man. We are then bid to reciprocate God's love, as the Torah states (Deuteronomy 6:5), "You shall love the Lord your God, with all your heart, with all your soul, and with all your might.[2]

◄§ Love that Depends on a Thing

There are two basic ways through which a person can come to the love of God.[3] He can contemplate all the good that God does, and realize how He constantly watches and sustains all creation.[4] When one thinks about this, he should feel an obligation to love God, just as one might love any other benefactor.[5] It was of such love that the Psalmist sung when he said (116:1), "I love God, because He has heard my voice and my prayer."[6]

Our sages likewise speak of this type of love when they teach us that we should love and praise God for every breath that He allows us

Collegiate Hashkafa Series—1973

to draw.[7] We must realize that God is continuously expressing His love for us, and reciprocate it toward Him.

This, however, is not the highest level of love. Our sages call it "love that depends on a thing."[8] When the thing is taken away, the love may also vanish. If one only loves God for the good He does, then he may abandon this love when things go badly.

⋐ Love that does Not Depend on a Thing

When a person understands God's true greatness, however, then he loves God for what He is and needs no other reason.[9] One way to achieve such love is simply to contemplate God's works and then go a step further and perceive what is behind it all.[10] An even deeper love comes from the observance and study of God's commandments. We see this in the scriptural sequence (Deuteronomy 6:5-6), "You shall love the Lord...and these words which I command you this day shall be on your heart."[11]

Love such as this comes under the category of what our sages call "love that does not depend on a thing." It therefore remains firm under all conditions, even when an individual is beset by evil. It is regarding such love that Scripture speaks when it says (Song of Songs 8:7), "Many waters cannot quench the love, nor can the floods drown it."

True love of God is the desire to do whatever possible to bring oneself close to Him, especially by understanding Him and His teachings.[12] The most intense earthly love between man and woman is merely a shadow of the love between God and man.[13] The Prophet expresses such love when he says (Isaiah 26:9), "With my soul I desired You in the night; with the spirit inside me, I have ardently sought You." The Psalmist also sings of such love and declares (42:3), "My soul thirsts for God—for the living God—when will I come and appear before God?"[14]

⋐ Expressing Love by Observing Commandments

Love in itself, however, is nothing unless it finds expression. Our primary expression of our love for God is in observing His commandments. The Torah therefore teaches us (Deuteronomy 11:1), "You shall therefore love the Lord your God, and keep His charge, His statutes, His ordinances, and His commandments."

Our sages teach us that God expresses His love for us in three basic ways, and that we must reciprocate this threefold bond of love.[15] The Prophet speaks of this when he says (Hosea 2:21-22), "I will wed You to me forever. I will wed You to me with right and justice, with love and mercy. I will wed You to me with faith...and know God." We forge this threefold bond with God through His commandments.

First of all, our bond of love implies that we have a strong desire to do God's will and continually seek out ways to serve Him. When we serve God out of love, we do not limit ourselves to the mere requirements of the Law, but go beyond them in seeking ways of drawing ourselves close to Him.[16]

The second thing that this bond of love implies is a strong enthusiasm in obeying God's commandments. Even the most difficult observances no longer seem burdensome, while the most trivial practices assume a high degree of meaning. All facets of religious observance then serve to strengthen this bond, and thus become a source of great joy. This is what the Psalmist meant when he sang (100:2), "Serve God with joy."[17]

Finally, this love implies a closeness to God in all walks of life. Observance is no longer a dry ritual or meaningless habit, but a means of bringing oneself close to God, and therefore, the most meaningful thing possible. It is of this that the Psalmist spoke when he said (73:28), "As for me, the nearness of God is my good."[18]

One who truly loves God does not serve Him out of any hope of reward, but for His own sake alone. Our sages thus teach us, "Do not be like servants who serve their master in order to receive a prize."[19]

This is the most perfect way of serving God. To expect reward for one's good, however, is not considered a shortcoming and one who serves God for no other reason than to receive reward is still considered perfectly righteous.[20] The only condition is that one not regret his good if the reward is not immediately forthcoming.[21] One must have faith that God will ultimately reward all good.[22]

All wordly riches, passions and honors are nothing compared to the ultimate bond of love between God and man. The Psalmist thus sang (73:25), "Whom have I in heaven but You? And having You, I desire nothing else on earth."[23]

Although love for God exceeds all else, one should avoid asceticism as a way of life. Our sages therefore teach us that it is forbidden to abstain from this world completely.[24] The way of the tzaddik (righteous man) is to use even worldly things as a means to bring himself close to God.[25]

If one truly loves God, then he loves Him more than his possessions, his family, and even his very own self. He is therefore willing to sacrifice anything required by God, even life itself.[26] To the Jew, this bond of love with God was even more precious than life.

There is no reward greater than that of one who serves God out of love.[27] Our sages therefore teach us that no accuser on high can speak evil against one who truly loves God.[28] The reward for such love comes directly from God Himself.[29]

❧ Israel and Torah; Creation's Purpose

Of all the peoples on earth, God set aside the Jews as His special representatives. It was this mutual bond between God and Israel that was to serve to bring about His ultimate purpose in creation. God sealed this bond of love by giving us His commandments, as we say in our evening prayers (*Ahavas Olom*), "With an infinite world of love have You loved the house of Israel, Your people. You taught us Your Torah, Your commandments, Your code and Your way." Our sages likewise teach us that "God wanted to do good to Israel, and therefore gave them Torah and commandments in abundance."[30]

The essence of the Torah are its commandments, *mitzvos* in Hebrew. The very word *mitzvah* comes from a root meaning "to bind."[31] This is because every commandment or *mitzvah* serves to draw us close to God and strengthen this bond of love.

There are basically two types of commandments. In some places, the Torah says "you shall do" something. This is a positive commandment or *mitzvas asei*. In other places, the Torah says "you shall not do" something. This is a negative commandment or *mitzvas lo saaseh*.

◄§ The Number of the Commandments

There is a tradition that the Torah contains 248 positive commandments and 365 negative ones. This adds up to a total of 613 commandments in the Torah.[32]

Of course, many of these commandments deal with laws of purity and sacrifice that were only applicable when the Temple or *Beis HaMikdash* stood (and will again apply when it is rebuilt) in Jerusalem. Therefore, of all the commandments, only 369 apply today, of which 126 are positive, and 243 are negative. Even of these, however, many only pertain to special cases or circumstances. The total number of commandments which apply under all conditions is 270, of which forty-eight are positive, and 222 negative.[33]

All the commandments, including their laws and interpretations, were given to Moses during the forty days that he spent on Mount Sinai.[34] The Torah thus states (Exodus 24:12), "God said to Moses: Come up to Me into the mountain, and stay there. I will give you tablets of stone and the Torah and commandments which I have written, that you may teach them." Our sages comment that this teaches that everything was given to Moses at Sinai.[35]

There were, of course, many commandments that had been known at earlier times. Thus, there were the seven universal commandments given to Adam and Noah.[36] Later, circumcision was given to Abraham, and a special dietary law not to eat the sciatic tendon (*Gid HaNasheh*), to Jacob.[37] We are likewise taught that Judah instituted levirate marriage (*yibum*).[38] Furthermore, there is a tradition that the detailed laws of marriage and divorce were given to the Jews while they were still in Egypt, having been revealed through Amram, the father of Moses.[39]

There were also other laws given to the Jews before they reached Mount Sinai. The rules of the Sabbath were initially given to them when they first received the manna.[40] Likewise, the laws regarding the honor due one's parents, as well as certain judicial regulations, were given at Marah, shortly before the Jews arrived at Sinai.[41]

Still, the final authority of all the commandments was their revelation at Sinai.[42] As soon as the Jews entered into this covenant with God, they were absolved from all previous commandments, and bound by the Torah as revealed by Moses.[43] It is for this reason that we do not learn any laws from things that happened before the revelation at Sinai.[44]

This is a most important point. The Torah may have embodied earlier laws, and itself may have been written over the forty-year period that the Jews spent in the wilderness. Still, all its commandments became binding at one instant—the moment that they were revealed and accepted at Mount Sinai.[45] We therefore cannot say that Judaism in any way evolved as a religion. It all came into being at once with the revelation at Sinai.[46]

✌ An Oath and a Covenant

The Jewish people accepted the Torah through both an oath and a covenant. The oath was taken by all Israel, and made the commandments eternally binding on all future generations.[47] The covenant consisted of circumcision, which took place in Egypt, and then of immersion in water and a special sacrifice.[48]

Whenever a non-Jew converts to Judaism, he essentially duplicates this oath and covenant. He must accept upon himself the commandments, undergo ritual immersion in a *mikveh*, and if he is a male, also undergo the ritual of circumcision. In this manner, he enters into the covenant in the same way that all Jews did originally.[49]

It was this oath and covenant that established the special relationship between God and the Jew for all generations. The Torah spells it out, saying (Deuteronomy 29:9-14):

> You are all standing before the Lord your God...to enter into the covenant an oath that the Lord your God is making with you today. The covenant is to make you His people this day, that He may be your God, as He promised you, and as He swore to your fathers, Abraham, Isaac and Jacob. It is not with you alone that I am making this covenant and oath, but also with those who are not here this day.[50]

When we speak of the Jews as a "chosen people," we use the term primarily because we were "chosen" to be the recipients of God's Torah and commandments. Thus, for example, we say in the blessing before the Torah, "Blessed are You...Who chose us from all peoples, and gave us His Torah."

The Torah and its commandments are therefore only binding on the Jews. The Torah itself thus says (Deuteronomy 33:4), "Moses commanded us the Torah, an inheritance of the congregation of Jacob."[51] The Psalmist likewise said (147:19-20), "He declared His word to

Jacob, His rules and laws to Israel; He has not done so to any other nation..."[52]

It is for this reason that the laws appearing in the Torah are not binding upon the non-Jewish world. The only exception are those universal laws, which tradition teaches us were given to the entire human race. In order to be universally binding, however, even these must be redundant in the Torah.[53] There is therefore no case where the law is stricter for a non-Jew than it is for a Jew.[54] There are a few exceptions to this rule, but in all such cases, a specific exception is made for the Jews where the law is stated.[55]

◄§ Eternality of the Commandments

One of the foundations of our faith is the affirmation that the commandments were given for all times.[56] We are therefore forbidden to add or subtract from their number, as the Torah states (Deuteronomy 13:1), "All this word which I command you, you shall observe to do. You shall not add to it, nor diminish from it."[57]

The Jewish religion was therefore determined by the Torah for all times. We may not add any commandments to it, nor subtract any from it. Even to interpret a commandment so as to add a law not included in tradition is forbidden.[58]

In order that the Torah be a living way of life, God gave to such bodies as the Sanhedrin the power to legislate new laws as they were required. This legislation includes everything that we call "rabbinical law" or *mitzvos derabbanan*. The above rule, however, implies that even the Sanhedrin had to be most careful in distinguishing between their legislation and true Biblical law. We thus find many major differences between rabbinical laws (*derabbanan*) and laws appearing in the Torah (*deoraisa*).[59]

◄§ The Ten Commandments; Essence of the Torah

The covenant was sealed with the giving of the Ten Commandments.[60] These commandments were publicly declared by God, inscribed on two tablets, and placed in the Ark of the Covenant.[61] The Torah thus says (Deuteronomy 4:13), "He proclaimed to you His covenant, which He commanded you to keep—Ten Commandments—and He wrote them on two tablets of stone."[62] The Ten Commandments thus served as an introduction to the other commandments, and contained the essence of the entire Torah.[63]

The Ten Commandments contain the main elements necessary for the religious and ethical survival of the Jewish people, and are therefore considered pre-eminent.[64] The first five deal with religious necessities, such as belief in God, the negation of idolatry, respect for God's name, a Sabbath commemorating God's creation, and the survival of tradition through honor of parents. The second five, on the other hand, deal with moral necessities, such as respect for life, chastity and property, the pursuit of honest judgment, and the subjugation of man's covetous desires.[65] Although the Ten Commandments were formally given at Mount Sinai, the concepts contained in them formed the basis of even the Patriarchs' dedication to God.[66]

Although the Ten Commandments are of primary importance they only constitute a small part of the Torah. There were, however, many people, who out of ignorance or malice, refused to accept all the commandments, and claimed that only these ten were actually given by God.[67] It was largely because of such people that the reading of the Ten Commandments was deleted from the daily service.[68] Since the Ten Commandments were so important, they were originally made part of the daily liturgy, but when people used this as "proof" that these were the only commandments, our sages decreed that they should never be included in any public service.[69] The Ten Commandments may be of cardinal importance, but still, all 613 commandments of the Torah were given by God and are essential to Judaism.

◄§ Observing the Commandments; Because Such is God's Will

The main significance of the commandments is the fact that they were given by God Himself. They are therefore the only means through which we can approach God and fulfill His purpose in creation.[70]

Furthermore, it is the commandments that make Judaism more than a mere religious philosophy.[71] Because of them, Judaism is a way of life involving action and observance, and not a mere confession of faith.[72]

Many of the commandments may seem very logical. On the other hand, there are many laws and rules that seem to defy logic. One should not observe the commandments because logic demands it, but simply because they were given by God.[73] There is only one logic required, and that is the relationship of the commandments to their Giver. This is higher than any possible human wisdom, as the Torah teaches us (Deuteronomy 4:6), "Therefore observe and do them (the commandments) for this is your wisdom and understanding in the sight of the nations."[74]

The commandments should not only supersede one's logic, they should even transcend one's personal tastes. We do not keep the commandments because they suit our fancy, but because God told us to. Our sages thus teach us that one should not say, "I will not eat pig because it disgusts me." Rather, one should say, "I would enjoy pork, but I will not eat it because God has commanded me not to."[75]

Ultimately, we therefore keep the commandments precisely because they are commandments—laws decreed by God. It is forbidden to think of them as anything else. Thus, one may not keep any commandment as a superstitious luck charm.[76] Our sages furthermore teach us, "The commandments were not given for our material pleasure."[77]

Eidos, Chukim and Mishpatim

Most of the commandments fall into two main categories. There are some laws whose reason is immediately obvious because they are necessary for the preservation of society. These laws are known as *mishpatim*, literally translated as "judgments." They include most moral laws, and make up the entire ethical structure of Judaism.[78]

The second category includes laws for which there is no apparent reason. These consist of ritual laws, and their main function is to strengthen the bond between God and man. These laws are called *chukim*, usually translated as "statutes" or "rules."[79]

There is also a third category, however, that falls between these two. These are commandments that have no moral basis, but still have the logical purpose of strengthening Judaism by reminding us of important religious truths or events in our history. This third group includes the various holidays and such commandments as Tefillin and the Mezuzah. These are called *eidos*, and are literally translated as "witnesses" or "testimonies." These are the commandments that bear "witness" to important concepts in Judaism.[80]

Understanding the Reason for Each Commandment

There are many *chukim* for which absolutely no reason is given. Even in these cases, however, we still strive to understand the benefits and symbolism of such commandments.[81] Furthermore, even where the basic reason for a commandment is known, we attempt to understand the logic involved in its detailed laws.[82]

Even when we think that we know the reason for a law, however, we can never be sure that this is its ultimate reason. Therefore, we cannot depend on any such reason to change or restrict any law.[83] This is even true where the reason is specified in the Torah, since there may be other reasons that are not revealed.[84] It is also possible that the laws involve other factors, not readily ascertainable by our own logic and experience.[85]

We therefore see that there are two basic ways of looking at the commandments, the legal and the philosophical. While we may be able to find philosophical reasons for many laws, we do not mix this into our discussions of actual law. For this, there is a legal process of *halachah*, with an inherent logic of its own.

There is also another area where we do not mix logic and law. It is forbidden to hold God to any reason that we may attempt to give for His commandments. In the Talmud we find a striking example of this. The Torah commands us (Deuteronomy 22:6), "If you come upon a bird's nest...do not take the mother with its young. Send away the mother, and then you may take the young for yourself." This patently seems to be a case where God is showing us that we must have mercy on all His creatures. Nevertheless, the Talmud teaches us that if one prays, "Have mercy on us, just like You have mercy on a bird's nest," then he must be stopped.[86] This is not a proper prayer. We might think that the reason for this commandment is "mercy," but all of our reasoning really falls short of the infinite meaning in the commandment.[87]

It is for this reason that God did not include the reasons for the commandments in the Torah. These were not revealed to any mortal in this world, other than to Moses himself.[88] God knew that if He revealed all the reasons, human nature along with imperfect understanding would lead people to make unwarranted personal exceptions to the commandments.[89] A person might think that he understood the reason fully, and feel that a particular commandment did not apply to him. The very fact that no reasons are given teaches us that we must obey the laws as commandments of God, and not because of any reasoning that our limited intellect may devise.

This therefore teaches us that we must observe all of God's commandments with equal care.[90] To profess to believe in a divinely-revealed Torah, and at the same time to choose to observe commandments according to one's own judgment, is to claim to be greater than their Giver.[91]

⊸§ God's Ultimate Purpose for Giving the Commandments

We know that God is absolutely perfect, and therefore has no needs. It is therefore obvious that He did not give us the commandments to benefit Himself in any way. This is what Scripture means when it says (Job 35:7), "If you are righteous, what do you give Him? What does He receive from your hand?"[92]

We therefore see that God's motive in giving the commandments was purely altruistic, for the sole good of the recipients. The Torah thus teaches us (Deuteronomy 10:13-14), "Keep God's commandments...for your own good. Behold, the heavens belong to the Lord your God...and the earth and everything in it." The Torah is saying just this. Since everything in heaven and earth belongs to God, He does not need our observance. We must therefore keep the commandments for our "own good."[93]

To the best of our understanding, God's ultimate purpose in creation was to do good.[94] The commandments were given as the means through which God would transmit this good, and are therefore primarily for the benefit of those who observe them.[95] Our sages therefore teach us that "the commandments were only given to purify God's creatures."[96] The Torah echoes this when it says (Deuteronomy 6:24-25), "The Lord commands us to keep all these laws...for our everlasting good. It is charity to us that we can observe and keep these commandments before the Lord our God, as He commanded us."[97]

Since the commandments were given for man's ultimate benefit, they might have been made difficult enough to present a challenge, but not so difficult as to make their observance impossibly burdensome.[98]

The Torah thus teaches us (ibid. 30:11), "This commandment which I bid you today is not too hard for you, neither is it far off."[99] Our sages similarly teach us that "God did not give the Torah to ministering angels."[100] God realized the fallibility of man when He gave the commandments, and conceived them in such a way that man should be able to abide by them. Our sages thus declare, "God does not act like a tyrant toward His creatures."[101]

People may complain, "It's hard to be a Jew," but this is not completely true. The most difficult commandments are not those directed toward God, but those involving our fellow man.[102] But here, it is not God who makes the commmandments difficult, but the inherent evil nature of man himself.

The main benefit of the commandments is in the realm of the spiritual. Observance of the commandments is ultimately the means through which a person brings himself close to God.[103] As such, they are like nourishment to the soul.[104] They strengthen man's soul, and at the same time, fortify him spiritually.[105]

Sin, on the other hand, is what separates a person from God. The Prophet thus told us (Isaiah 59:2), "Only your sins have separated between you and your God."[106] Sin is therefore like poison to the soul.[107] The prohibitions in the Torah were given to us by God in order to protect us from this poison of sin.[108]

God's purpose in creation was to do good, and ultimately, this good is given as a reward for observing the commandments. On a universal scale, therefore, the commandments serve to fulfill God's purpose in creation.[109] In doing so, they also enhance God's relationship with His universe.[110]

God's Relationship with the Universe

God created things in such a way that man's good must come as a result of his own action, and therefore, He deals reciprocally with man. When man does something to awaken his own awareness in God, then God awakens him further from above.[111] Our own deeds are therefore the means that generate the spiritual closeness that is our ultimate reward.[112]

On a greater scale, the commandments lead to a manifestation of God's unity in the universe, even in this material world.[113] Through Israel's observance of God's commandments, His position becomes strengthened in this world. It is of this that the Psalmist is speaking when he sings (Psalm 68:35), "Give strength unto God—upon Israel His pride."[114] Although the average person might not realize it, the commandments thus serve the highest purpose in God's ultimate plan.[115]

If a person were to understand the true spiritual nature of the world, including the ultimate meaning of good and evil, then he would readily understand the significance of all the commandments. It was in this manner that the Patriarchs understood and observed the Torah even before it was given.[116] For the same reason, the true significance of all the commandments will be obvious in the World to Come, when all truth will be revealed.[117]

✑§ Additional Benefits of Commandment Observance

Although the main benefit of the commandments lies on a purely spiritual plane, it also provides a great many mundane benefits.

First of all, a great number of commandments deal with man's relationship with his fellows and are necessary for the preservation of a harmonious society.[118] Thus, when Hillel was asked to provide a single rule summarizing the Jewish religion, he replied, "What is hateful in your eyes, do not do to another."[119] Rabbi Akiba similarly taught that the prime rule of the Torah is the commandment (Leviticus 19:18), "You shall love your neighbor like yourself."[120] Scripture thus teaches us (Proverbs 3:17), "Its ways are ways of pleasantness, and all its paths are peace."[121]

The ritual commandments serve the purpose of sanctifying our lives and bringing us close to God.[122] They penetrate every nook and cranny of our existence, hallowing even the lowliest acts and elevating them to a service to God.[123] There are a multitude of laws covering such everyday things as eating, drinking, dressing and business, and these sanctify every facet of life, constantly reminding us of our responsibilities toward God.[124]

Every commandment therefore serves to make us more holy and Godly.[125] It is for this reason that before observing many commandments, we recite a blessing containing the words, "Who has made us holy through His commandments."[126] The Torah likewise teaches us (Numbers 15:40), "That you remember and keep all My commandments, and be holy unto your God."[127]

The many rituals associated with daily life also serve to teach us self-discipline.[128] Our sages thus teach us that "when Israel is involved with the Torah and *mitzvos*, they master their urge (*yetzer*) and are not mastered by it."[129] The Torah likewise speaks of this when it says (ibid. 15:39), "You shall remember...all of God's commandments, and not stray after your heart and eyes, by which you would be led astray."[130]

The commandments also serve to maintain the identity of the Jewish people and keep them from assimilating. In relation to many laws, God thus tells us (Leviticus 20:24), "I am the Lord your God, Who has set you apart from the other peoples."[131] The many rituals also provide opportunities for communal observance and fellowship, through which individuals can identify with the Jewish community as a whole.[132]

The Jewish people are also unified by the commandments that remind us of our unique history and heritage. We thus find the constant reminder (Deuteronomy 16:3), "That you should remember the day when you left Egypt all the days of your life."[133] Remembering our unique history also serves to remind us of our unique responsibilities.

The commandments also serve in an educational capacity, transmitting God's teachings from one generation to the next.[134] The Torah thus tells us (ibid. 31:13), "That their children, who have not known, may hear and learn to fear the Lord your God."[135] The Psalmist similarly states (78:5-6), "He laid a solemn charge on Jacob, and established a law in Israel, which He commanded our fathers to teach their sons, that it may be known to a future generation, to children yet unborn; and these would repeat it to their sons in turn."

It is only such a constant transmission of tradition that can guarantee the continuity of our faith and therefore this is a most important reason for the commandments.[136] They act as a survival mechanism for Judaism, enabling it to retain its strength, even through the harshest persecutions.[137] Indeed, this may be the strongest of all proofs of the divine nature of the commandments, if any such proof is needed. As long as the Jews kept the commandments, they remained strong for over a hundred generations. A single generation's lapse, on the other hand, has led to both the spiritual and physical decay of the Jewish people.

Above and beyond all the meager reasons that our puny minds can give for God's commandments, there still exists an infinite depth known only to God. This is what God taught His Prophet when He declared (Isaiah 55:8-11):

> For My thoughts are not your thoughts,
> and your ways are not My ways...
> As the heavens are higher than the earth,
> so are My ways higher than your ways,
> and My thoughts than your thoughts.
> But as the rain and snow come down from heaven
> and do not return there
> Until they have watered the earth, making it blossom
> and bear fruit,
> giving seed to sow and bread to eat.
> The word that comes from My mouth is the same:
> It shall not return to Me void;
> It shall accomplish My purpose,
> and succeed in what I sent it to do.[138]

1. Zohar 1:10b, 1:230b, 2:166b, Sefer HaBris 2:13. Also see Emunos VeDeyos 1:4 end, 3:0, Or HaShem (Crescas) 2:6:2, Sefer HaYashar #1, Pardes Rimonim 2:6, Etz Chaim, Shaar HaKelallim #1, Reshis Chochmah, Shaar, HaTshuvah 1, Sh'nei Luchos HaBris, Bais Yisrael (Jerusalem 5720) 1:21b, Shomrei Emunim (HaKadmon) 2:13, Derech HaShem 1:2:1, Likutei Moharan 64; Moreh Or #1.

2. Yad, Yesodei HaTorah 2:1, Sefer HaMitvos, positive #3, Sefer Mitzvos Gadol, positive #3, Zohar 3:263b. Also see Chinuch 418, Ibn Ezra on Exodus 20:1.

3. Zohar 1:12a, Chovos HaLevavos 10:2, Shnei Luchos HaBris 1:74b; Commentary on Yad, Yesodei HaTorah 2:1.

4. Reshis Chochmah 2:9 (New York, 5728) p. 82c; Sefer Mitzvos Gadol, loc. cit.

5. Sefer Chasidim 31.

6. See Radak, Midrash Tehillim, and Yalkut (82:874) ad loc.

7. Devarim Rabbah 2:26, from Psalm 150:6. Cf. Radak ad loc.

8. Avos 5:16. Cf. Tanna DeBei Eliahu Rabbah 28 (Jerusalem, 5723) p. 109a, Zohar 1:12a; Sifri, Rashi, and Yalkut (1:837) on Deuteronomy 6:5.

9. Emunos VeDeyos 2:13, Moreh Nevuchim 3:51. Cf. Kuzari 4:5.

10. Yad, Yesodei Hatorah 2:2 and Hagohos Maimonios ad loc; Sefer HaMitzvos loc cit. and Kinas Sofrim ad loc; Chinuch loc. cit., from Sifri. Tshuvos HaRambam 347, Sefer Chasidim 14, Reshis Chochmah 2:5 (63d).

11. Rashi, Sifri, Yalkut (1:839) ad loc.

12. Yad, loc. cit. Cf. Moreh Nevuchim 1:30, Charedim, positive 1:5.

13. Sefer Chasidim 14. Cf. Charedim, positive 1:6; Yoma 54a.

14. Chovos HaLevavos 10:1, Reshis Chochmah 2:1 (51c).

15. Cf. Bereshis Rabbah 80:6, Reshis Chochmah 2:3 (59b), Mesilas Yesharim 19.

16. Cf. Tanna DeBei Eliahu Rabbah 16 (78a), 28 (108b); Yerushalmi Berachos 9:5 (67a), Reshis Chochmah 2:1 (51b).

17. Cf. Deuteronomy 28:47, Ikkarim 3:33, Reshis Chochmah (52a), Rokeach, Shoresh Ahavas HaShem.

18. Radak ad loc. Cf. Ramban on Deuteronomy 11:22, Charedim positive 1:10, Yad, Tshuvah 10:3.

19. Avos 1:3, Sifri on Deuteronomy 11:13, Rashi ibid., Nedarim 62a; Yad, Tshuvah 10:1-4, Yoreh Deah 246:21 in Hagah, Sefer Chasidim 63, Reshis Chochmah 2:1 (51b), Shnei Luchos HaBris 1:79b.

20. Pesachim 8a, Rosh HaShanah 4a, Baba Basra 10b; Tosefos Yom Tov on Avos 1:3, Yad, Tshuvah 10:5.

21. Tosafos, Pesachim 8b 'SheYizkeh,'' Rosh HaShanah 4a 'U'VeShevil,' and Maharsha ad loc., Avodah Zarah 19a 'Al Menas.'' Tikunei Zohar 30 (73b), quoted in Reshis Chochmah 2:1 (51c). Also see Chinuch 428; Sotah 14a, Maharitz Chayos, Maharsha 'Omar Lo') .

22. Cf. Avos DeRabbi Nassan 5:2, Sefer Chassidim 301.

23. Shnei Luchos HaBris 1:79b, Chovas HaLevavos 9:2.

24. Taanis 22b, 11a and Tosefos ad loc. 'Amar,'' Yerushalmi Kidushin 4:12 (48b) Tanna DeBei Eliahu Rabbah 14 (72b); Yad, Deyos 1:4, Emunos VeDeyos 10:4. Cf. Yerushalmi Peah 8:8 (37b), Yerushalmi Nedarim 9:1 (29a). Also see Orech Chaim 571:1.

25. Mesilas Yesharim 13, Likutei Amarim (Tanya) 1:7 (11a) ff. Cf. Zohar 3:263b, Moreh Nevuchim 3:51, Yad, Deyos 3:1,2.

26. Berachos 61b, Zohar 1:12a, Sefer Mitzvos Gadol, positive 3, Sefer Chassidim 14, Reshis Chochmah 2:1 (52b). Also see Genesis 22:12.

27. Sotah 31a, Sifri on Deuteronomy 6:5, Yalkut 1:837, Avos DeRabbi Nassan 5:1, Tanna DeBei Eliahu Rabbah 28 (108b), Rashi on Deuteronomy 7:9.

28. Sefer Chassidim, end of 164. Cf. Avodah Zarah 35b, Zohar 1-174b.

29. Reshis Chochmah 2:2(55a).

30. Makkos 3:16 (23b).

31. Likutei Moharan 4:6. Cf. Berachos 6b, Shabbos 30b, Rashi ad loc. 'Litzvos.'

32. Makkos 23b, Targum J. on Genesis 1:27, Mechilta on Exodus 20:2 (67a), Sifri 2:76, Bereshis Rabbah 24:5, Sh'mos Rabbah 33:8, Shir HaShirim Rabbah 1:13, Tanchuma Ki Tetze 2, Pirkei deRabbi Eliezer 41 (98a), Pesikta 12 (101a), Zohar 1:170b. Also see Shabbos 89a, Yebamos 47b, Nedarim 25a, Shavuos 29a, Minachos 43b, Rashi ad loc. 'Shekulah.'' Tosafos, Minachos 39a 'Lo,' Rashi on Genesis 32:5, Numbers 15:9. For a detailed discussion of this number, see Ramban on Sefer HaMitzvos, Shoresh #1 (la ff), Shnei Luchos 3:3bff. See also Bamidbar Rabbah 13:15, 18:17.

33. *Shnei Luchos HaBris* 3:1b, in note quoting *Megillas Sesarim,* also quoted in *Pri Megadim,* introduction to *Orach Chaim;* also quoted in letter before introduction to *Minchas Chinuch* (Sentry Press, New York, 5722) p.iv. In *Sefer HaMitzvos,* end of positive 248, however, we find 60 such positive commandments listed.

34. Cf. *Sotah* 37b, *Chagigah* 61, *Zebachim* 115a, *Sifra* (105a), Rashi, Ramban, on Leviticus 25:1, *Sifra* (115d) on Leviticus 27:34; *Sefer HaMitzvos, Shoresh* 1, from *Makkos* 23b.

35. *Berachos* 5a.

36. *Sanhedrin* 56b, *Tosefta Avodah Zarah* 9:4, *Bereshis Rabbah* 16:9, *Devarim Rabbah* 2:17, *Shir HaShirim Rabbah* 1:16, *Pesikta* 12 (100b), *Zohar* 1:35b; *Yad, Melachim* 9:1, *Moreh Nevuchim* 1:2, *Kuzari* 3:73 (75b).

37. "The Jew," elsewhere in this volume.

38. Genesis 38:8. In *Pesikta* 23(100b), *Shir HaShirim Rabbah* 1:17, we find an indication that this was an actual commandment. Other sources, however, write that Judah instituted this of his own accord, see *Bereshis Rabbah* 85:5, *Vayikra Rabbah* 2:9; Ritva, Maharitz Chayos on *Yebamos* 5b.

39. *Yad, Melachim* 9:1; *Tshuvos Makom Shmuel* 23, Maharitz Chayos on *Sotah* 12a. Cf. *Mechilta* on Exodus 18:1 (57b), *Meir Eyin* ad loc. #28. Also see *Yerushalmi Kiddushin* 1:1 (2a), *Bereshis Rabbah* 18:8, *Yad, Melachim* 9:8, *P'nai Yehoshua* on *Tosafos, Kiddushin* 43 'LeKulo Alma.'

40. *Sanhedrin* 56b, *Targum J., Mechilta* (46a), *Yalkut* (1:257), Rashi on Exodus 15:25. *Seder Olom.* Cf. *Pirkei DeRabbi Eliezer* 18 (42b), *Tosafos, Shabbos* 87b 'Ka'asher," Turey Zahav, Yoreh Deah 1:0.

41. Ibid. Rashi, loc. cit. however, omits parental honor, and substitutes the Red Cow (Numbers 19). This is also disputed by Rabbi Eliezer HaModai in *Mechilta* loc. cit. For a discussion of other laws given before Sinai, see *Yebamos* 5b, *Megillah* 6b.

42. Rambam on *Chulin* 7:6, Maharitz Chayos, *Berachos* 13a, *Yebamos* 5b, *Sanhedrin* 56b, *Makkos* 23b, Cf. *Mishneh LaMelech,* on *Yad, Melachim* 10:7, *Tshuvos Makom Shmuel* 22.

43. Rashi, *Sanhedrin* 59a 'LaZeh.' Cf. *Sanhedrin* 71b, *Yad, Melachim* 10:4.

44. *Yerushalmi Moed Katan* 3:5 (14b), *Tosafos. Moed Katan* 20a 'Mah," Bechor Shor ad loc., *Yad, Avel* 1:1, Aruch "Shachar,' Maharitz Chayos, *Yoma* 28b, *Taanis* 28a, *Moed Katan* 20a, *Nazir* 15b, *Chulin* 16a.

45. Cf. *Eruvin* 21b, Maharitz Chayos ad loc.

46. *Kuzari* 1:81 (49a).

47. *Shavuos* 29a, *Nedarim* 25a. See also *Nedarim* 8a, *Nazir* 4a, *Yad, Nedarim* 3:7, *Shavuos* 11:3, *Sifsei Cohen, Yoreh Deah*

119:22, *Tshuvos Nodeh BeYehudah, Orach Chaim* 1:38, *Tshuvos Shaagas Aryeh* 60, Maharitz Chayos, *Nedarim* 8a, *Nazir* 4a, *Tshuvos Rambam* 170. See further, Rashi, Ramban, on Deuteronomy 27:26, Maharsha, *Shavuos* 29a, 'KeSheHishbia,' Rashash, ibid., HaGra, Yoreh Deah 228:99.

48. Cf. Joshua 5:5, *Yebamos* 71b, *Kerisos* 9a, *Tosafos* ad loc. 'VeK'siv.' Radal (on *Pirkei DeRabbi Eliezer*) 29:1, 29:49; Ramban, Rashba, *Yebamos* 46a 'SheKen,' Rambam, *Igeres HaShmad.* p. 6. See also Exodus 24:8, *Yebamos* 46a, *Tosefos Yom Tov* on *Pesachim* 8:8.

49. *Kerisos* 9a, *Yad, Issurey Biah* 13:1.

50. Ramban, Abarbanel, Bachya, *Yalkut* (1:560) ad loc., *Tanchuma Netzavim* 3, *Yerushalmi Nedarim* 3:1 (8b).Also see Deuteronomy 26:18, 27:9, Jeremiah 31:32; Deuteronomy 5:2.

51. *Sifri, Yalkut* (1:552) ad loc., *Sanhedrin* 59a.

52. Ibn Ezra ad loc., *Chagigah* 13a, *Tshuvos Chacham Tzvi* 26, Maharitz Chayos on *Baba Metzia* 61a.

53. *Sanhedrin* 59a, *Tosafos, Avodah Zarah* 5b 'Minayin," *Zebachim* 68b 'VeSheNismis," *Chulin* 23a 'Tamoos.' Also see *Tosafos, Baba Kama* 55a, 'LeMinehu.' Cf. *Tshuvos Rashbash* 543, *Tshuvos Chacham Tzvi* 26, *Sheilas Sholom* (Yeshiah Berlin) #10; Maharsha on *Tosafos, Chagigah* 2b 'Lo,' Maharitz Chayos, *Chagigah* 11b, *Baba Kama* 55b, *Baba Metzia* 61a, *Sanhedrin* 56b. Cf. *Kuzari* 3:73(75b).

54. *Sanhedrin* 59a.

55. Ibid. *Tosafos* ad loc. 'Leika.'

56. *Thirteen Principles of Faith* #9.

57. *Yad, Mamrim* 2:9, Raavad ad loc., *Sefer HaMitzvos,* negative 313, 314, *Sefer Mitzvos Gadol* 364, 365, *Chinuch* 454, 455. Cf. Deuteronomy 4:2. However, some hold that this only applies to the addition of positive commandments, but not negative ones. Cf Raavad, *Chinuch,* loc. cit.

58. *Yad,* loc. cit., *Minchas Chinuch* 454. Cf. *Bereshis Rabbah* 7:2, *Bamidbar Rabbah* 18:3, *Koheles Rabbah* 7:43, *Tanchuma, Chukas* 6, *Pesikta* 4 (35b).

59. *Yad,* loc. cit. Ramban on Deuteronomy 4:2 end; *Pri Megadim,* introduction 1:35; *Amudei Yerushalmi, Megillah* 1:5 (7a), Maharitz Chayos, *Megillah* 14a.

60. Exodus 20:2-14, Deuteronomy 5:6-18. Although both versions contain somewhat different wording, we are taught that both were given in a single act of Divine speech. See *Shavuos* 20b, *Rosh HaShanah* 27a, *Yerushalmi Nedarim* 3:2 (89a), *Yerushalmi Shavuos* 3:8 (17b); *Mechilta* (69a). Rashi, on Exodus 20:8, *Sifri* 2:233, *Tosafos, Baba Kama*

54b 'Behemtecha.' Ibn Ezra on Exodus 20:2 writes that the Exodus version was written on the first set of tablets, while the Deuteronomy version was written by Moses on the second set. This view is supported in Baba Kama 55a, cf. Pinto (Riff) ad loc. (in Eyin Yaakov #15), P'nai Yehoshua ibid.; Rabbi Reuven Margolius, HaMikra VeHaMesorah #1. In Sh'mos Rabbah 47:10, however, we find the opinion that both sets contained exactly the same wording, cf. Exodus 34:1, Ibn Ezra ad loc.

61. See Kuzari 1:87 (52b), Moreh Nevuchim 2:46. For a discussion how they were written on the Tablets, see Yerushalmi Shekalim 6:1 (25a), Mechilta on Exodus 20:14 (70b), Sh'mos Rabbah 47:10, Shir HaShirim Rabbah 5:12. For a discussion of how God wrote the tablets, see Moreh Nevuchim 1:46.

62. Cf. Mechilta to Exodus 20:16 (71b). Also see Deuteronomy 5:22, Rambam, Tosefos Yom Tov on Tamid 5:1, Maharsha on Berachos 11b 'VeKaru.'

63. We are therefore taught that the Ten Commandments include all 613. Cf. Bamidbar Rabbah 13:15, Shir HaShirim Rabbah 5:12, Yerushalmi Shekalim 6:1 (25a), Yalkut 1:358, 1:825, Rashi on Exodus 24:12, Kuzari 1:87 (52b). We are likewise taught that the Decalogue contained 613 letters, alluding to the 613 commandments. Cf. Bamidbar Rabbah 13:15, 18:17.

64. Regarding the pairing of the commandments, see Mechilta to Exodus 20:14 (70b).

65. Ikkarim 3:26.

66. Cf. Yalkut 1:276 end, quoting Midrash Abkir.

67. Yerushalmi Berachos 1:5 (9b); Rashi, Berachos 12a 'MiPney,'' Magen Avrahem 1:9, Turey Zahav 1:5.

68. Berachos 12a, Rambam, Bertenoro on Tamid 5:1.

69. They may, however, be read privately. See Orach Chaim 1:5 in Hagah, Beer Heitev 1:11, Mishneh Beruah 1:16, Tshuvos Rashba 184, Tshuvos Bais Yaakov 155, Tshuvos Sh'vus Yaakov 2:44.

70. Kuzari 1:79 (47a), 1:98 (66b), 2:46 (54b), 3:23 (31b).

71. Kuzari 4:13 (830a).

72. Kuzari 1:115 (75b). Cf. Avos 3:15, Bertenoro, Tosefos Yom Tov ad loc. 'VeHakol.' Also see Ramban, Toras HaAdam, Shaar HaGamul (Jerusalem 5715) p. 72; Mechilta on Exodus 12:6 (5a).

73. Chayei Adam 68:18. Cf. Rosh HaShanah 16a, Maharitz Chayos ad loc., Rambam on Makkos 3:16, Chovas HaLevavos 3:3.

74. Rashi ad loc. Cf. Sifra on Leviticus 18:3 (86a), Moreh Nevuchim 3:31.

75. Sifra (93d), Yalkut (1:626), Rashi on Leviticus 20:26; Rambam, Shemonah Perakim #6, Reshis Chochmah, introduction on Perek HaMitzvos (240c), Shnei Luchos HaBris, "Maamar HaSheni." 1:78b, Cf. Sifri 2:28.

76. Yad, Tefillin 5:4. Cf. Avodah Zarah 11a, Minachos 33b, Rashi, Pesachim 4a 'Chovas,'' Hagahos Maimonios, Tefillin 1:11 #7, Maharitz Chayos, Baba Metzia 101b.

77. Rosh HaShanah 28a, Nedarim 16b; Yad, Shofar 1:6, Ran, Nedarim 15b 'VeHah' end, Ibid. 35b 'U'Melamdo,'' Magen Avraham 233:6, Sifsei Cohen Yoreh Deah 215:2, 221:4, Mishneh Berurah 58:12; Tshuvos Menachem Azariah 31, Tshuvos Nodeh BeYehudah, Orach Chaim 2:1333, Tshuvos Shaagas Aryeh 60, Maharitz Chayos, Gittin 55, Nedarim 15b, 16b, 35b, Pri Megadim, introduction 4:5.

78. For a discussion of the two categories, see Yoma 67b, Maharitz Chayos ad loc., Sifra on Leviticus 18:4 (86a), Bamidbar Rabbah 19:3, end, Pesikta 4 (38b), Yalkut 1:577; Rambam, Shemonah Perakim #6; Yad, Meila 8:8 Moreh Nevuchim 3:26; Rashi on Genesis 26:5, Leviticus 18:4; Ramban on Leviticus 16:8), Emunos VeDeyos 3:2 (54a), Kuzari 2:48 (55a), Ikkarim 1:17, Reshis Chochmah, introduction to Perek HaMitzvos (240c).

79. See Rashi, Ramban, on Numbers 19:1, Bamidbar Rabbah 19:4, Pesikta 4 (40b).

80. See Ramban on Deuteronomy 6:20, Radak on 1 Kings 2:3.

81. Yad, Temurah 4:13, Teshuvah 3:4 Mikvaos 111:12; Moreh Nevuchim 3:26, 3:31, Ramban on Leviticus 19:19, Deuteronomy 2:6, Chinuch 545, Ibn Ezra on Exodus 20:1, Tosefos Yom Tov on Berachos 5:3; Etz Yosef on Vayikra Rabbah 27:10, Devarim Rabbah 6:1, Mahartiz Chayos on Sotah 14a.

82. Tosafos, Sotah 14a, Chulin 5a, "Keday," Gitten 49b 'R. Shimon.' Maharam ad loc., Tosefos Yom Tov on Sanhedrin 8:6, 10:5. Cf. Baba Kama 79b, Baba Metzia 3a, Maharitz Chayos on Rosh HaShanah 16a, Milchamos HaShem (Rambam), Rosh HaShanah (Rif 11a) 'Veod.'.

83. Yerushalmi Nazir 7:2 (35a), Maharam Di Lanzano, Shiurei Korban ad loc., Shiltei Giborim Avodah Zarah (Rif 6a) #1, Shnei Luchos HaBris, Torah SheBaal Peh, K'lal Drushim VeAgudos (3:241a); Terumas HaDeshen 108, Shiurei Berachah, Yoreh Deah 183:1. Actually, we find in the Talmud that Rabbi Shimon does derive laws from logical reasons, but this opinion is rejected by the majority. Cf. Baba Metzia 115a, Kiddushin 68b, Yoma 42b, Yebamos 23a, Sotah 8a, Gittin 49b, Sanhedrin 16b, 21a, Minachos 2b; Rashi, Kidushin 20b "Lefi," Sanhedrin 112a

'MiPney,' Maharitz Chayos *Sanhedrin* 70a; *Chinuch* 591, HaGra on *Even HaEzer* 16:2; *Choshen Mishpat* 97:4, *Turei Zahav* ad loc.; *Teshuvos Makom Shmuel* 32; Rashash Maharitz Chayos on *Baba Metzia* 115.

84. *Lechem Mishneh, Loveh U'Malveh* 3:1, however, states that according to Rambam, we decide like Rabbi Shimon in such a case. Cf. *Kesef Mishneh, Issurei Biah* 12:2. This, however, is nevertheless not the accepted opinion. Cf. *Even HaEzer* 16:1 in *Hagah, Bais Shmuel, Turey Zahav* 16:1, HaGra ibid. 16:2. Also see *Minachos* 65a, b; *Toras HaShelamin Yoreh Deah* 183:4.

85. A good example of this is the regeneration of the hymen of a child under three, *Niddah* 5:4 (44b) *Kesubos* 11b. This depends on the lunar, rather than the more logical solar calendar. Cf. *Yerushalmi, Kesubos* 1:2 (4a), *Yerushalmi Nedarim* 6:8 (823b), *Yerushalmi Sanhedrin* 1:2 (6a), *Magid Mishneh, Ishus* 2:21, *Kol Yehudah* (on *Kuzari* 3:41 (850a) 'Lo.'

86. *Berachos* 5:3 (833b), *Tosefos Yom Tov* ad loc., *Megillah* 4:9 (25a); *Yerushalmi Berachos* 5:3 (40a), *Yerushalmi Megillah* 410 (33a), *Yalkut* 1:920; *Yad, Tefillah* 9:7, *Moreh Nevuchim* 3:48, Rambam on Deuteronomy 22:6, *Chinuch* 545, *Tiferes Yisroel* Maharal 6; *Etz Yosef* on *Vayikra Rabbah* 27:10, *Devarim Rabbah* 6:1. Also see Genesis 18:25.

87. See note 138.

88. *Bamidbar Rabbah* 19:4, *Pesikta* 4 (39a), *Yalkut* 1:759.

89. *Sanhedrin* 21b, *Sefer HaMitzvos*, negative 365, *Moreh Nevuchim* 3:26, Maharitz Chayos, *Shabbos* 12b.

90. Cf. *Avos* 2:1.

91. Nissan Mindel, *The Commandments* (Kehot, New York 1964) p. 6 quoting *Moreh Nevuchim* 3:31.

92. Cf. *Yerushalmi Nedarim* 9:1 (29a), Ramban on Deuteronomy 22:6, *Chinuch* 545, *Nefesh HaChaim* 2:4, *Shomer Emunim (HaKadmon)* 2:11 #4. Also see *Job* 22:3, Psalm 16:2. Radak ad loc.

93. Rashi, Ramban, ad loc., *Chinuch* 95.

94. See Volume 2 of this series, ''Free Will and the Purpose of Creation.''

95. *Derech HaShem* 1:2:2-4, *Mesilas Yesharim* 1 (3b). Cf. *Makkos* 3:16 (23b), *Sh'mos Rabbah* 30:16, *Vayikra Rabbah* 30:12, *Reshis Chochmah.* Introduction to *Perek HaMitzvos* (239d).

96. *Bereshis Rabbah* 44:1, *Vayikra Rabbah* 13:3, *Tanchuma Sh'mini* 8, *Midrash Tehillim* 18:25, *Yalkut* 2:121; *Moreh Nevuchim* 3:26, *Avodas HaKodesh* 2:3, *Shnei Luchos HaBris, Shaar HaGadol* (1:48b), *Tiferes Yisroel* (Maharal) #7.

97. *Moreh Nevuchim* 3:27, Ibn Ezra on Exodus 20:1 end, Ramban on Deuteronomy 22:6. Cf. Jeremiah 32:39.

98. *Sh'mos Rabbah* 34:1, *Sefer Chassidim* 567, from *Job* 37:23.

99. Ramban ad loc., *Akedas Yitzchak* 77, *Ikkarim* 4:25.

100. *Berachos* 25b, *Yoma* 30a, *Kiddushin* 54a, *Meila* 14b. Cf. *Shabbos* 89a.

101. *Avodah Zarah* 3a.

102. *Sefer Chassidim* loc cit.

103. *Zohar* 3:31b, 3:86b, 3:128a, *Likutei Amarim* 1:4 (8a), *Nefesh HaChaim* 1:6, note 'VeYadua.'

104. *Zohar* 1:24a, 3:99b, *Nefesh HaChaim* 2:6, *Anaf Yosef, Yoma* 28b (in *Eyin Yaakov* #23). Cf. *Sh'mos Rabbah* 30:18, *Tanchuma, Mishpatim* 3. Also see *Koheles Rabbah* 2:26, 3:16, 5:24, 8:16. Cf.Isaiah 3:10, *Zohar* 3:29b, 3:227a end, 3:24b end.

105. *Shnei Luchos HaBris, Bais Chochmah* (1:26b). Cf. *Yoma* 39a.

106. Rambam, *Shemonah Perakim* #8, *Reshis Chochmah* 1:7 (22b), *Nefesh HaChaim* 1:18.

107. *Zohar* 3:99b, 3:232a end, *Tikunei Zohar* 20 (47b), *Nefesh HaChaim* 2:7.

108. *Shnei Luchos HaBris, Bais Chochmah* (1:26b). Cf. *Shabbos* 49a, 130a. Also see *Devarim Rabbah* 8:4, *Reshis Chochmah*, introduction to *Perek HaMitzvos* (239c, d).

109. For discussion see *Shnei Luchos HaBris, Shaar HaGadol* 1:46b ff. Also see *Elemah Rabosai* (RaMaK) 1:1:2, *Shomer Emunim (HaKadmon)* 2:75.

110. *Eichah Rabbah* 1:35, *Yalkut* 1:744; *Zohar* 1:61a, 2:32b, 2:58a, 2:65b; *Shnei Luchos HaBris, Shaar HaGadol* 1:47b, *Nefesh HaChaim* 1:3. Cf. *Zohar* 2:155a.

111. *Zohar* 1:35a, 1:82b, *Nefesh HaChaim* 1:6. Cf. *Yoma* 39a, *Shir HaShirim Rabbah* 6:4, Rashi on Song of Songs 7:2 end; *Berachos* 6a.

112. *Ohav Yisroel (Ekev)* on Deuteronomy 8:3.

113. *Zohar* 2:85b, 2:118a, 2:162b, 2:165a, *Tikunei Zohar* 70 (131a), *Nefesh HaChaim* 1:6, *Likutei Amarim (Tanya)* 1:4 (8b).

114. *Zohar* 2:23b, *Nefesh HaChaim* 1:3.

115. Cf. *Berachos* 6b.

116. Cf. *Avos DeRabbi Nassan* 33:1, *Bereshis Rabbah* 61:1, 95:2, *Bamidbar Rabbah* 14:7, *Tanchuma VaYigash* 11, *Midrash Tehilim* 1:13; Ramban on Genesis 26:5, *Nefesh HaChaim* 1:21, *Anaf Yosef* on *Yoma* 28b (in *Eyin Yaakov* #23). Regarding their actual observance, see *Kiddushin* 4:13 (82a), *Yoma* 28b, Maharsha, Maharitz Chayos, ad loc., *Yerushalmi Kiddushin* 4:12 (48b), *Bereshis Rabbah* 49:6, 64:4, 95:2, *Vayikra Rabbah* 2:9, *Tanchuma Lech Lecha* 1, 11, *Behar* 1; *Midrash Tehillim* 1:13, *Lechem Mishneh, Melachim*

9:1, Maharitz Chayos on *Taanis* 4a. Cf. *Berachos* 26b. Regarding the details of circumcision, see *Tosafos, Yebamos* 71b *'Lo,'* Maharitz Chayos ad loc., *Zohar* 1:163b, Radal (on *Pirkei DeRabbi Eliezer*) 29:49, note #8. Regarding Noah, see Rashi on Genesis 7:2, *Baalei Tosafos* ibid.

117. *Bamidbar Rabbah* 19:4, *Pesikta* 4 (39a), *Yalkut* 1:759.

118. Cf. Rashi, *Shabbos* 31a "DeAlaich," *Kuzari* 2:48 (55b). The commandments are thus divided into two categories: *Bain Adam LeMakom,* between man and God, and *Bain Adam LeChavero.* Cf. *Yoma* 8:9 (85b), Rambam on *Peah* 1:1, *Birkei Yosef, Orach Chaim* 606:1, *Zohar* 2:106b.

119. *Shabbos* 31a.

120. *Sifra* (89b), Rashi, ad loc. *Yerushalmi Nedarim* 9:4 (30b), *Bereshis Rabbah* 24:8, *Yalkut* 1:40, quoting *Midrash Abkir, Yalkut* 1:613.

121. Cf. *Yad. Shabbos* 2:3.

122. See note 70.

123. Cf. *Minachos* 43b; *Sifra* on Leviticus 8:16 (42a), *Bamidbar Rabbah* 10:3, 17:7, *Shir HaShirim Rabbah* 6:4, *Tanchuma Sh'lach* 14 *Ki Tavo* 4. Also see *Berachos* 62a.

124. *Chovas HaLevavos* 8:3 #21, Ibn Ezra on Deuteronomy 5:18 end, *Moreh Nevuchim* 3:35 #9, 3:44.

125. *Mechilta,* Rashi, Ramban, on Exodus 22:30; Ramban on *Sefer HaMitzvos, Shoresh* 4 (41b).

126. *Nefesh HaChaim* 1:6, note *'VeZeh.'*

127. Cf. *Berachos* 12b.

128. Rambam, *Shemonah Perakim* #4, *Moreh Nevuchim* 3:35 #13. Cf. *Chovas HaLevavos* 3:3.

129. *Avodah Zarah* 5b.

130. Cf. *Berachos* 12b.

131. *Bamidbar Rabbah* 10:3, *Shir HaShirim Rabbah* 6:4. Cf. *Avodah Zarah* 31b, 36b.

132. *Moreh Nevuchim* 3:42, *Emunos VeDeyos* 3:2 (854b). Cf. *Yerushalmi Chagigah* 3:6 (21a), *Yerushalmi Baba Kama* 7:7 (33b), Maharitz Chayos, *Niddah* 34a.

133. Cf. *Kuzari* 3:10 (12b).

134. *Berashis Rabbah* 1:1, *Yalkut* 2:942.

135. Cf. Exodus 12:26, 13:8, 13:14, Leviticus 23:43.

136. *Shir HaShirim Rabbah* 1:24, *Tanchuma VaYigash* 2, *Midrash Tehillim* 8:4.

137. *Kuzari* 3:10 (12b).

138. *Emunos VeDeyos* 3:2 (55a).

The Structure of Jewish Law

ᴥᔓ Uniformity in Law and Practice

I T IS GOD'S WILL that there be a certain degree of uniformity in Jewish practices as well as in the interpretation of the Law. The Torah thus states (Numbers 15:16), "There shall be one law and one ordinance for you."[1] Therefore, even when we have no formal central authority such as the Sanhedrin, God has provided us with guidelines to insure the continuance of Judaism as a unified religion. These guidelines constitute the structure of Jewish Law or Halachah.

The unique relationship between God and Israel assures us that we will always be able to ascertain the manner in which He desires that we observe His commandments. The Torah thus says (Deuteronomy 4:29), "You shall seek the Lord your God...and you shall find Him, if you search after Him with all your heart and with all your soul." This relationship also guarantees that we will always collectively obey His will in the long run, and the Psalmist thus said (94:14-15), "God will not cast off His people, nor will He forsake His inheritance. For judgment (of the Law) will return as far as righteousness, and all upright men will follow it."

Any practice, decision or code that is universally accepted among the Jewish people is therefore assumed to represent God's will, and is binding as such. Even when a decision is initially disputed, the commonly accepted opinion becomes binding as law.[2]

Collegiate Hashkafa Series—1974

The Talmud and the Shulchan Aruch

The Talmud was accepted by all Israel, and is therefore the final authority with regard to all questions of religious law.[3] Such universal acceptance is a manifestation of God's will, and therefore, one who opposes the teachings of the Talmud is like one who opposes God and His Torah.[4] All later codes and decisions are binding only insofar as they are derived from the Talmud.[5]

There were other works that were written prior or contemporary to the Talmud, and these are likewise very important for the understanding of our laws, beliefs and history.[6] These were all known to the compilers of the Talmud, however, and it is therefore assumed that whenever the Talmud disputes these other works, it does so for a definite reason.[7] We therefore ignore decisions found in the Jerusalem Talmud,[8] Midrashim and Tosefta[9] whenever they disagree with the Talmud.[10] There are, however, certain particular cases, where because of long-established custom, the opinions of these other works are accepted even when they disagree with the Talmud.[11]

Although all opinions found in the Talmud are equally sacred,[12] there is always one binding opinion wherever questions of actual practice are concerned.[13] This final opinion is known either from the Talmudic discussion itself, or from later traditions.[14]

Where a dispute merely involves questions of theology or history,[15] however, and has no practical consequences,[16] then any opinion found in the Talmud is equally acceptable.[17] Similarly, no final decision is usually rendered between conflicting opinions in the case of laws that are no longer in effect.[18]

The generation following the completion of the Talmud initiated the period of the Saboraim.[19] These were sages who carefully re-edited the Talmud, inserted minor additions, and around 540 c.e., put it in its present form.[20] The Saboraim flourished until 689 c.e., codifying rules for deciding between conflicting opinions found in the Talmud.[21] These rules were based upon Talmudic traditions and accepted by all Israel, and therefore remain unchallenged.

Following the Saboraim came the period of the Gaonim, which lasted until the death of Rav Hai Gaon in 1038. Like the Saboraim, the Gaonim headed the great academies of Sura and Pumbedisa in Babylonia, which had been founded in Talmudic times, and were recognized and accepted as the centers of authority on all matters of religious law.[22] Since the decisions of the Gaonim were both universally accepted and based on traditions preserved in the academies, they cannot be refuted by any later authority, without incontestable proof.[23]

With the closing of the great Babylonian academies, there ceased to be any formally acknowledged center of Jewish authority. Numerous codes, however, based on the Talmud and the decisions of the Gaonim were compiled by leading authorities, and these achieved almost universal recognition. Most noteworthy among these were the codes of

Rabbi Yitzchak Alfasi (*Rif*: 1013-1103), and Rabbi Asher ben Yechiel (*Rosh*: 1250-1328), as well as the *Mishneh Torah* of Moses Maimonides (*Rambam*: 1135-1204).[24] This period is known as that of the *Rishonim* or "first codifiers."

The work that was most widely accepted, however, was the *Shulchan Aruch* written by Rabbi Yosef Karo (1488-1575), which took into account almost all of the earlier codes.[25] Since the *Shulchan Aruch* followed the Sephardic, or Southern European and Near Eastern religious practices, a gloss was added to it by Rabbi Moshe Isserles (*Rama*: 1520-1572), including all the Ashkenazic or Northern European customs.

With the publication of the *Shulchan Aruch*, the period of the *Rishonim* (first codifiers) came to an end, and that of the *Acharonim* (later codifiers) began. The opinions of the *Rishonim* gained almost universal acceptance through the *Shulchan Aruch*, and therefore, later authorities could not counter them. While the *Acharonim* may decide between opinions found among the *Rishonim*, they do not dispute them without overwhelming proof.

The *Shulchan Aruch* did not consist of the individual opinions of Rabbis Yosef Karo and Moshe Isserles, but rather, of a compilation of those opinions found in the works of the *Rishonim*, which had gained universal or very wide acceptance. Because of the absolute universal acceptance of the *Shulchan Aruch*, its decisions are considered universally binding, unless otherwise indicated by the authorities of succeeding generations.[26]

The *Shulchan Aruch* became the standard of Jewish religious law, and therefore, it became the subject of many commentaries which expounded, and occasionally disputed, its views. Most noteworthy of these were the *Magen Avraham* of Rabbi Avraham Abele Gombiner (1665),[27] the *Turei Zahav* (*TaZ*) of Rabbi David ben Shmuel HaLevi (1646),[28] the *Sifsei Kohen* (*Shach*) of Rabbi Shabbatai ben Meir HaKohen (1647),[29] the *Chelkas Mechokek* of Rabbi Moshe ben Yitzchok Lima (1670),[30] the *Bais Shmuel* (*Bash*) of Rabbi Shmuel ben Uri Shraga Pheobus (1689),[31] and the *Sefer Meiras Eynayim* (*SeMA*), of Rabbi Yehoshua ben Alexander HaKohen Falk (1606),[32] All of these were printed alongside the *Shulchan Aruch*[33] and almost universally accepted.[34]

Besides this, however, there were literally hundreds of accepted authorities, both among the commentators on the *Shulchan Aruch* and among the writers of responsa. These applied the Law to individual cases, and thus set binding precedents. Over the years, various compilations of these later opinions have been published, the most noteworthy being the *Kitzur Shulchan Aruch* ("Abridged *Shulchan Aruch*" or "Code of Jewish Law") by Rabbi Shlomo Gantzfried (1804-1886).

The opinions found in any code or responsum that is generally accepted is considered an absolutely binding precedent.[35] A recognized religious authority, however, may dispute such a decision, either on the basis of adequate Talmudic proof,[36] or an unequivocal tradition that a particular decision was not generally accepted.[37] In all such cases, it is preferable to follow the rulings of a living authority, as the Torah states (Deuteronomy 17:9), "You shall come... unto the judge who shall be in those days."[38]

Deciding Debated Decisions

In every generation, there are certain rabbis, who, because of their great scholarship and piety, are generally accepted as the religious leaders and authorities, as the Torah states (Deuteronomy 17:10), "You shall observe and do all that they teach you."[39] Even though this command-ment refers specifically to the Sanhedrin, it also applies to the religious leaders of every generation.[40]

Just as a religious leader must be outstanding in wisdom and scholarship, so must he be distinguished in piety and observance. The Prophet thus tells us (Malachi 2:7), "They shall seek the Law from his lips, for he is an angel of the Lord of Hosts." Our sages comment on this that we should only seek interpretation of the Torah from a rabbi who resembles an angel in piety and holiness.[41] Therefore, if an individual is not outstanding in piety and observance, he is worthy of neither the prestige nor the authority of a religious leader, even though he may be a great religious scholar.[42]

An unopposed decision, whether given by a contemporary religious leader or found in an accepted code, should be accepted, even though it is not mentioned by other authorities.[43]

Where there is a dispute between two equal authorities, whether they are contemporary to each other or not,[44] we decide as in the case of any other questionable circumstance.[45] For this reason,[46] if the case involves a law found in the Torah (deoraisa), the stricter opinion must be followed,[47] whereas if it involves a law enacted by the sages (derab-banan), the more lenient opinion may be accepted.[48] This same rule also applies in cases where there is equal reason to forbid something as to permit it, and therefore, no final decision is possible.[49] If one has ab-solutely no basis at all for a decision, however, the question remains completely open, and the stricter course must be taken in all cases.[50]

In the case of law found in the Torah (deoraisa), the stricter opi-nion is always followed, even when it is that of the lesser of the two authorities.[51] Where rabbinical law (derabbanan) is concerned, however, the opinion of the greater authority should be followed, whether it is stricter or more lenient.[52]

The religious leader who is most universally accepted is always considered the greatest authority, even if others exceed him in scholar-ship. If two authorities have an equal following, however, then the one generally recognized as a superior scholar is considered the greater.[53] While age and experience count to some degree, that in itself is not enough to distinguish an authority.[54]

It is forbidden for a disciple to oppose his teacher,[55] and therefore, we never follow the opinion of one who opposes his master,[56] even though the disciple may have the stricter opinion, and even in the case of a law of the Torah.[57] This is only true, however, during the lifetime of the teacher, but after his death, his students are counted as independent authorities.[58] Similarly, a disciple who surpasses his master in scholarship is no longer subservient to his opinion.[59]

We are commanded (Exodus 23:2), "You shall incline after a majority."[60] Even though this commandment relates specifically to the Sanhedrin, it also applies to any controversy between religious leaders.[61] In particular, if an individual opinion is opposed by that of the majority, the former must be completely ignored.[62]

Therefore, if two factions oppose each other in a question of law, the opinion of the side with the greater number of sages must be followed.[63] If it is well established, however, that the smaller group is superior in wisdom and scholarship, its opinions must be followed, since the smaller group represents a greater quantity of scholarship.[64]

Some maintain that in order to constitute a clear majority, the larger faction must all agree regarding their reasons as well as with respect to their decision.[65] Therefore, in a case involving Torah law, a lenient decision of the majority can only be followed if they all agree as to its reason.[66] Otherwise, the two are considered as being equally balanced, and therefore, as in all similar cases, the stricter opinion must be followed. In any case, if the entire group is able to discuss the case, then the larger one is considered as a clear majority even when its members disagree as to the reasons for their decision.[67]

When two factions have the opportunity to actually debate a question, the majority opinion must be followed, even when it is more lenient.[68] In such a case, one who follows even a stricter opinion of the minority is guilty of violating the commandment to "incline after a majority,"[69] and is worthy of dire punishment.[70] Where there is no actual debate between the factions, however, as in the case of written opinions, one may follow the stricter opinion of the minority, since they might be able to convince the majority in actual debate.[71]

When rabbinical laws (derabbanan) were legislated by the Sanhedrin, a condition was made that any valid opinion could be followed in cases involving great monetary loss.[72] Therefore, when a question of rabbinical law involves the possibility of great monetary loss, one may even follow the lenient opinion of a minority, a lesser scholar opposing a greater one, or a disciple opposing his master.[73] The only condition here is that the lenient opinion be viable insofar as the stricter one has not been universally accepted.[74]

Religious law depends on precedent rather than on historical scholarship.[75] Therefore, we usually follow the most recent valid decision,[76] even though it might dispute an earlier majority.[77] However, a later authority is only followed when he is known to be fully aware of the earlier decisions[78] and worthy of disputing them,[79] and he must refute them with clear and unambiguous proof rather than with mere logic.[80]

This, however, is only true when the earlier opinion is generally known and codified. When the earlier opinion is not generally known, it can be assumed that the later authority would have accepted it if he had been aware of it, and the earlier opinion can be followed.[81]

✑§ The Rabbi of a Community

When a community accepts a duly-qualified rabbi as their religious leader, his decisions are binding in all cases.[82] He may even reverse the decisions of his predecessors,[83] even though his opinions may be the more lenient.[84] If the community rabbi is a recognized religious leader, he must be followed even when he disagrees with the majority of his contemporary authorities.[85]

In all such cases, the rabbi must depend on his own judgment, secure in the promise of Divine guidance.[86] It is thus written (II Chronicles 19:6), "Consider what you do, for you judge not for man, but for the Lord, and He is with you in giving judgment."[87]

The authority of a community rabbi, however, depends upon his general acceptance. Other religious scholars living in the community may therefore follow stricter opinions according to their own judgment.[88] The only condition is that they do not openly oppose the community rabbi,[89] or publicly show their dissent.[90]

Similarly, if there are many sages in the community who disagree with the rabbi, he should yield to the opinion of the majority.[91] This only applies, however, where the majority are all the rabbi's equal in wisdom and scholarship. Under no condition should the rabbi yield to the laity in any question of religious law, no matter how great their number.

In rendering a decision, a rabbi must carefully consider all its aspects.[92] He must strive to find a precedent for his decision in the opinions of earlier authorities.[93] He should not base his decision on the mere actions of a previous authority,[94] unless he thoroughly understands the issues, and knows that the reason for that action was completely unambiguous.[95] Where an action is accompanied by a formal decision, however, it is considered the most valid of precedents.[96]

Just as a rabbi must not permit something that is forbidden, he must also be careful not to forbid something that is permitted. Therefore, if a rabbi must forbid something because of a question or custom, he must carefully state his reason, in order not to establish an erroneous precedent. Similarly, if he must permit something because of an emergency or in the case of great loss, he must clarify his reason for that particular case.[97]

A rabbi should be careful not to render an unusual or anomalous decision.[98] In cases where he must do so, he should be most careful in explaining his reasons.[99] Any uncommon decision, depending on subtle or esoteric reasoning, should not be publicized, lest it lead to erroneous conclusions.[100] It is for this reason that we find many cases where something is permitted only in the case of a scholar,[101] and which may not be taught to the ignorant.[102]

When an authority renders a decision in a case where there is no clear precedent, he must strive to substantiate his case as strongly as possible.[103] After he is positive of his conclusion, he may even make use of dubious proofs to strengthen his decision.[104] This is the reason why many proofs accompanying a decision may appear to be far from conclusive. In extreme cases, one may even ascribe the decision to a great religious leader in order that it may be generally-accepted,[105] even though this would be a forbidden breach of truth in any other circumstances.[106]

When a rabbi is asked to decide a question of law, it is assumed that his opinion will be accepted as binding. Therefore, a case which he forbids is considered intrinsically prohibited,[107] and it cannot be permitted by another rabbi.[108] The initial decision can only be overturned if it can be proved that the initial judgment was erroneous.[109]

Since the initial decision renders the case intrinsically forbidden, it cannot be overturned by even a greater sage,[110] or by a majority rule.[111]

An erroneous decision, however, cannot render a case intrinsically forbidden. Therefore, if a second rabbi is able to show that the original decision can be refuted by generally accepted authorities or codes,[112] he may reverse the original decision.[113]

Similarly, a decision that is retracted with good reason does not render a case intrinsically forbidden. Therefore, if a second rabbi is able to show that common practice traditionally opposes the initial decision,[114] even though it may have been disputed among earlier authorities,[115] he may convince the first rabbi to retract his decision and permit the case in question.[116] Without such a clear tradition, however, logic alone is not considered sufficient reason for a rabbi to reverse even his own decision.[117]

Although a case is rendered intrinsically *forbidden* on the basis of a mere decision, it is not considered intrinsically *permissible* until the decision is actually acted upon. Therefore, as one rabbi permits something in a certain case, a second rabbi can pursue a stricter course and forbid it.[118] Once the decision has been acted upon however,[119] a second rabbi should refrain from reversing the initial decision,[120] unless he has clear proof that it is erroneous.[121]

A case only becomes intrinsically forbidden when there is a valid intrinsic reason for a particular ruling. However, when it is forbidden only as a stringent measure due to lack of permissive evidence, it does not become intrinsically forbidden. In such a case, the decision can be reversed on the basis of individual judgment alone.[122]

A decision can only render a case intrinsically forbidden when it is initially unopposed. If two or more rabbis are present when the case is presented, however, any initial decision can be disputed and reversed as long as it has not been accepted.[123]

A decision can only render the particular case under consideration intrinsically forbidden. Therefore, although a decision may establish a precedent,the precedent is not absolutely binding, and it can be ignored according to the judgment of rabbis deciding similar cases.[124] If it is known, however, that a case was forbidden specifically to safeguard a religious law, its precedent should be respected in all similar decisions.[125]

In order to prevent dispute, one should not present a case before a rabbi without informing him[126] of all previous decisions associated with it.[127]

Although the Law demands a certain degree of uniformity in Jewish practices, it does recognize geographical differences, and therefore allows different communities to follow varying opinions in relatively minor questions of religious law. Where there is no geographical or similar justification for varying practices, however, such differences are liable to be associated with ideological divergences, and are therefore forbidden. Therefore, within a single community, the Law requires a high degree of uniformity in religious practice.[128]

The Torah states (Deuteronomy 14:1), "You are children of the Lord your God; you shall not cut yourselves (lo sisgodedu).'' We are taught that just as it is forbidden to mutilate a human body, so is it prohibited[129] to mutilate the body of Judaism by dividing into factions,[130] thereby disaffirming the universal Fatherhood of God and the unity of His Law.[131]

It is therefore forbidden for members of a single congregation to form factions, each following different opinions or practices.[132] Similarly, it is forbidden for a single rabbinical court to give a split decision.[133] Where a city has more than one congregation, however,[134] or more than one rabbinical court, the following of each is counted as a separate community, and they may follow different opinions and practices.[135] Nevertheless, it is forbidden for a community to split into two congregations primarily because of a dispute over law or practice.[136]

It is prohibited for members of a single community to follow different opinions even when this does not result in any dissension.[137] Where the differences in practice also result in strife and conflict, however, they are also guilty of violating the commandment (Numbers 17:5), "You shall not be like Korah and his company," who caused strife among our people.[138]

Therefore, if a community does not have a regular rabbi, whose opinions would be universally binding, all questions regarding practice must be discussed and debated until an agreement regarding a uniform practice is reached.[139] Whenever a clear majority exists, they can compel the minority to abide by their decisions and practices.[140] In the absence of a clear majority, however, the dispute must be treated like any other question of practice, where the stricter opinion is followed in questions of Torah laws, and the more lenient one where rabbinical law is concerned.[141]

The prohibition not to divide into factions only applies to cases involving obvious questions of law. It does not apply, however, to cases that merely involve a question of custom[142] or commitment.[143] Similarly, one may unobtrusively follow a stricter opinion in a case where it is not obvious that he is dissenting from the accepted practice of his community.[144]

One is not guilty of forming a separate faction when he has a valid reason for following a different practice than that of the community at large.[145] Therefore, one is permitted to follow a stricter opinion because of his station[146] or origin.[147] When people from different communities form a new community, however, they must all agree to abide by a common practice[148] regarding all questions of law.[149]

The essence of the practice of religious law depends on the affirmation that the consensus of Jewish opinion represents the will of God, as long as it is not clouded by such ulterior motives as the desire for conformity or profit. Any decision or practice that is instituted exclusively to serve God therefore joins the mainstream of Jewish tradition, and partakes of the authority of the Torah itself. Accordingly, we are taught that whatever an earnest scholar may innovate at any time has already been spoken at Sinai.[150]

1. *Kuzari* 3:38 (42b), Rambam on *Megillah* 2a.
2. *Baba Kama* 100a, 117b, *Sanhedrin* 6a, 33a, *Bechoros* 28a, according to *Yad, Sanhedrin* 6:2, *Chosen Mishpat* 25:2; cf. *Shach* ad loc. 25:8, also see *Seforim* 14:19.
3. *Baba Metzia* 86a, *Yad,* Introduction, *Choshen Mishpat* 25:1, in *Hagaos Hagra* ad loc. 25:6.
4. *Iggeres Rav Sherira Gaon,* quoted in introduction to *Shaarei Tzedek.*
5. Cf. *Rashbam, Baba Basra* 13a "ad," *Tosefos Yom Tov, Shei'is* 4:10.
6. Cf. *Maharitz Chayos, Gittin* 7a, 17a.
7. Cf. Rashi, *Taanis* 16a "VeLama," *Nazir* 20b "Hashta," *Niddah* 8a (end) "VeOmar," *Maharitz Chayos, Tannis* 16a, *Nazir* 20b, *Baba Kama* 60a.
8. *Bereshis Rabbah* 31:3, Rif, *Eruvin* 35b, *Migdal Oz,* on *Yad, Shofar* 1:5, *Kesef Mishneh* on *Yad, Nedarim* 6:17 end, *Bais Yosef, Orach Chaim* 59 end, *Yad Melachai,* "Klalei Shnei HaTalmudim" 2.
9. *Yerushalmi Peah* 2:4 (13a), *Yerushalmi Chagigah* 1:8 (7b), *Rashbam, Baba Basra* 130b "ad," *Ran, Nedarim* 40b "U'le'inyan," *Tshuvos Rashba* 1:335, *Tosefos Yom Tov, Berachos* 5:4, *Tshuvos Radbas* 3:647, *Tshuvos Noda Bihudah (Tinyana) Yoreh Deah* 161, *Beer Yaakov, Even HaEzer* 119, *Yad Malachi* 72, *Maharitz Chayos, Nedarim* 40b.
10. *Tosafos, Berachos* 48a "VeLes." However, where they do not disagree with the Talmud, they can be accepted, *Maggid Mishneh,* on *Yad, Shabbos* 18:2, *Bach, Orach Chaim* 124, *Mayim Chaim* 1b, *Lechem Yehudah* 14b end, *Yad Malachi,* "Kelalei Shnei HaTalmudim" 4.
11. *Tosafos, Berachos* 18a "LeMachar," *Pesachim* 40b "Avel," *Megillah* 32b "Rosh," *Baba Basra* 74a "Piskei," *Avodah Zarah* 65b "Avel," *Magen Avraham* 690:22, quoting Rabbi Isaac Stein on the *Sefer Mitzvos Gadol* (S'mag).
12. *Gittin* 6b, *Eruvin* 13b, *Ritva* ad loc.; *Yerushalmi Berachos* 1:4 (9a), *Yerushalmi Yebamos* 1:6 (9a), *Yerushalmi Sota* 3:4 (16a). *Yerushalmi Kiddushin* 1:1 (4a); Rashi, *Kesubos* 47a "Ma," *Tosafos Yom Tov,* introduction, *Avodah Hakodesh, Shaar HaTachlis* 23, *Sh'nei Luchos HaBris,* "Bais David' (Jerusalem 57201) 139b, *Chagigah* 3b, *Bamidbar Rabbah* 14:11. Cf. *Pirkei DeRabbi Eliezer* 18 (42a). Also see *Tosefos Shantz* on *Eduyos* 1:5.
13. Cf. *Yerushalmi Sanhedrin* 4:2 (21b), *Midrash Tehillim* 12:14. Also see *Avodah Zarah* 7a, *Choshen Mishpat* 25:2 in *Hagah.*
14. Cf. *Mavo HaTalmud; Meor HaGadol, Sanhedrin* (Rif 12a) end, Rosh, *Sanhedrin* 4:6.
15. Cf. *Yerushalmi Shevi'is* 1:1 (1a), Rambam on *Sefer HaMitzvos, Shoresh* 3 (39b), *Maharitz Chayos, Chagigah* 6b.
16. Cf. *Yoma* 5b, *Maharitz Chayos* ad loc., Rosh, *Chulin* 1:23, Rashi, *Chulin* 17a "SheHichniso." Also see *Maharitz Chayos, Sotah* 2a, *Baba Kama* 2b.
17. Rambam on *Sotah* 3:5, *Sanhedrin* 10:3, *Shavuos* 1:4; *Iggeres Techiyas HaMesim* (in *Igros U'Tshuvos HaRambam,* Jerusalem 5721) pp. 11, 15; *Tosafos, Yoma* 5b, *Chagigah* 6b "Mai," *Sanhedrin* 15b "Shor," Rashash, *Shabbos* 62a, *Maharitz Chayos, Yebamos* 86b, *Makkos* 23b *Tosefos Yom Tov, Sotah* 3:5, *Makkos* 3:16. See, however, *Rabbeinu Chananel, Sanhedrin* 22a, where he renders a decision in such a case. Carefully compare *Gittin* 6b and *Eruvin* 13b.
18. Rashi, *Zevachim* 45a "Omar," *Tosafos, Zevachim* 45a, 87a, *Sanhedrin* 51b, "Hilchasa." *Minachos* 45b, 52b, "Halacha," *Shabbos* 133a "VeTenan," *Yoma* 13a "Halacha," *Tosefos Yeshenim* ibid.; *Mahari Kolon, Shoresh* 165 (p. 179a), *Kenesses HaGedolah,* "K'llalei HaGemara' 99, *Magen Avraham* 218:3, *Tshuvos Chavas Yair* 94, *Tshuvos Panim Meiros* 2:51, *Yad Malachi* 234.
19. The initial work of redacting the Talmud was done by Rav Ashi (352-427 c.e.), together with his school in Babylonia. It was completed by his son, Mar bar Rav Ashi (Tovyomi) and Meremar, and concluded in 505 c.e.
20. *Iggeres* Rav Sherira Gaon; *Machzor Vitri* p. 484.
21. *Sefer HaKaballah.*
22. *Iggeres Rav Sherira Gaon;* Introduction to *Yad.*
23. Rosh, *Sanhedrin* 4:6.
24. Cf. Introduction to *Bais Yosef; Shnei Luchos HaBris,* "Torah SheBaal Peh" 3:249b.
25. The "Prepared Table." Following the *Tur* ('Pillar') of Rabbi Yaakov ben Asher (c. 1300), this work was divided into four parts: *Orach Chaim* ("The Path of Life") dealing with blessings, prayers and festivals; *Yoreh Deah* ("Instructor of Knowledge") dealing with Kashruth and other ritual laws requiring expert decision; *Even HeEzer* ("The Stone of Help") dealing with the laws of marriage and divorce; and *Chosen Mishpat* ("The Breastplate of Judgment") dealing with rabbinical courts, property and monetary transactions.
26. *Tshuvos Chavas Yair,* additions (p. 262),

quoted in *Pischei Tshuvah, Choshen Mishpat* 25:2; *Nesivos HaMishpat* 25:20, quoting *Thumim* ibid., *Tshuvos Tzemech Tzedek* 9 (end), *Avodas HaGershoni* 48, *Shaar Ephriam* 113 (end of p. 81).

27. "Shield of Abraham" on *Orach Chaim*.

28. "Rows of Gold" on all four sections called *Magen David* (Shield of David) on *Orach Chaim*.

29. "Lips of the Priest" on *Yoreh Deah* and *Choshen Mishpat*.

30. "Portion of a Lawgiver" on *Even HaEzer*.

31. "House of Samuel" on *Even HaEzer*, up until Chapter 126.

32. "Book that Enlightens the Eyes." on *Choshen Mishpat*.

33. Other widely accepted codes are the *Chayei Adam* and *Chochmas Adam* of Rabbi Avraham Danzig (1810 c.e.), the *Kitzur Shulchan Aruch* of Rabbi Shlomo Gantzfried (1870 c.e.), and the *Mishnah Berurah* of Rabbi Yisrael Meir Kagan (known as the *Chafetz Chaim*; 1906). None of these, however, were as universally accepted as those mentioned in the text.

34. *Shem HaGedolim; Tshuvos Chavas Yair*, loc. cit.

35. Rosh, *Sanhedrin* 4:6, *Choshen Mishpat* 25:1, *Terumas HaDeshen* 241, 271, *Kenesses HaGedolah*, abridged rules (in *Orach Chaim*) 64, *Pri Megadim*, "Rules of Decisions" (in *Yoreh Deah*) No. 6. Cf. *Eruvin* 41a.

36. Rosh, loc. cit, *Choshen Mishpat* 25:1 in *Hagah*. If one does not agree with the logic of a decision, however, but does not have ample proof to dispute it, he may not do so. *Pischei Tshuvah, Choshen Mishpat* 25:3.

37. Ibid., *Sema* 25:2, *HaGra* 25:7.

38. Rosh, loc. cit, from *Rosh HaShanah* 25b; cf. *Tosafos* ad loc. "*SheHaYamim*." See *Sifri* (153), *Yalkut* (911), Rashi ad loc., *Chinuch* 495 end, *Rashash, Yoma* 80a.

39. Cf. *Yad, Mamrim* 1:1, *Sefer HaMitzvos*, positive commandment 111.

40. *Chinuch* 495, *Minchas Chinuch* 496; *Chayei Adam* 127:1. Cf. *Maharitz Chayos, Shabbos* 3b, *Rambam* on *Shabbos* 1:4.

41. *Moed Katan* 17a, *Chagigah* 15b; *Yad, Talmud Torah* 4:1, *Yoreh Deah* 246:8, *Shach* 246:8.

42. *Yoma* 72b, *Yoreh Deah* 243:3.

43. *Chulin* 7a, *Kenesses HaGedolah* (in *Orach Chaim*) 60.

44. *Yad, Mamrim* 1:5.

45. Rif, *Pesachim* 12a; *Tshuvos Rashba* 253.

46. *Avodah Zarah* 7a, *Tosafos* ad loc. "*BeShel*". *Yad*, loc. cit., *Choshen Mishpat* 25:2 in *Hagah, Shach*, "*Kitzur Hanagos Horaos Issur VeHetzer*' (*Yoreh Deah* 242) No. 2. *Yad Malachi* 82,83.

47. Cf. *Baba Basra* 57b, *Rashbam* ad loc. "*LeChumra*," *Kesubos* 73b, *Gittin* 63b, *Nedarim* 53a, *Chulin* 134a, *Niddah* 25a.

48. *Shabbos* 34a, *Eruvin* 5b, 45b, *Betza* 3b. See "Love and the Commandments" elsewhere in this volume.

49. Rif. *Shabbos* 30a, Rosh, ibid. 6:16, *Hagahos Maimonios* on *Yad, Chametz U'Matzah* 2:16 No. 1. Cf. *Sefer Yereim* "*Amud HaBiah*" 217 (p.99a); *Kesef Mishneh* on *Yad, Sefer Torah* 9:15, *Tzitzis* 1:18 end, *Shabbos* 28:3, *Yom Tov* 19:8, 6:10, 8:3; *Tamim Deyim* 242 (p. 71a) *Pri Chadash, Orach Chaim* 672:2, *Yoreh Deah* 110 "*Kelalei S'fek S'fekah*" 17; *Yavin Shemua* 288, *Yad Malachi* 634, *Eliahu Rabba U'Zutta* (p. 44d).

50. Radbaz 205, Rashdam, *Orach Chaim* 165, *Tshuvos Chava Yair* 94, *Pri HaAdamah* (p40c), *Mikveh Yisroel* (p. 16b), *Tshuvos Zaken Aaron* 24 (end), *Yad Malachi* 82, 83. Cf. *Berachos* 51a (end).

51. *Shach* op. cit. No. 2, from *Yad, Mamrim* 1:5, where we see that no distinction is made between a greater and lesser scholar.

52. *Shach* loc. cit, from *Avodah Zarah* 7a; *Choshen Mishpat* 25:2 in *Hagah*.

53. *Hagahos Ashri* (on Rosh) *Avodah Zarah* 1:3, *Sema* 25:18, *Shach*, loc. cit.

54. *Shach*, loc. cit. Cf. *Baba Basra* 142b.

55. *Eruvin* 63a, *Berachos* 31b, *Yoma* 53a; *Yerushalmi Shevi'is* 6:1 (16a), *Yerushalmi Gittin* 1:2 (5b), *Sifra* on *Leviticus* 10:1, *Pesikta* 26 (172a), *Yad, Talmud Torah* 5:2, *Yoreh Deah* 242:4.

56. *Mavo HaTalmud; Yad Malachi* 38, 39, *Tshuvos Zaken Aaron* 3 (8b). Cf. *Niddah* 14b, *Kiddushin* 42b, *Sanhedrin* 29a.

57. *Shach* loc. cit.

58. Ran, *Succos* (Rif 1a) "*U'LeRabbi*," *Sh'nei Luchos HaBris* 3:249a. Also see Rosh, *Baba Metzia* 1:49, *Eruvin* 2:4; *Halichos Olam* 5:3, *Kerisos Yemos Olam* 3:6, *Yam Shel Shlomo, Baba Kama* 2:15, *Yad Malachi* 17.

59. *Shach*, loc. cit.

60. Cf. *Baba Metzia* 59b, *Tosafos, Baba Kama* 27b "*Ka Mashma Lan*," *Maharitz Chayos* ad loc., *Get Pashut*, rules, *Ketzos HaChoshen, Kuntres HaSefekos* 6:2.

61. *Chinuch* 78. Cf. *Yerushalmi Sanhedrin* 4:2 (12b), *Midrash Tehillim* 12:14. Also see *Chulin* 11a, *Sefer HaMitzvos*, positive commandment 175, *Yad Malachi* 296.

62. *Berachos* 9a, 37a, *Shabbos* 60b, 130b, *Betza* 11a, *Yoma* 36b, *Yebamos* 40a, 46b, 47a, *Baba Kama* 102a, *Avodah Zarah* 7a, *Bechoros* 37a, *Niddah* 30b, 49a, *Kenesses HaGedolah* (in *Orach Chaim*) 47.

63. *Choshen Mishpat* 25:2. Cf. Rambam, introduction to *Mishneh*, that this even is true when 1000 oppose 1001. Also see *Tshuvos*

Rashba 253, Kenesses HaGedolah (in Orach Chaim) 92; Niddah 10b.

64. Chinuch 78, from Yebamos 14a, cf. Maharsha ad loc., Minchas Chinuch 78:1, Tshuvos Rashba 263, Kenesses HaGedolah (in Orach Chaim) 39.

65. Shach op. cit. "U'Kasav," Choshen Mishpat 25:19, Rabbi Akiba Eiger ad loc. in Choshen Mishpat 25:2, however, this is disputed. See Tshuvos Shaar Ephriam 10:8, Get Pashut 122:8, Bais Ephriam, "Kuntres HaSefekos' 39:13, Tshuvos Maharit 2:19, Tshuvos Noda Bihudah (Tinyana) Choshen Mishpat 3, HaGra, Choshen Mishpat 25:21.

66. Shach op. cit. No. 7.

67. Beer Hetev, Choshen Mishpat 25:12.

68. Shach op. cit. "U'Mashma."

69. Minchas Chinuch 78:6. 70. Berachos 1:3 (10b), Yerushalmi Berachos 1:4 (8b), Yerushalmi Yebamos 1:6 (9a), Yerushalmi Sotah 33:4 (16a), Yerushalmi Kiddushin 1:1 (4a), Mesilas Yesharim 20 (30b).

71. Minchas Chinuch 78:1 (end), Get Pashut, Kuntres HaKelalim, end.

72. Shach op. cit.

73. Eruvin 46a, Niddah 6b, 9b, Choshen Mishpat 25:2 in Hagah, Tshuvo Rashba 203, Shach op. cit. No. 2,3, Kenesses HaGedolah (in Orach Chaim) 92.

74. Eruvin, Niddah loc. cit.

75. Cf. Baba Basra 142b.

76. Choshen Mishpat 25:2 in Hagah, quoting Maharik Shoresh 84; Rosh, Sanhedrin 4:6. Cf. Mavo HaTalmud; Rif, Berachos 31b, Ran, Succos (Rif 1a) "LeRabbi," Shnei Luchos HaBris 3:249b, Yad Malachi 168, 194.

77. Kenesses HaGedolah (in Orach Chaim) 39, Ram Alshakar 93, Binyamin Zeev 126, Yad Malachi 169, Pri Magadim, introduction to Yoreh Deah, Rule No 8, Pischei Tshuvah, Choshen Mishpat 25:8. Also see Raavad, Eduyos 1:5, Shach op. cit. "VeKi Tomar."

78. Choshen Mishpat 25:2 in Hagah, Shach ad loc. 25:21, Tshuvos Maharam Alshich 39 (61b).

79. Shach op. cit. No. 8, Choshen Mishpat 25:21, Nesivos HaMishpat 25:20.

80. Pischei Tshuvah, Choshen Mishpat 25:3, 25:8, Tshuvos Moshe Rothenberg, Yoreh Deah 60. See notes 36, 37.

81. Choshen Mishpat 25:2 in Hagah, quoting Maharik Shorsh 96. Cf. Shabbos 61a, Rosh, Berachos 3:35. Also see Tomas Yesharim 16, Kenesses HaGedolah (in Orach Chaim) 44.

82. Choshen Mishpat 25:2 in Hagah, from Tshuvos Rashba 253. Cf. HaGra ad loc. 25:22, Shabbos 130a, Yebamos 14a, Also see Kenesses HaGedolah 93, Pri Chadash, "Rules Regarding Customs," (Orach CHaim 496) No. 11.

83. Choshen Mishpat ibid. from Eruvin 41a.

84. Bach, Choshen Mishpat 25, Shach 25:20. Cf. Shiltei Giborim, Avodah Zarah (Rif 1a) No. 3.

85. Pri Chadash, loc. cit. end.

86. Baba Basra 131a, Sanhedrin 6b, Niddah 20b.

87. Sanhedrin 6b, Rashbam, Baba Basra 131a "VeAl."

88. Pri Chadash, quoting Rashba loc. cit.

89. See Tosafos, Pesachim 51a "ly", Shach, Yoreh Deah 214:7.

90. See Yad, Yom Tov 8:20, Rosh, Pesachim 4:4, Magen Avraham 468:11, Rav Shulchan Aruch 468:13.

91. Pri Chadash, loc. cit, from Berachos 37a, Tosefta 4:12. Also see Berachos 9a.

92. Avos 1:1.

93. Kenesses HaGedolah (in Orach Chaim) 59. Cf. Tshuvos Mahari Weil 164.

94. Baba Basra 130b.

95. Kenesses HaGedolah 63, Binyamin Zeev 131, Tshuvos Rivash 301.

96. Cf. Shabbos 21a, 136b, Baba Basra 83b, 130b, Niddah 65b.

97. Shach, op. cit. No. 8.

98. Yoreh Deah 242:10, Hagahos Maimonios on Yad, Talmud Torah 5:3 No 6. Cf. Sanhedrin 5b, Niddah 20b (top), Berachos 3b (end), Eruvin 13b; Avos 1:11, 2:4, Maharitz Chayos, Yoma 40b.

99. Shach, Yoreh Deah 242:17, Shiyurei Berachah ad loc.; Pri Megadim (Introduction to Orach Chaim) "Order of Decisions" 1:10.

100. Shabbos 12b, Minachos 36b; Baba Kama 30b, Maharitz Chayos ad loc., Yad, Tefillin 4:14, Yom Tov 4:9. Also see Taanis 26b, Nedarim 23b, Pesachim 30b, Succah 34b, Maharitz Chayos, Chulin 12a, 15a, Yad Malachi 191 (28b).

101. Nedarim 14a, Baba Metzia 71a, Tosafos, Baba Kama 99b "Manacha," Maharitz Chayos ad loc.

102. Minachos 99b, Nedarim 49a; Rashi, Taanis 13a "KeSheAmru."

103. Yerushalmi Berachos 2:3 (14b), Nimukei Yosef, Baba Kama (Rif 30a) "Gemara," Maharitz Chayos, Yoma 32a.

104. Nimukei Yosef loc. cit.

105. Magen Avraham 156:2, from Eruvin 51a, Pesachim 112a, Rashi, Rashbam ad loc. "Hisla," cf. Birkei Yosef, Yoreh Deah 242:24, quoting Tshuvos HaGeonim 324; Tanna DeBei Eliahu Rabbah 4 (31b), Ramasayim Tzofim ad loc. 4:2; Makor Chesed (on Sefer Chasidim) 977:2. Also see Shabbos 115a, Rashi ad loc. "Asa," Pesachim 27b, Gittin 20a.

106. Yerushalmi Nazir 7:1 (34 top), Berachos 27b, Mesechta Kalla (end), Hagra ad loc. No. 3; Yoreh Deah 242:24.

107. Ran, *Avodah Zara* (Rif 1b) "*HaNishal*," quoting Raavad, Rashba, *Chidushei HaRan*, Ritva, Meiri on *Avodah Zarah* 7a. Others, however, hold that the reason for this law is in order to maintain the respect and dignity of the first rabbi, Ran loc. cit, *Shiltei Giborim* ibid. No. 3.

108. *Chulin* 44b, *Niddah* 20b, *Berachos* 63b: *Yorah Deah* 242:31 in *Hagah Hagahos Maimoni* on *Yad*, *Mamrim* 1:5 No. 1. Cf. *Avodah Zarah* 7a. *Tosefta Eduyos* 1:3, *Yerushalmi Shabbos* 19:1 (86b).

109. See note 113.

110. Ran loc. cit., Rivesh 379, *Maadnei Melech*, *Chulin*, p. 151b. Those who abide by the second reason given in note 107, however, maintain that a greater sage or a majority can reverse such a decision. Ran loc. cit., *Maharik Shoresh* 171, *Shach*, *Yoreh Deah* 242:53, *Beer Hetiv* 242:34, *Divrei Chamudos* (on Rosh) *Chulin* 3:7 No. 24, *Radbaz* 56, *Yad Malachi* 2:232 (147a). Cf. *Yebamos* 97b, Rashi, *Chulin* 59b "*VeHizihru*."

111. For the same reason as above.

112. Cf. *Sanhedrin* 6a, 33a; *Yad, Sanhedrin* 6:1, *Choshen Mishpat* 25:1.

113. *Yoreh, Deah* loc. cit., *Tosafos, Avodah Zarah* "*HaNichal*," Rosh 1:3, Ran, loc. cit. *Chulin* (Rif 9b) "*Chacham*," Cf. *Bechoros* 28b., *Sanhedrin* 33a. Also see *Tshuvos Zaken Aaron* 2, 183, *Yad Malachi* 2:225 (147b).

114. Cf. *Niddah* 20b, *Tosafos* ad loc. "*A'Garmi*," *Tosafos, Chulin* 44b "*Haichi*," Rosh, *Chulin* 3:7. Others, however, hold that tradition alone is not enough, see Ran, *Chulin* (Rif 9b) "*Rabba*," *Shach*, *Yoreh Deah* 242:55, *Beer Hetiv* 242:34. Also see *Shiltei Giborim*, loc. cit. *Tshuvos Mishkenos Yaakov* 59, *Pischei Tshuvah*, *Yoreh Deah* 242:18, *Tshuvos Ran Ashkenazi* 53, *Mikveh Yisrael* 62a, 69b, *Yad Malachi* 2:231 (147a), *Hagra*, *Yoreh Deah* 242:72.

115. *Tosafos, Avodah Zarah*, loc. cit, *Anshei Shem* on Ran, *Avodah Zarah* loc. cit. Cf. *Choshen Mishpat* 25:2.

116. Ran, loc. cit, *Shach*, *Yoreh Deah* 242:58. Others, however, maintain that in such a case the decision cannot be reversed at all. Ran, *Chulin*, loc. cit,. *Shach*, *Choshen Mishpat* 25:14 No. 17. 18. A third opinion does not even require that the decision be retracted by its originator in such a case. *Tosafos, Avodah Zarah* loc. cit. *Hagra*, *Yoreh Deah* 242:72. Also see *Tshuvos Panim Meiros* 1:2. *Pischei Tshuvah*, *Yoreh Deah* 242:19.

117. Rosh, *Avodah Zarah* 1:3, *Shach*, *Yoreh Deah* 242:58, *Beer Hetiv* 242:36, *Maadnei Melech*, *Chulin* p. 151c. Those who hold that the reason is for respect, however (note 107), maintain that the originator can retract his deci-

sion in any case.

118. *Berachos* 63b, *Tosafos, Avodah Zarah* loc. cit, *Hagra*, *Yoreh Deah* 242:77. See *Shiltei Giborim* loc. cit, that according to those who maintain that the reason is because of respect for the first rabbi, there is no difference between a decision to permit and one to forbid.

119. *Taz, Yoreh Deah* 242:18. This essentially answers the objections of the *Nikudas HaKesef* ad loc., and *Beer Hetiv*, *Yoreh Deah* 242:37.

120. *Yoreh Deah* loc. cit, Rosh, *Avodah Zarah* 1:3, from *Yerushalmi Shabbos* 19:1 (96b). Others, however, maintain that even such a case may be reversed, cf. *Hagahos Maimonios*, loc. cit, *Sefer Mitzvos Gadol (S'mag)*, positive commandment 111, *Yam Shel Shlomo*, *Chulin* 3:18, Rivash 379. Also see *Tshuvos Radbaz* 362.

121. *Tshuvos Radbaz* 362, 393, *Pischei Tshuvah* 242:20.

122. Cf. *Bais Lechem Yehudah*, *Yoreh Deah* 242:31, *Atzei Levonah*, ibid.

123. *Tosefos, Avodah Zarah* loc. cit, *Schach*, *Yoreh Deah* 242:52.

124. *Yoreh Deah* loc. cit, quoting *Maharik Shoresh* 172. Cf. *Eruvin* 41a, *Hagra*, *Yoreh Deah* 242:78. Also see *Tshuvos Mabir* 1:156, *Rashdam*, *Orach Chaim* 17, *Yad Malachi* 2:224 (147a), *Tshuvos Shivaz Tzion* 25, *Pischei Tshuvah*, *Yoreh Deah* 242:21.

125. *Yam Shel Shlomo*, *Chulin* 3:18, *Shach*, *Yoreh Deah* 242:60, *Beer Hetiv* 242:38. Cf. *Mordecai*, *Chulin* 611.

126. *Tosafos, Avodah Zarah* loc. cit, Rosh 1:3, *Yoreh Deah*, loc cit.

127. *Avodah Zarah* 7a, *Tosefta Eduyos* 1:3, *Yerushalmi Shabbos* 19:1 (86b).

128. Cf. *Yebamos* 14a.

129. Some hold that this is a Biblical Prohibition, *Pri Megadim*, *Eshel Avraham* 493:6, from *Kesef Mishneh* on *Yad, Avodas Kochavim* 12:14. However, *Minchas Chinuch* 467, quoting *Yesh Seder LaMishneh*, writes that this is only a rabbinical prohibition. This also appears to be the opinion of *Sefer HaMitzvos*, negative commandment 45.

130. *Sifri* (96) ad loc., *Yalkut* 1:891; *Yebamos* 13b, *Yad, Avodas Kochavim* 12:14, *Sefer HaMitzvos*, negative commandment 45, *Sefer Mitzvos Gadol (S'mag)*, negative 62 *Chinuch* 467; *Orach Chaim* 493:3 in *Hagah*.

131. Rashi, *Yebamos* 13a "*Lo*," Ritva ibid.

132. *Chinuch* 467, *Pri Chadash*, *Orach Chaim* 493:3 (end), quoting *Kesef Mishneh*, loc. cit.

133. *Yebamos* 14a, *Yad*, loc. cit, cf. *Kesef Mishneh*, *Lechem Mishneh* ad loc.

134. *Magen Avraham* 493:6, quoting *Tshuvos Rabbi Eliahu Mizrachi* 1:37, *Pri Chadash*, "Rules regarding Customs" (in *Orach Chaim* 496) No. 20.

135. *Yebamos* 14a, *Rosh* 1:9.

136. *Shach,* op. cit. rule No. 10.

137. *Rav Shulchan Aruch* 493:7 (end). Cf. *Hagahos Ben HaMechaber, Minchas Chinuch* 467.

138. *Sefer HaMitvos* loc. cit.

139. *Chinuch, Shach,* loc. cit.

140. *Magen Avraham* 493:6, *Pri Chadash,* op. cit. No. 21. Cf. *Hagahos Maimonios* on *Yad, Tefillah* 11:1 No. 2, *Shiltei Giborim, Yebamos* (*Rif* 3b) No. 1, *Tshuvos Rashdam* 1:20, *Tshuvos Radach* 2:13, *Tshuvos Moshe Alshich* 29, *Yad Malachi* 2:356 (151a).

141. *Chinuch, Shach,* loc. cit. See notes 47, 48.

142. *Yebamos* 13b, *Rashba* ad loc: *Eshel Avraham* 493:6; *Hagahos Ben HaMechaber* loc. cit. *Magen Avraham* 493:6, however, holds that this is only the initial supposition of the *Gemara,* but it is rejected at the conclusion of the discussion. He also maintains that this is indicated by the wording of the *Yad,* loc. cit. Cf. *Tosafos, Pesachim* 14a "*Sh'toi,*"

Yerushalmi, Pesachim 1:5 (5b).

143. *Magen Avraham* 493:6, *Tomas Yesharim* 168, 170, *Yad Malachi* 2:354 (151a).

144. *Yam Shel Shlomo, Yebamos* 1:10, *Karban Nesanel* (on *Rosh*) *Yebamos* 1:9 No. 4; *Eshel Avraham* 493:6, *Hagahos Ben HaMechaber* loc. cit. This opinion also appears to be shared by *Tosafos, Yebamos,* "*BiM'komo,*" and "*Lo.*" However, *Magen Avraham,* loc. cit., also disputes this opinion.

145. *Rosh, Yebamos* 1:9.

146. Cf. *Shabbos* 142b, *Moed Katan* 11b, 12b, *Baba Metzia* 73b, *Avodah Zarah* 8b; *Tshuvos Divrei Yosef* 45, *Yad Malachi* 6 (2b).

147. *Magen Avraham* 493:6, *Kenesses HaGedolah, Orach Chaim* p. 122. *Yoreh Deah* 64; *Yad Malachi* 2:355 (151a).

148. *Magen Avraham* 493:6. Cf. *Rashi, Succah* 44a. "*LeDedahu,*" *Kapos Temarim* ad loc. *Maharitz Chayos, Yebamos* 14a.

149. But not by questions of custom, *Magen Avraham* loc. cit.

150. *Yerushalmi, Peah* 2:4 (13a).